# SISTERS
## OF
# RICHARD
# III

*In the meantime, the duke of Clarence before-named, brother to king Edward, had been fully reconciled to the king by the mediation of his sisters, the duchesses of Burgundy and Exeter, of who, the one without the kingdom, and the other within it, entreated the duke to make peace with his brother.*

*Croyland Chronicle*

*To my next generation of strong women: my beautiful daughter, Chloe, and my equally beautiful nieces, Megan and Amy.*

## Acknowledgements

I would like to send my thanks to Matthew Lewis, who pointed me in the direction of the Colchester connection with regards to the Princes in the Tower and his kindness in answering emails from a woman he had never heard of! Many thanks, also, to the team at Pen and Sword: Sarah-Beth Watkins, Laura Hirst, Lucy May and my editor, Michelle Higgs, for your professionalism and friendliness in all our interactions.

And lastly to my family, with love.

# SISTERS
# OF
# RICHARD
# III

## THE PLANTAGENET DAUGHTERS OF YORK

### SARAH J. HODDER

PEN & SWORD
**HISTORY**

AN IMPRINT OF PEN & SWORD BOOKS LTD.
YORKSHIRE – PHILADELPHIA

First published in Great Britain in 2024 by
**PEN AND SWORD HISTORY**
An imprint of
Pen & Sword Books Ltd
Yorkshire – Philadelphia

ISBN 978 1 39906 386 9

Typeset in Times New Roman 11.5/14 by
SJmagic DESIGN SERVICES, India.
Printed and bound in the UK by CPI Group (UK) Ltd.

Pen & Sword Books Limited incorporates the imprints of Atlas, Archaeology,
Aviation, Discovery, Family History, Fiction, History, Maritime, Military,
After the Battle, Military Classics, Politics, Select, Transport, True Crime,
Air World, Frontline Publishing, Leo Cooper, Remember When,
Seaforth Publishing, The Praetorian Press, Wharncliffe Local History,
Wharncliffe Transport, Wharncliffe True Crime and White Owl.

*For a complete list of Pen & Sword titles please contact*
**PEN & SWORD BOOKS LIMITED**
George House, Units 12 & 13, Beevor Street, Off Pontefract Road,
Barnsley, South Yorkshire, S71 1HN, England
E-mail: enquiries@pen-and-sword.co.uk
Website: www.pen-and-sword.co.uk

or

**PEN AND SWORD BOOKS**
1950 Lawrence Rd, Havertown, PA 19083, USA
E-mail: uspen-and-sword@casematepublishers.com
Website: www.penandswordbooks.com

# Contents

# Introduction

In 1483 one of England's most controversial kings took the throne of England. In becoming Richard III, he would defy all loyalty that he had seemingly shown to his family thus far and seize the throne of England from its rightful heir – his young nephew Edward. From that moment his reputation was sealed and he would become known to history as a usurper and a probable child murderer, after both his nephews – Edward and his younger brother Richard – disappeared into the Tower, never to be seen again and presumed murdered on their uncle's orders. Richard would rule England for a mere two years before his death would bring about one of the most famous eras in British history, that of the Tudors.

Today there are societies and individuals that look to rehabilitate Richard's reputation, to look at why he took the actions he did and to consider if the fate of his nephews was wrongly attributed to him. This book will also take us through the events of 1483–85 but from a different viewpoint. It will look at events as they occurred through the lives of Richard's sisters, Elizabeth and Margaret of York. It will also look at how they, alongside their elder sister, Anne of York, navigated the reign of Edward IV, as well as their young lives during the period we know as the Wars of the Roses, and their later adult lives as they assumed new roles during the Tudor era.

Of course, our three women of York were sisters to not one, but two kings of England. The daughters of Richard, Duke of York and his wife, Cecily Neville, they were sisters to Edward IV and Richard III. As young women they watched from the periphery as their father challenged England's anointed king and lost his life; as their brothers fought for the throne of England, first as a cohesive group before eventually turning on each other; and as their own brother, Richard, brought to an end 300 years of Plantagenet rule, making way for an England under the reign of a new Tudor dynasty.

But like many women, they were not just bystanders to these events; they have their own story to tell. Anne of York was married to a Lancastrian who sided against her father and brothers, before finding later happiness, albeit briefly, with her second husband. Elizabeth of York married John de la Pole and became the mother of eleven children who would become thorns in the side of the Tudor kings. Margaret of York became Duchess of Burgundy, a hugely influential woman in her adopted kingdom although she never stopped supporting her family back in England. Between them they witnessed and contributed to one of the most turbulent times in English history, yet they have naturally been overshadowed by their more famous brothers. This is their story.

Note: In an era when Elizabeth, Anne and Margaret were common names, it is often hard to distinguish one from another. For the purposes of this book, I have called the York sisters Anne of York, Elizabeth of York and Margaret of York. They were, in their later years and after their marriages, also known as Anne, Duchess of Exeter; Elizabeth, Duchess of Suffolk; and Margaret, Duchess of Burgundy. The daughters of Edward IV and Elizabeth Woodville were also known as 'of York' – for instance, their eldest daughter, Elizabeth, was known as Elizabeth of York. When discussing Edward's daughters within this book, I will call them Princess to avoid confusion.

# Chapter 1

# A brief descent of the crown
## Edward II to Henry IV

The York family, of which Anne, Elizabeth and Margaret were a part, was intricately connected to the English royal family even before two York sons gained the ultimate seat of power. From Athelstan, the first king to rule all of England, through to William the Conqueror and beyond, the story of England's ruling elite requires a book all to itself but, to completely understand the world within which our three York girls lived, it is useful to travel back a few centuries to see how events shaped the world they were born into.

Our three York girls were Plantagenet women, a name their father adopted as his family surname in the fifteenth century, possibly to emphasise his connection to England's ruling dynasty. The rule of the House of Plantagenet began in England in 1154, when Henry II, the son of the Empress Matilda and Geoffrey Plantagenet, Count of Anjou, succeeded to the English throne; it would continue for the next 300 years before it ended with the death of King Richard III on the battlefield at Bosworth.

Arguably one of England's greatest Plantagenet kings was Edward III and it is the descent of numerous families from Edward's five sons that formed the core of the power struggles during the late 1400s. With five sons and four daughters who survived to adulthood, it is supposed that many of us alive today will in some way be descended from this great English king. In his studies of genetics, scientist Adam Rutherford argues how it is almost impossible for anyone with a predominantly British ancestry not to be.[1] But the lines of descent were of course closer and less intertwined at this point in English history with just under 100 years having passed between Edward's rule and that of Henry VI, the first Wars of the Roses king.

Edward III's reign began over a century and a half after Henry II took the throne, and with a rule spanning some fifty years, it made Edward not only one of England's greatest kings but also one of its longest. But his path to power was not a straightforward one. When he ascended the throne in 1327, aged just 15, it was not upon the death of his father but rather by an organised rebellion undertaken by his mother, Isabella of France, and her alleged lover, Roger Mortimer.

Edward's father, Edward II, had ruled England for twenty years in what can only be described as a rather turbulent reign. Born in 1284, he became king in 1307 at the age of 23. His ability to make enemies and his seeming lack of concern that he had done so led to him being deposed in January 1327. Many of the troubles that arose during his rule sprang from his tendency to forge close relationships with some within his court, seemingly to the detriment of others. The ability to form a close friendship is typically an admirable quality, but arguably less so in a leader when displaying an outward show of favouritism to just a few subjects will inevitably breed anger and resentment in others.

Edward II's most prominent and controversial relationship was with a squire named Piers Gaveston, the son of one of his household knights, who had joined his household in 1300. The two men were so close that his position as Edward's favourite not only provoked discontent among his barons but it also offended the French royal family, who felt this relationship showed a lack of respect towards his French wife, Queen Isabella.

The exact nature of Edward's relationship with Gaveston has never been fully determined. Both men were married, but there was suspicion that they were also lovers. Either way, the leading nobles, men such as the Earl of Lancaster, the king's cousin, were unhappy at the favours awarded to Gaveston, a man they considered inferior in all ways. Christopher Marlowe penning his play, *Edward II*, in the late sixteenth century gives voice to the Earl of Lancaster to impart the view of many of the earls and barons at that time:

> Earl of Lancaster [to the king]: My lord, why do you thus incense your peers, that naturally would love and honour you but for that base and obscure Gaveston? Four earldoms have I, besides Lancaster – Derby, Salisbury, Lincoln, Leicester. These will I sell, to give my soldiers pay, Ere Gaveston shall stay within the realm.[2]

Lancaster was a man held in high regard by many. He was also an exceedingly rich man with an income of around £11,000 a year from his lands, almost double that of the next wealthiest baron. Very much estranged from his cousin the king, many other powerful magnates sided with him. As tensions rose, Edward quickly came to realise that to safeguard his own position he would have to appease his barons. He agreed to exile Gaveston, arranging for him to be sent across the sea to take up the position of Lieutenant of Ireland. But, although he had done as his nobles asked, he saw this as a temporary measure and the plan was always to bring his favourite back as soon as the climate allowed.

And before too long, Gaveston did indeed return, this time even more self-important and confident than before he left. For Edward's barons, already deeply concerned about the king's ability to lead, Gaveston's renewed presence became a catalyst for a set of wide-ranging reforms that they persuaded Edward to agree to. Known as the Ordinances of 1311, Edward's agreement to accept these reforms once again appeased the barons, but only in the short term. The continued arrogance displayed by Gaveston kept tensions simmering and they eventually boiled over in 1312, when a group of men, led by the Earl of Lancaster, seized Gaveston and executed him. Edward was furious and so began several years of armed confrontation between the king and his men.

Either unwilling or unable to learn lessons from the past, Edward would later go on to replace Gaveston with another favourite, in the shape of a man named Hugh Despenser the Younger, the son of the Earl of Winchester. Joining Edward's court as a chamberlain sometime around 1318/19, he very quickly became a close friend and adviser to his king and once again rumours abounded that they may have been lovers. And once again the barons resented the preferential treatment showered upon Despenser by the king and in 1321 they seized the Despensers' lands, forcing Despenser and his father into exile. In response, Edward revoked the Ordinances of 1311 and began a military campaign, capturing and executing his cousin Lancaster. With all this in-fighting, Edward's reign was never destined to end successfully but when the end came, it was brought about not by his enemies but someone he may never have suspected: his wife and queen, Isabella.

Marlowe also features Queen Isabella in his work, portraying her as an unhappy queen, robbed of affection from her husband by his lover, Gaveston:

> So well hast thou deserved, sweet Mortimer, As Isabel could
> live with thee for ever. In vain I look for love at Edward's

hand, Whose eyes are fixed on none but Gaveston. Yet once more I'll importune him with prayer: If he be strange and not regard my words, My son and I will over into France, and to the King my brother there complain, How Gaveston hath robbed me of his love: But yet I hope my sorrows will have end, And Gaveston this blessed day be slain.[3]

In reality, Isabella remained true to her husband during Gaveston's lifetime, although it no doubt pained her to be on the outskirts of her husband's affections, and it was only during Edward's alliance with the Despensers that she began to ally herself elsewhere.

The Mortimer that Marlowe mentions in the play is a man named Roger Mortimer, a rich baron who held many estates in the Welsh Marches and Ireland following his marriage to the wealthy heiress Joan de Geneville. Mortimer was the 1st Earl of March, a title that would one day find its way down to Richard Plantagenet, Duke of York, and later his son Edward. Born around 1287, Mortimer was eight years older than Isabella, who was born around 1295. When Hugh Despenser was awarded lands belonging to Mortimer by the king, Mortimer became involved with the king's enemies, leading an unsuccessful revolt which ended in him being captured and imprisoned in the Tower of London. Just over a year later he made a daring escape from the Tower and fled across the sea to France where he would soon be joined by Queen Isabella.

When Mortimer began his relationship with the queen is unknown; perhaps their affair had begun in England or perhaps they didn't meet until they were together in France. Marlowe, of course, infers a connection between them during Gaveston's lifetime. What is clear is that in 1323, Queen Isabella obtained her husband's permission to go to France, reportedly to meet with her brother, King Charles IV. Whilst at the French court she joined Mortimer and the pair openly became lovers. Isabella then refused to return to England until the Despensers were removed from their position as the king's favourites. As a married woman, her quite public liaison with Mortimer was met with dismay, even at the French court of her brother, and the pair were forced to relocate to Flanders where they obtained assistance for an invasion of England with the help of Count William of Hainault. A marriage treaty was also agreed between the count's daughter, Philippa and a young Prince Edward, who had travelled to France with his mother.

The queen and Mortimer returned to England in 1326, accompanied by Prince Edward and a small army. Enemies of the Despensers welcomed their return and moved to join them. King Edward, realising the strength of his enemies, fled to Wales. He was eventually captured and forced to relinquish his crown in January 1327 in favour of his 14-year-old son. The old king was moved as a prisoner around several English castles before meeting his end in Berkeley Castle on 21 September 1327. Rumours that he met a violent death flourish, with the writer of the *Croyland Chronicle* recording:

> Edward, being then a youth, but fifteen years of age, was solemnly crowned at Westminster, and raised to the throne of England on the feast of the Purification of the blessed Mary, his father being still kept in prison. However, shortly after this, they conveyed the old king to Berkeley Castle, where, as many were forming plans for his liberation, he died a horrible death.[4]

With the full agreement of the English nobles, a teenage Prince Edward was crowned King Edward III at Westminster on Christmas Day, amidst great celebration:

> And thus as it was agreed by all the nobles, so it was accomplished; and then was crowned with a crown royal at the palace of Westminster beside London the young King Edward third, who in his days after was right fortunate and happy in arms. This coronation was in the year of our Lord MCCCXXVI, on Christmas Day, as and then the young king was about the age of sixteen; and they held the feast till the Conversion of Saint Paul following.[5]

The marriage deal that his mother and Mortimer had struck with Count William of Hainault also came to fruition, and the teenage Philippa left for England in 1327, escorted by her uncle, John Hainault. They arrived in London in December 1327 where Philippa was greatly welcomed by the people of the city. Edward and Philippa's marriage was celebrated in York Minster on 24 January 1328.

By 1330, Edward was old enough to assume independent rule and in a revealing glimpse of his loyalty towards his father, he took his revenge on Mortimer, arresting him and charging him with treason and the murder of Edward II. Mortimer was subsequently executed. Edward spared his mother and she was allowed to live freely as the dowager queen until the end of her life; she lived until her early sixties.

Edward III's marriage to Queen Philippa was hugely more successful than that of his parents. During their long marriage, the couple had at least thirteen children together. There were five daughters: Isabella, Joan, Blanche, Mary and Margaret and at least eight sons, three of whom died in infancy. Of their surviving sons who lived to adulthood, their eldest son, born in 1330, was also named Edward. He was more famously known as the Black Prince for reasons undetermined, perhaps in reference to the colour of his armour or his prowess on the battlefield. His other brothers were Lionel of Antwerp, Duke of Clarence (born 1338); John of Gaunt, Duke of Lancaster (born 1340); Edmund of Langley, Duke of York (born 1341); and Thomas of Woodstock, Duke of Gloucester (born 1355). Their birth dates and positions as Edward's sons would become of great importance in later claims to the throne. Although hugely dedicated to his wife Philippa, Edward's reign did bring the appearance of one Alice Perrers into our history books, his long-term mistress whose reputation as a scheming, power-grabbing and domineering woman has made her famous long after her passing.

After a long and successful reign, Edward III died in June 1377, leaving a glowing legacy as recorded by Walsingham:

> Among all the world's Kings and Princes he had been a glorious king, benevolent, merciful and magnificent. His nickname was 'man of grace' on account of that singular grace in which he excelled. In this gift of grace of exceptional quality given him by heaven, he surpassed all his predecessors.[6]

After his death the throne should have passed to his eldest son, Edward the Black Prince, but he had predeceased his father in 1376, his death widely attributed to dysentery contracted during his many trips to the battlefields of France. Some fifteen years before his death, Edward had married Joan of Kent and it was to their son, a young boy named Richard, that the crown would pass to in 1377, giving England a 10-year-old king who would be known as Richard II.

As Richard was still very much a minor, the rule of the country during his first few years as king was mainly overseen by his uncles, John of

Gaunt and Thomas of Woodstock. But as he grew into his kingship, Richard began to surround himself with young men of his own age, and a little like his great-grandfather Edward II, he began to lavish gifts on his favourites, causing hostility amongst other courtiers. Young knights of the chamber such as James Berners, Michael de la Pole and Robert de Vere, Earl of Oxford, were part of Richard's inner circle and felt the benefits that closeness to the king could bring. A contemporary description of Richard describes his lavishness:

> King Richard was of the common stature, his hair yellowish, his face fair and rosy, rather round than long, and sometimes flushed; abrupt and somewhat stammering in his speech, capricious in his manners, and too apt to prefer the recommendations of the young, to the advice of the elder, nobles. He was prodigal in his gifts, extravagantly splendid in his entertainment and dress, timid as to war, very passionate toward his domestics, haughty and too much devoted to voluptuousness. So fond of late hours, that he would sometimes sit up all night drinking.[7]

By 1388 Richard was close to being viewed as a tyrant by those not in his inner circle and a group of men calling themselves The Lords Appellant decided to take action. The name they chose denoted the 'bringers of trial proceedings against royal favourites'[8] and their aim was to force the king to agree to the trial of five of his favourites in what would become known as the Merciless Parliament that assembled in February 1388. The men who formed the Lords Appellant were Richard's uncle Thomas of Woodstock, Duke of Gloucester; Richard Fitzalan, Earl of Arundel; and Thomas Beauchamp, Earl of Warwick. They were later joined by Richard's cousin, Henry Bolingbroke, Earl of Derby (a son of John of Gaunt) and Thomas de Mowbray, Earl of Nottingham. As a result of their protestations, many of Richard's favourites were imprisoned or forced into exile, and although Richard seemingly accepted this, he would bide his time until almost ten years later, when he moved to arrest Gloucester, Arundel and Warwick. The Kirkstall chronicler certainly believed that there was a connection between these arrests and the events of the Merciless Parliament almost a decade before, reporting that Richard 'then called to mind his former humiliations'.[9] The estates of the three detained lords were confiscated and many were handed over to Richard's supporters.

Richard's cousin, Henry Bolingbroke, was not arrested with the other men, but tensions blew up again in 1398, when a remark made by Thomas de Mowbray, Duke of Norfolk, was reported by Henry to the king as treasonous. Mowbray denied the remark and protested his innocence, and to bring the matter to a conclusion, Bolingbroke and Mowbray agreed to a duel. Yet before the duel could take place, Richard decided to banish them both from the kingdom to avoid further bloodshed.

A year later Henry's father, John of Gaunt, died, and Richard was still hesitant to allow his exiled cousin to come home to claim his lands and the Duchy of Lancaster. To remove the need for Henry to return, the king cancelled the documents that would allow Bolingbroke to inherit. But it did not have the desired effect; instead a furious Bolingbroke hastened back to England, landing at Ravenspur and determined to claim what was his. As he made his way down the country towards London, he quickly gained support. What began as a mission to reclaim his inheritance of the Duchy of Lancaster soon became a quest for a much bigger prize. With the support of the Earl of Arundel, Bolingbroke began a military campaign; his ultimate aim nothing less than the throne itself. Capturing and imprisoning Richard, the king was forced to abdicate and Bolingbroke had himself crowned king of England. Winning the support of most of the nobles, many of whom had been unhappy with Richard's reign, he was crowned King Henry IV on 13 October 1399 at Westminster Abbey.

Richard II remained in the tower for some weeks before being moved to a safer location. The new king was initially willing to let him live, but it soon became clear that a living king in captivity would always be a figurehead for insurrections and it is believed that Richard died in February the following year at Pontefract Castle. There were rumours that he had somehow escaped captivity and survived for many years more, but they were never given much credence. Richard was initially buried in Kings Langley although when Bolingbroke's son came to the throne as Henry V, he allowed the reburial of Richard in the tomb that he had commissioned for himself in Westminster Abbey. His tomb was opened in 1871 and his remains suggested that he had been a man almost 6 feet in height.[10]

With the accession of Henry IV, a new line of descent for the English crown had begun, stemming from Edward III's third son, John of Gaunt, Duke of Lancaster. The House of Lancaster would continue on the throne unchallenged for the next two generations until the reign of Henry VI, when it would face opposition once more.

# Chapter 2

# All branches lead to Edward III

Anne, Elizabeth and Margaret of York were born in the mid-fifteenth century into an England that had been ruled over by Bolingbroke's grandson, Henry VI, for the last twenty or more years. Their own personal story, however, also began many years before their births. Each and every one of us has a lineage, a family tree with its roots deep into the earth and branches that divide and divide again and wind their way back through centuries past. Our own stories are deeply rooted in our ancestry; the lives and choices of those who came before us lead us to understand our own place in the world. And for the York sisters, their ancestry was illustrious indeed. Rich with the trappings of royalty and the desire for power, and full of love and duty, treachery and loyalty, both their paternal and maternal lineage stretched back to Edward III and then back further through England's royal tapestry.

If they ever looked back through their family tree, Anne, Elizabeth and Margaret would have seen an abundance of formidable women in their lineage including some of England's greatest queens. The She-Wolf Isabella of France (an intended defamation for Edward II's queen), the kindly Philippa of Hainault and the remarkable Eleanor of Aquitaine were all ancestors. Closer to them in time, they may have learned about the lives of their grandmothers, Joan Beaufort and Anne Mortimer.

But understandably, their first role model when looking for female influence in their lives would have been their mother, Cecily Neville. Cecily, described by Amy Licence in her 2014 biography as 'a famous beauty of her age',[1] was the youngest daughter of the great Neville family. In reference to her strikingly good looks she was known as 'The Rose of Raby'; Raby Castle being her childhood home and the place that she was born. At the time of her birth in May 1415, her father Ralph Neville was well into his second marriage. He had had at least eight children with his first wife, Margaret Stafford, as well as at least thirteen children with Cecily's mother, Joan Beaufort. Cecily was born into the heart of an extensive family. And as the youngest daughter of a very large group of siblings all fighting for their place in the world, there was every chance she would grow up quite insignificant, well married perhaps, but unnoticed by history. But fate had other ideas for Cecily as this old ballad written about her conveys:

> A gracious lady!
> What is her name, I thee praie tell me?
> Dame Cecile, Sir.
> Whose daughter was she?
> Of the Erle of Westmoreland, I trowe the yengist,
> And yet grace fortuned her to be the highest.[2]

Cecily's fortune, entwined with that of her future husband and sons, would propel her to become one of history's remembered figures, more so than many of her other siblings, and her daughters would be part of that story with her.

As grandchildren of the Neville family, the York sisters' ancestry could be traced back through their mother, their grandfather, Ralph Neville, Lord of Raby and Earl of Westmorland, and then back to at least the time of Henry II in the twelfth century when an Alan de Neville was working as a chief justice of the forests under King Henry. Before that, the Neville name is thought to have begun in France, perhaps from Neuville-sur-Touques or Calle de Neu Ville as far back as the ninth century,[3] and members of the Neville family made their way to England in the retinue of William the Conqueror. There is mention of a Gilbert Neville who may have been a steward of William the Conqueror and a minor landholder in Lincolnshire in 1086, but there is no evidence to corroborate this. But in 1163, there was certainly an Alan de Neville working in an administrative position for the king, and he was likely the first of the Nevilles to raise the family name by bringing the clan into the sphere of the Crown.[4]

In his role as chief justice, Alan would have been involved in royal business in a much wider sense than just his forestry duties. Records show that he authorised expense payments to the Sheriff of Yorkshire for the costs involved in transporting prisoners to Nottingham for forest offences, and he also approved the Sheriff's expenses for the transportation of pigs from York to Doncaster for the king's use. By all accounts he was also quite a forceful figure, prepared to do whatever he considered necessary to further his cause, no matter the cost. The writer of the *Battle Abbey Chronicle* certainly remembered him as a man not to be messed with: 'There was in his times one Alan de Neville, the chief of the king's foresters, who, by the power granted him, most maliciously vexed various provinces of England with innumerable and unusual prosecutions. And, as he neither feared God nor regarded man, he spared neither ecclesiastical dignities nor secular.'[5]

Working to further his own career, Alan strove to please his king, showing no compassion or leniency to either the clergy or the common man when going about his business. The chronicler concluded that 'thus, to please an earthly monarch, he was not afraid to offend the King of Heaven'. But as is the fickleness of kings, Alan's dealings did not, in the end, gain him the respect of King Henry for when Alan was on his deathbed and the brethren of a nearby monastery approached the king to request a share of Alan's wealth, the king was heard to say 'his wealth is going to be mine. You may have his corpse. The devils of hell may have his soul'.[6]

Future generations of Nevilles did, however, continue to build on the foundations that Alan had begun and they remained involved in royal forest administration for the next 300 years. In addition, many Nevilles also forged successful marriages which played a huge part in contributing to the fortunes of the whole family. After crossing the sea from Normandy, the earliest Nevilles had settled in Lincolnshire, but by the mid-twelfth century branches of the family had moved to Essex and Yorkshire. As they moved up the social ladder they were able to move into larger residences, notably Brancepath Castle in Yorkshire and Raby Castle in Durham.[7] By the late 1300s, the Nevilles of Raby had become one of the two most powerful families in the north, equal only to the Percy family of Northumberland. The years of royal service by the family were finally recognised by Richard II when he elevated Ralph de Neville, Lord of Raby, to the title of Earl of Westmorland in 1397.

The Nevilles had worked their way up to power by gaining favour with England's royal family, but through their mother's maternal line the York sisters could trace their lineage directly back to royalty itself, by way of the tenacious Katherine Swynford, their great-grandmother. Born Katherine de Roet in the mid-fourteenth century, Katherine spent much of her adult life embroiled in notoriety and scandal as an adulteress due to her relationship with John of Gaunt. The York sisters' grandmother (Cecily's mother) was Joan Beaufort, the third of four children born sometime around 1377 to Katherine and Gaunt during their affair which lasted over a quarter of a century before they would eventually marry. This relationship connected Anne, Elizabeth and Margaret back through Gaunt to Edward III.

John of Gaunt, the third son of Edward III, was charismatic, chivalrous and arguably one of the most important noblemen of his time, as well as one of the richest. Born in 1340, he was perhaps nine or ten years older than Katherine, whose exact birth date is unknown. She and her sister Philippa arrived at the English court with their father. When he died, a kindly Queen Philippa took the two girls into her care, which means they were probably brought up alongside Gaunt and his siblings within the royal household.

Raised under the watchful eye of the queen, Katherine and Philippa grew up to be accomplished ladies – well-educated and well-mannered. But even with a royal upbringing, they were not of noble lineage and whether or not the young Katherine and John had established any sort of friendship or connection whilst they were young, Katherine would never have been deemed a suitable bride for this prince of the realm. When John of Gaunt did marry in 1359, to a young woman named Blanche of Lancaster, both Katherine and Philippa were given roles serving in her household, a position they would have considered an honour. In the early 1360s Katherine would also marry – to a young gentleman named Hugh Swynford who was a knight in the service of John of Gaunt. Her sister, Philippa de Roet, married around the same time; her husband was a young man named Geoffrey Chaucer, who at that time was a young page in the household of the Black Prince but destined to become one of England's most famous writers and poets. Philippa and Geoffrey's granddaughter, Alice Chaucer, would later connect to the York family through the marriage of her son to Elizabeth of York, creating a further line of descent from the de Roet girls to the Yorks.

In 1368, Blanche of Lancaster unexpectedly died; she was only around 22 years of age. Gaunt was said to be devastated at the loss of the woman he had been married to for nine years and who had borne him seven children during their time together including the future Henry IV. Chaucer, another admirer of Blanche's, wrote his first major poem after her death, 'The Boke of the Duchesse', which is widely believed to have been based on Blanche. Possibly even commissioned by Gaunt himself, the poem captures Blanche as a lady who surpasses all others and cements her reputation as a woman of great beauty with a kind and open temperament, respected and loved by all. There is no evidence that John and Katherine were in any sort of relationship during his first marriage, and when her mistress's household disbanded, Katherine returned to the home she shared with her husband Hugh at Kettlethorpe. Gaunt, still only 28 years old, was back on the marriage market.

For the next three years Gaunt remained a single and eligible man until in 1371 his path crossed with the 17-year-old Constance of Castille. Constance and her sister, Isabella, were the daughters of King Pedro of Castille and since his death they had been living in exile in the village of Bayonne in France under the protection of Gaunt's elder brother, the Black Prince. As a foreign princess, Constance was a highly suitable match and the union most certainly appealed to Gaunt's chivalrous side. Constance was fighting for the right to inherit her father's throne, and Gaunt was fully aware that if he assisted her in reclaiming the throne of Castille, he would gain himself a kingdom in the process. After their marriage, in September 1371, the couple returned to England and took up residence at Hertford Castle.

That same year Katherine also became a widow when her husband Hugh died whilst overseas in Gaunt's retinue. To compensate Katherine for the death of her husband in his service and perhaps to help out a young woman he had befriended from childhood, Gaunt secured her a place in the household of his new wife at Hertford. Not long after this, most likely in the spring of 1372, it is believed their affair began. In the summer of 1372, Constance gave birth to her first child; just a few months later Katherine retired to her home at Kettlethorpe where she also bore Gaunt a child. She gave birth to a son and the boy was named John after his father and given the surname Beaufort.

Katherine and Gaunt would continue their affair for the next nine years, discreetly at first, but after a while they made less effort to hide it. Katherine's reputation as one of history's fallen women would be sealed in March 1378 when she was seen openly riding around Gaunt's Leicestershire estates with her lover holding her bridle; presumably this was seen as a sign of over-familiarity between the pair. The chronicler, Walsingham, would publicly condemn the Duke for being seen outside 'with his unspeakable concubine, a certain Katherine Swynford', terming him 'abominable in the eyes of god' for flaunting his mistress so openly.[8] As was the lot of many women who stepped outside the bounds of female propriety, Katherine herself would become vilified as a witch and a whore; the writer of the *Anonimalle Chronicle* declaring her a she-devil and an enchantress, and Froissart delivering perhaps one of the milder insults, deeming her a woman of light character.[9]

Refusing to be cowed, the pair continued their liaison despite the widespread disapproval. But their relationship would eventually become unsustainable when, in 1381, the Peasants' Revolt threw the country into chaos. Taking root in Essex in May that year, the uprising was centred in the south-eastern counties of England and was led by a man named Wat Tyler. By 1381, Edward III had been dead for four years and Richard II had just imposed a new Poll Tax on the country. Just thirty years after the Black Death had ravaged the country, many were struggling. Furious about this new, imposed tax that only added to their suffering, the men and women of the south decided to take matters into their own hands. As a group of men marched on London determined to destroy property and take the lives of anyone related in some way to the ruling elite, Gaunt, uncle to the king, was in Scotland with the English army, and therefore powerless to defend his loved ones and property. The historian Dan Jones writes that in the 'worst crisis of order the country had ever known … the most experienced and powerful noble in the land was left exiled and impotent'.[10] When the protestors reached Gaunt's London home, the Savoy Palace, they burnt it to the ground. Thankfully Katherine was not in residence at the time.

With this threat putting other members of the wider royal family into danger, Gaunt attempted to restore respect and confidence in the king and his leading nobles. He was forced to publicly confess his adultery with Katherine and acknowledging his mistakes, he openly split with his beloved mistress. In what may have been an additional blow to Katherine, he also confessed to infidelity with 'many others in his wife's household',[11] although it is, of course, entirely possible that she already knew that he was not fully faithful to her; for a start he was a married man. By the time of their break-up, Katherine and Gaunt had four children together. Publicly renounced, Katherine was left to bring them up on her own and to pick up the pieces of her life. Whatever her private feelings, she quietly and with dignity returned to her home to concentrate on her children. How long they actually stayed apart is unknown; perhaps they resumed their relationship discreetly but during their time apart Katherine would remain close to Gaunt's children from his marriage to Blanche, particularly his eldest son, Henry Bolingbroke, and his wife Mary. Gaunt never earned his kingdom of Castille, and during the last few years of his marriage to Constance they lived separate lives, with Constance dying in 1394. By January 1396, Katherine and Gaunt had wed; she had been in love with the duke for over a quarter of a century and had finally got her man. The couple appealed to the Pope to pronounce on the legitimacy of their children and in September 1396 he proclaimed their marriage valid and their Beaufort children legitimate. Their union was also acknowledged by King Richard II.

By 1396, Joan Beaufort, Cecily's mother, was 17 years old and already a widow; her first husband, Robert Ferrers, had died just three years into their marriage. But now a recognised daughter of the powerful John of Gaunt, she became a highly desirable marriage prospect and, in 1397, she married the 32-year-old Ralph Neville. Gaunt, pleased with his daughter's new husband, settled a handsome annuity of over £200 on the couple for life.[12]

Although the king had recognised their Beaufort children, they were nevertheless excluded from the line of succession, but it would be through this Beaufort line that a later Henry VII made his claim to the throne. Henry's mother, Margaret Beaufort, was a future granddaughter of Gaunt and Katherine's eldest son, John Beaufort, and through her marriage to a Welshman named Edmund Tudor, their son Henry would one day be the last male of the House of Lancaster through the Beaufort line to John of Gaunt, and thus descended from Edward III himself.

With the mighty Nevilles and the indomitable Beauforts in their lineage, Elizabeth, Anne and Margaret of York were already connected to England's ruling house, yet it was through their father that their family's real link to the English royal family, and to the subsequent power that they would claim, came about. Their father was, of course, Richard Plantagenet, Duke of York, and through both his mother, Anne Mortimer, and his father, Richard of Conisburgh, Richard's family tree also wound its way back to Edward III. It was these lines of descent that would one day lead him to challenge an anointed king in a power struggle that would define English history.

Richard of York's most direct line back to King Edward was through his mother, but as this took him back through a female descendant of

Edward III, it was considered a weaker link. Richard's mother, Anne, was the great-granddaughter of Lionel, Duke of Clarence, Edward's second eldest son to survive to adulthood. Lionel had fathered only one daughter with his wife Elizabeth, named Philippa, presumably in honour of his mother, the queen. Philippa of Clarence married one of the Mortimer Earls of March – Edmund, the 3rd Earl. A union between their eldest son Roger and a Lady Alianore Holland led to the birth of Anne Mortimer.

Anne Mortimer had married Richard of Conisburgh in secret in 1408. Together they had three children: Isabel, Henry and Richard. Born on 22 September 1411, Richard would never get to know his mother as tragically she died shortly after his birth.

Richard's lineage back to Edward III through his paternal line was slightly more fractured and also through a more junior line. His father, Richard of Conisburgh, was a younger son of Edmund of Langley, the 1st Duke of York. In theory the dukedom should never have been his to inherit as the younger son of a younger son. But circumstances conspired that in 1415, when he was just 4 years old, Richard found himself the sole living male in his family, inheriting the title of Duke of York from his uncle, and becoming the third duke to bear that name.

The rank of duke had been invented by King Edward III for his sons and, during his lifetime, he created his three eldest sons Dukes of Cornwall, Clarence and Lancaster respectively. Later, in 1377, after Richard II had ascended the throne, it was he who awarded his uncle Edmund Langley (Edward's fourth son) the title of Duke of York[13] and later, in 1385, his other uncle, Thomas of Woodstock, was promoted to Duke of Gloucester.

Before becoming a duke, Edmund of Langley had been known as the Earl of Cambridge, a title he had been awarded in 1362, just a few years prior to his father's death. Ten years later, on 11 July 1372, he had married Isabella of Castille, the younger sister of Constance who had married John of Gaunt. It was also during the mid-1370s that Edmund came into possession of Fotheringhay Castle, beginning its long association with the York family.

Edmund and Isabella had three children together: Edward of York (born 1373), Constance of York (born 1374) and Richard of Conisburgh, Earl of Cambridge (born c.1385). After Isabella's death, Edmund married for a second time to a lady named Joan Holland, but this marriage produced no issue.

Edmund died at Kings Langley on 1 August 1402, aged 61 years old, and the title of Duke of York immediately passed to his eldest son Edward. A later exhumation of a body presumed to be Edmund in 1877 by Professor George Rolleston revealed a fragment of grey/red hair near the skull. Author Matthew Lewis, in his biography of Richard, Duke of York, reasonably suggests that if this hair fragment did indeed belong to Edmund, it could be the source of the flame-red hair found in the Tudor line of Henry VIII and Elizabeth I, Edmund's three and four-times great-grandchildren.[14]

Edward, the 2nd Duke of York, maintained a good relationship with his cousin, Henry IV, and Henry's son, Henry V, who he accompanied to France in 1415 as part of the English retinue that fought at Agincourt. Sadly, it was here that Edward's life ended; he was one of the few English casualties that day. He was in his early forties when he died, and his body was brought back across the channel and buried beneath the step leading to the choir in the church of St Mary and All Saints, Fotheringhay.[15]

As Edward had produced no issue from either of his marriages, when he died the title Duke of York should have passed to his younger brother, Richard of Conisburgh, but just a few months before Edward's death in 1415, Conisburgh managed to get himself executed for treason. As a younger son, he was not particularly wealthy and it may have been in the hope of some sort of financial gain that he decided to involve himself in a plot to remove King Henry V from the throne and replace him with his brother-in-law, Edmund Mortimer, 5th Earl of March. Mortimer, brother to Conisburgh's late wife, Anne, could also claim descent from Edward III, but he seemingly had no desire to make a grab for power as it was he who revealed the plot to the king. Conisburgh was subsequently arrested and beheaded on 5 August 1415. A few months later, in October of that year, Edward Duke of York died and all his lands and wealth passed to his nephew, Richard Plantagenet, who was just 4 years old when he became the third Duke of York.

Initially the young orphaned boy was handed into the care of a man named Robert Waterton[16] and the York estates were placed under the control of the Crown. Although Richard's father had been executed, he was never attainted, so the lands were to be held in trust until he reached his majority. When, in 1422, Henry V died, his son, who would now become Henry VI, was just a babe in arms. Around this time,

Richard's wardship was sold to Ralph Neville for 3,000 marks,[17] and Richard moved to the Neville home of Raby Castle where he entered the sphere of a young girl named Cecily, an encounter that would shape the rest of his life and the future of England.

Arriving at Raby Castle as a young boy on the cusp of becoming a teenager, there may not have been an instant connection between Richard and his future bride, Cecily. The age difference between them – Richard was around 11 years old, Cecily just 7 – was small in number but vast in maturity, and it is likely that Richard would have been interested in more grown-up pastimes than spending a lot of time with a young girl. How much of a friendship they had or whether they spent any time together at all is now lost in the annals of time.

Raby Castle itself, Cecily's childhood home, was a large and striking house for the young Nevilles to grow up in with plenty of outside space for them to run around and be children in. Describing Raby in the early 1500s, Leland wrote: 'there [be] 3 long parkis to Raby [castle], whereof 2 be plenished with dere. The middle park hath a lodge in it; and thereby is a chace, bearing the name of Langely, and hath fallow dere; it is a 3 miles in length'.[18] Leland also notes that the castle was the largest in the north of England and a visit centuries later by King James I saw him declare that Raby was the 'fairest in his dominions'.[19] Even today Raby Castle stands tall and magnificent, still one of the fairest medieval buildings in the country.

Situated a mile north of the village of Staindrop, a previous owner, John de Neville, had obtained a licence in 1379 to 'make a castle of his manor of Raby, and to embattle and crenelate its towers' giving the castle its imposing appearance. Crenellating the house meant the owner had permission to add battlements and, as this then fortified the property, permission had to be sought first from the Crown. The hub of the home was always the great hall and the one at Raby was said to measure an impressive 120 feet long by 36 feet wide. The west end of the hall was crossed by a gallery which was used for music and theatre, and at certain times a band of minstrels would surely have provided entertainment there for Cecily, Richard and the extensive Neville family that inhabited Raby.[20] Perhaps Anne, Elizabeth and Margaret ran around this great hall as children, during a visit to their mother's family home?

Just a few years after arriving at Raby, in January 1425, Richard's uncle, Edmund Mortimer, died. As he also left no children to inherit, his Marcher territories on the Welsh borders and the Earldom of March now became another part of Richard's inheritance. His ever-increasing wealth and his numerous titles lent him a promising future as one of England's most powerful men. As one of the king's closest kin, when he reached around 16 years old, it was decided that he should hasten to London to join the king's household. On 22 March 1428 a letter was sent to Raby from the king and his council requesting his presence.[21] The king himself was still only 6 years old, but the council, headed up by the king's uncles John, Duke of Bedford, and Humphrey, Duke of Gloucester, had decided that Richard, a young man who was clearly going to be rich and powerful when he was of age, would be better treated as a close and trusted relation to the king than left to his own devices.

Whether Cecily and Richard were betrothed by the time he packed his bags and left Raby is unclear. In her biography of Cecily Neville, Amy Licence suggests that it would have been around the time that Cecily reached the age of 13, which was about 1428; perhaps the betrothal took place just before Richard left for court. They had certainly married by 1 August 1429 when a grant was made to 'Richard, Duke of York, and Cecily his wife, noblewoman' to choose a portable altar. If they hadn't already, it would soon be time for them both to leave Raby Castle and set up a home of their own. The York family had begun.

# Chapter 3

# A young family of York

With the banks of the River Nene to the south and surrounded by extensive lands which included two large deer parks, Fotheringhay Castle was perched atop a small hill with beautiful views across the Northamptonshire countryside and nearby Rockingham hunting forest. A typical motte and bailey castle, it had come into the possession of Edmund Langley, the 1st Duke of York, in 1377 and he had spent much time and money enlarging the castle, rebuilding the keep and adding a great pond, which would have been used by the castle occupants for the provision of fresh fish. Ownership of the castle transferred to Richard of York as part of his inheritance, and Fotheringhay would very quickly become Richard and Cecily's favoured property after their marriage and the place they would make their primary residence. Many years later, Cecily's will would demonstrate her attachment to Fotheringhay throughout her life; she left books, ecclesiastical vestments and a great canopy of state made of crimson cloth of gold to the collegiate church of St Mary and All Saints, just a stone's throw from the castle.[1]

The castle had begun life as a single stone tower, with two chapels, a great hall, chambers and the kitchen all situated within the bailey. Access was via a drawbridge across a moat. In a later century, well after the Yorks had left the safety of its walls, Fotheringhay would become most famous as the prison of Mary, Queen of Scots, who was held here from 1586–87, until her execution in the great hall. By the time it was demolished in 1625, the castle had changed considerably, each of its occupants making their own additions to the once simple tower. The very last description of the castle in its glory tells us of a double moat that had been constructed, using water from the River Nene and the brook on the eastern side. A set of stairs just past the drawbridge led up to some 'fair lodgings' and then rose again to the wardrobe.

The great hall, which bore witness to many scenes of the House of York over the years and that would also be the last place Mary Queen of

Scots would ever gaze upon on this earth, was described as 'wonderful spacious'. Other rooms that merited a mention included the chapel, goodly lodgings, a great dining room and a large room 'well garnished with pictures'. Outside the main dwellings was a buttery, large brewhouses and bakehouses, and 'houses convenient for offices'.[2]

But the Fotheringhay that Richard and Cecily first came to know would have been a much simpler construction and it was here that on Monday, 10 August 1439, they were joined by the first new member of the York family when Cecily gave birth to a baby girl. They named her Anne.

With infant death a common occurrence, babies were baptised as soon as possible after birth. Anne, within days of her arrival into the world, would have been christened in one of the two chapels contained within the inner bailey of the castle, or perhaps in the nearby church of St Mary and All Saints.

If the christening happened at the latter, she would have been carried by her godparents and accompanied by other family members out of the castle grounds through the main gatehouse on the north-west side. They would have continued in procession across to the parish church which had been rebuilt by the first two dukes and then, as now, contained the mausoleum of the House of York. Anne's mother, Cecily, would not have been part of the christening party as she would be completing her lying-in period. As custom dictated, she would remain in her confinement room until approximately a month after the birth, when she would have then been churched and allowed to return to normal life.

The collegiate church of St Mary and All Saints stood between the River Nene and the Willow Brook, and also offered idyllic views across the countryside. The church was built by King Edward III, who also built a college on the south side of the building. Construction work had begun again in 1434 when Richard, Duke of York, commissioned a parish church to be built on the western side, which may have still been in progress at the time of Anne's christening. Arriving at the church, the gathered guests would have been greeted by Richard Wancourt, clergyman of the parish since 1437, who would have conducted the christening service. After the ceremony, if the returning party had glanced up at the castle's grey keep as they approached the drawbridge, they would have seen the York family badge of the falcon and fetterlock proudly displayed above them.[3] This was the York family heartlands and on this day in August 1439, the family of York were blessing their first child and giving thanks for her safe arrival into the world.

By the time Anne of York was born, Richard and Cecily had been married for over a decade, but it seems that thus far they had not been blessed with a child. There is a possibility that Anne was not their first child, and suggestions that the couple had borne another earlier daughter, whom they had named Joan, cannot be proved or denied. If Joan had existed, she was most likely named after Cecily's mother, but her birth is unsubstantiated and she certainly did not survive. Indeed, there may have also been other miscarriages or stillbirths that went unrecorded. Or Anne may simply have been their first child; christened with a name that was surely in tribute to Richard's mother, Anne Mortimer.

Friar Osberne Bokenham of the Augustinian priory of Clare, in his poem which details the children born to Cecily and Richard, seems to concur that Anne was their firstborn:

> Sir aftir the tyme of longe bareynesse
> God first sent Anne, which signyfieth grace,
> In token that al her hertis hevynesse
> He as for bareynesse wold fro hem chace
> Harry, Edward and Edmonde, eche in his place
> Succedid; and after tweyn daughters came
> Elizabeth and Margarete, and afterward William.
> John aftir William next borne was,
> Which bothe be passed to goddis grace:
> George was next, and after Thomas
> Borne was, which sone aftir did pace
> By the pathe of dethe to the hevenly place
> Richard liveth yet: but last of alle
> Was Ursula, to him whom God list calle.[4]

Speculation as to why it took the couple so long to bear children from this distance of time is perhaps a fruitless task. Not all couples conceive immediately, they may have spent long amounts of time apart in the early years of their marriage, there could have been an underlying medical issue with one or both of them, and any number of other reasons. Cecily may even have suffered a chain of unrecorded miscarriages that befell many women during a time when medical expertise on pregnancy and childbirth was scant. Whatever the reason, baby Anne arrived safe and sound in the summer of 1439 giving her parents reason to rejoice.

The infant Anne's care would have involved many childhood rituals that we would simply find peculiar in the twenty-first century. Common advice for midwives and new mothers was that newborns should be covered in roses ground with salt, and that from birth their limbs should be swaddled to prevent them growing crooked. Two or three times a day they should be unbound and washed with a silk or linen cloth; in the winter with hot water and in the summer with lukewarm. If bathed, they should be anointed, using an oil with myrtle or roses, before being re-swaddled.[5]

When Anne was tiring, it would have been recommended that she was put to sleep in a dark place until her sight was 'gathered and joined' … 'too bright a light will hurt and divide the sight and may give [babies] a squint'. The position of her cradle was also important and 'should be positioned in such a place that neither the beams of the sun by day neither of the moon by night come in on the infant'.[6]

To encourage babies to feed, advice was given for the nurse or mother to rub the roof of the baby's mouth and its gums with a finger covered in honey to cleanse and comfort the inner part of the mouth and also to excite appetite. Families of a higher status such as Anne's would have employed a wet nurse to feed their babies. Wanting the best for their children, they would look to employ a woman who was well presented with a good diet for it was believed that any ailment that affected the child would come from the milk. Advice to avoid 'evil milk' was common and if the child did sicken, medicine was given to the nurse and not the child.[7]

Anne's first few years would have been spent in the nursery at Fotheringhay or at one of the other numerous properties owned by the Yorks. It was usual for the medieval household to be peripatetic and that didn't just include people; household goods would be loaded up onto carts to be moved on to another residence. This afforded families the luxury of being able to travel around the country, and also allowed thorough cleaning of the properties whilst the lord and lady were absent. Servants would also travel with the household, with a few remaining behind to clear and maintain the house, and older children would accompany their parents on horseback whilst younger children would be carried in litters. The duke's duties at court and on his many estates meant he travelled often during Anne's younger years. Depending on his intended length of absence, she would have either travelled with her parents or been left behind at Fotheringhay with her nurse whilst her parents attended their business.

Anne was not to remain an only child for long. Whatever the reason for her parents' long period of childlessness was seemingly no longer an issue as just under two years after her birth, Anne was joined by a younger brother. Henry Plantagenet, undoubtedly a much longed-for first son, was born at Hatfield on 10 February 1441. Why Cecily was at Hatfield is unclear – it was not a York property and at that time, the manor of Hatfield was one of the residences of the Bishop of Ely. In 1441 Cecily would have stayed at the old manor house; it would be another four decades before Cardinal John Morton (Bishop of Ely 1479–86) would begin work on building the present Hatfield Old Palace. The most likely explanation for Henry's birth at Hatfield was that Cecily was mid-journey. She may have been travelling to or from London when her labour pains arrived earlier than she had expected, causing her to seek the nearest place of refuge for her to give birth.

This first York son was named Henry after the king and recognising the compliment, King Henry sent jewels to Cecily to celebrate the new arrival. But baby Henry did not live long; whether it was days, weeks or months went unrecorded, but he had certainly died before 1445[8] and it's probable he did not even reach his first birthday. Anne, at just 18 months old, may never even have met this new baby brother whose life on earth was so short.

If Anne had been at Fotheringhay during her mother's unexpected stay at Hatfield, she would soon be joining her parents on a journey that would take her much further afield. Her father had just been offered the position of Lieutenant General of France, a post that was to last five years. Given the length of absence, both Cecily and Anne would travel with him across the English Channel.

By 1441, Henry VI, now a 20-year-old man, had been independently in charge of the country for the previous four years, assuming the reins of government in 1437 when he reached the age of 16. His uncle, John, Duke of Bedford, who had been responsible for English interests in France for much of Henry's minority had died in 1435, and Henry's trusted advisor, Richard Beauchamp, Earl of Warwick, who had held the post of Lieutenant of France and Normandy since 1473, had died in 1439. The king therefore needed someone reliable and capable to oversee the English territory across the sea.

Tensions between the French and English Crowns had existed for centuries. The king's father, Henry V, the great warrior, had earned a legendary reputation as a hero during his lifetime and to later generations, due to his unwavering zeal to reclaim French territory and bring it back under English control. Although not fully successful, his quest had culminated in the mighty Battle of Agincourt in 1415 that saw a small English army of an estimated 6,000 troops defeat a French army of around 60,000. In the subsequent Treaty of Troyes struck with the French king, Charles VI, Henry V had taken Charles' daughter, Catherine of Valois, as his bride, and had himself named heir apparent to the French throne. Henry died in August 1422, just a couple of months before he could claim that inheritance and when King Charles himself died in October that year, his son, disinherited by the treaty, immediately had himself crowned in Reims to become Charles VII.

But England's present king, Henry VI, was his father's antithesis in almost every way. Instead of being a strong and influential leader, it seems that Henry saw himself fulfilling the role of a kind father to his subjects, their mentor rather than their champion. A contemporary of Henry's, John Blacman, who served for a while as his chaplain and later became his biographer, described him as 'a simple man, without any crook of craft or untruth as is plain to all. With none did he deal craftily, nor ever would say an untrue word to any, but framed his speech always to speak the truth'.[9] The passion that his father had shown in invading France was not echoed by his son, although he recognised the need to protect the English-controlled territories across the sea. And who better to send to do that than his trusted kin, the Duke of York.

The York family's move to France had been somewhat delayed by Cecily's necessary stay at Hatfield, but once she had completed her lying-in period, they were ready to make the long journey down to the south coast and across the sea to their new home. On 6 May 1441 they began their journey, heading to Portsdown in Hampshire, where they would then set sail across the English Channel to the French port of Honfleur. Approaching the age of 2, toddler Anne had many aunts to fuss over her on the voyage, as the Yorks were accompanied by the Countesses of Oxford and Eu, as well as the Duchess of Bedford and her husband, better known to history as Jacquetta Woodville and her husband Richard

Woodville. The Woodvilles were returning to France, having previously lived there during Jacquetta's first marriage to the king's uncle, the Duke of Bedford. As an English duchess, after Bedford's death the gift of her marriage had belonged to the king. But Jacquetta had fallen in love with Woodville, a young soldier in her husband's retinue, and they had married in secret, returning to England to a heavy fine from Henry VI but eventually receiving his forgiveness.

Arriving in Portsdown on 16 May, the Yorks and their travelling party now had to make their way across the unpredictable strip of water that separated England from the continent. Their large entourage, which was also made up of some 30 knights, around 900 men at arms and 2,700 archers,[10] must have caused quite a commotion as they awaited the arrival of the ships that would transport them across the sea. No doubt the hustle and bustle caused by such a large amount of people must have provided a young Anne with a constant distraction to keep her occupied. The Yorks and their retinue remained in Portsdown for over a month, eventually setting sail around 25 June,[11] and landing in Normandy in late June 1441. Once on French shores, they began the last part of their journey to their final destination, the majestically beautiful town of Rouen and its castle on the banks of the River Seine.

Anne may have been too young to ever remember her arrival into Rouen, but those travelling with her may never have forgotten their first impression of the beautiful old town, essentially described as a river city. A later nineteenth century-visitor entering Rouen for the first time wrote:

> The effect which is produced upon the stranger who, for the first time, walks through the streets of Rouen is described by all travellers as remarkable and peculiar. The general arrangement of the city, the character of its architecture … all serve to convince him that he is decidedly in one of the most picturesque, though may not be in one of the most elegant, cities that he has ever seen.[12]

About 70 miles to the north-west of Paris, Rouen is situated in a beautiful valley, encircled to the north by lofty hills and the south by the river. The best viewpoint, according to these late Georgian travellers, was from St Catherine's Hill with its magnificent views across the whole town. By the early nineteenth century, it was no longer a walled city;

its walls and castles were levelled to the ground many years before 'and peaceful boulevards are now to be seen where formerly bristling ramparts frowned'. But in Anne's time the city would have been well defended by stone walls.

Once Anne and her family reached Rouen itself, they headed to the castle which was to be their home for the next five years. Today only the tower of Rouen Castle survives, but when the York family lived there, it was a large and comfortable residence furnished with royal apartments that Cecily and Richard would have occupied, alongside a nursery for Anne and any future siblings that she could expect to join her.[13] The castle itself was built by Philip Augustus in 1205. Circular in shape, it had six towers and two thick curtain walls. During his governance of France, the Duke of Bedford had also lived at the castle. Just a decade before the arrival of Anne and her family, it had been the prison of Joan of Arc, the young French heroine whose 'visions' of a French victory in the Anglo-French wars brought her to the attention of the English authorities and eventually led to her being burnt at the stake. After her death, Joan's ashes were cast into the River Seine. Rumours of her saintliness and miracles attributed to her, as well as her heroism in the face of the English army, led to her canonisation by the Roman Catholic church in 1920.

Within the defensive walls of this castle in the capital town of Normandy, the York family set up home in style. As they settled into life in Rouen, Anne's father was often away on military business and Anne would have spent much time in the company of her mother and the other women who had travelled with their husbands, who no doubt kept themselves entertained within the castle and town. Her mother, Cecily, was supposedly so extravagant that during their time in France, an officer of the household had to keep an eye on her expenditure. Their residence was so luxurious that it even boasted a cushioned privy. One of Cecily's purchases, that of lavishly jewelled dresses, may perhaps even have included clothes for the young Anne.[14]

Anne would spend the first ten months in Rouen as an only child, but after losing their first son in 1441, Cecily had quickly fallen pregnant again. In April 1442, Anne was joined by a new sibling when Cecily gave birth to her second baby boy. This new brother for Anne was born on Saturday 28 April 1442 in the royal quarters of the castle. He was named Edward.

Shortly after his birth, Edward was christened in the castle chapel, with Lady Saye acting as his godmother and Thomas, Lord Scales and an unidentified second man acting as his godfathers.[15] A local woman named Anne de Caux was brought in as his nurse and Edward would clearly become fond of her. Many years later, in 1474, this little boy, who no-one at the time could have predicted would go on to be King Edward IV, awarded her an annual pension of £20. This award was also continued by Richard III, illustrating perhaps how much of an integral part she would play in the lives of the York children.[16]

This first year in their Rouen life would later come back to haunt the whole family when, many years later, Edward's paternity would be called into question. Within weeks of arriving in Rouen at the end of June, the Duke of York had set out with the English army to Pontoise. He did not return until late August. There was, of course, no imagination rich enough in 1441/42 to predict that Edward would ever become king, and certainly no-one could have predicted that a son who had not even been born yet would make the accusations. But, in 1483, a York son, Richard, would claim that his brother, Edward, had been a bastard son, a product of his mother's relations with an archer named Blaybourne. Rumours that had apparently been in circulation before he ever dared utter them officially.

That this wasn't immediately discredited in 1483 is perhaps because the circumstances of the Yorks' first few months in Rouen meant that it could indeed have been a possibility. Edward's birth date of April 1442 would, working on a typical gestation period, indicate a conception date of late July or early August 1441. Having arrived in Rouen in late June, and York's subsequent departure just a couple of weeks later, it is indeed possible to argue that York could not have been with Cecily at the time of her supposed conception as he left in early July and did not arrive back until 20 August. To further demonstrate the argument, it is claimed that Edward's christening, which took place in a quiet ceremony in the castle chapel, unlike his later siblings born in France who would receive a cathedral christening, was done so to draw attention away from Cecily's indiscretion. Taking that into account, the rumours about Edward's parentage could indeed have been true. What these arguments don't consider is that a pregnancy term can, and does, of course, vary, and what is termed a 'normal' pregnancy can include the birth occurring a couple of weeks over or under a due date. If Edward was born two weeks late

28

or two weeks premature, then he could, of course, have been conceived either before York's departure or soon after his return. The Duke of York always acknowledged Edward as his son and, having already lost a son at Hatfield, the small no-fuss christening in the castle chapel could just have been a desire to see Edward baptised quickly; no doubt the loss of their first son was at the forefront of their minds. He may even have been a sickly baby, giving them even more cause for worry and making the need for a hastily arranged christening even more urgent.

Sickly or not, Edward survived and thrived, and he and 4-year-old Anne were joined a year later by another brother, Edmund, born on 17 May 1443. Then just over a year after Edmund's birth, Anne was joined by her first female sibling when on Monday, 21 September 1444, Cecily gave birth to her second daughter, whom they would name Elizabeth.

Edmund and Elizabeth's christenings were much larger and more lavish affairs with both being held in the nearby Rouen Cathedral; within the chapter book of the cathedral, there are records for the reception of Edmund's christening on 18 May 1443 and Elizabeth's on 22 September 1444.[17]

The beautiful old cathedral in Rouen stood majestically in the town and was described by our later Georgian visitors as 'a magnificent structure, of great extent, and highly ornamented'.[18] The cathedral and castle residents seemingly enjoyed a good relationship; another entry in the cathedral chapter book dated 30 October 1442 gives permission for the Duke of York to use ornaments and vestments from the cathedral to decorate the chapel of Rouen Castle in celebration of the feast of All Saints.[19] It seems the cathedral was also held in great esteem by a past resident of the castle, the Duke of Bedford, who left the chapterhouse a golden chalice garnished with gems, a pair of golden censers and a silver-gilt crucifix as gifts in his will. The duke was buried in the choir of the cathedral, and the canons reportedly took diligent care of his tomb, which was sadly destroyed in 1562, although his coffin was found in 1866 in its original position on the right side of the altar.

With just five years between Anne and Elizabeth, they likely formed a close relationship as they grew up. Their two male siblings, Edward and Edmund, would invariably have been brought up differently to their sisters, highlighting the different directions that their lives would be expected to go in. During their time in France, the Duke of York began looking into securing French estates for his second youngest son, Edmund, who, of course, was only an infant at this point. But the aim was to set him up in the future as a wealthy Norman landowner. For Edward, as York's eldest son and heir, he would, of course, inherit all of York's English estates and, during their time in France, York also initiated discussions with King Charles of France for a potential marriage between Edward and one of Charles' younger daughters. But for Anne and Elizabeth, their future would involve a good marriage, to whichever man their father chose for them; the expectation that they would become good wives and mothers, and bear sons to carry on another family name.

As the sisters grew up in Rouen, they would have enjoyed a typical medieval lifestyle similar to their English counterparts, albeit infused perhaps with the sophistication of the French culture. Although Elizabeth was probably too young to have any memories of their time in France, Anne, as a young child, may have loved this hustling, bustling town on the banks of the river that was their home for five years. Perhaps she remembered trips to the river itself which, much like the Thames, would have been a scene of great activity, with boats steered by watermen carrying their passengers back and forth as they went about their daily lives. Maybe Anne and her siblings were taken to the harbour, which would have been full of apprentices, local tradesmen and townspeople spilling out into the riverside streets from the local inns. Or perhaps they promenaded along the bank on the far side, the fashionable walkway of all the ladies of the town.[20]

Feasts and saints' days would also have been celebrated and, along with All Saints in October for which the castle was decorated with items from the cathedral, Anne and her siblings may also have celebrated Epiphany and eaten the French Galette des Rois ('king cake') – a traditionally French dessert served in French households on 6 January. Recipes for the Galette varied over the years, but the idea was that dividing up the cake would 'draw the kings' to the Epiphany. The interior of the Galette contained a single charm, la fève, which was traditionally a broad bean, and whoever found the charm would become king or queen for the day. In celebration of the feast of Epiphany, the ships in the harbour would have been all lit up and the tradesman in the town would have sent gifts to their customers.[21]

What must have been a memorable event for the York siblings took place in early 1445 when a future queen of England came to stay. As part of the peace talks which had taken place between England and France, a marriage had been agreed between King Henry VI and Margaret of Anjou, a daughter of René, Duke of Anjou, a favourite of Charles VII. Temporarily resting during her journey towards her new life in England, Margaret spent two weeks at Rouen Castle over Easter. The York children would surely have met their new queen and although Elizabeth was not even a year old, Anne may certainly have remembered such an auspicious occasion. When Margaret was rested and ready to travel again, the Duke of York accompanied her on her onward journey to Honfleur, where she would make the sea crossing to England.

And it was a journey that Anne, Elizabeth and their siblings would soon be making themselves when York's tenure in Rouen ended in September 1445. The whole family, including their French nurse, Madame De Caux, arrived back in England by Christmas. During the journey back to England, Cecily would have been in the early stages of another pregnancy and on Tuesday, 3 May 1446, Anne and Elizabeth welcomed another sister when their mother gave birth to a baby girl. She was christened Margaret, almost certainly in honour of their recent house guest, the new English queen, Margaret of Anjou.

Although the family were now back in England, Margaret's actual birthplace is unknown. The most obvious location would be their main home at Fotheringhay, but some reports note that baby Margaret was baptised at Waltham Abbey.[22] The Duke of York would often travel into London and although he would later be gifted Baynard's Castle to use as his London base, it is likely that before then he would have stayed at various guest houses along his route into the capital, such as that at Waltham Abbey.[23] It is therefore quite possible that Cecily was travelling with her husband and gave birth to Margaret at the Abbey.

As well as gaining a new sister, 1446 was to be a momentous year for Anne for another reason. Just a few short months before the birth of Margaret, Anne had been married to her cousin, Henry Holland, fulfilling the marriage contract that had been agreed between the two families in August 1445. The Hollands were not a significantly rich family, but they were another of the king's closest relatives. Henry was the son of John Holland, Earl of Huntingdon and Duke of Exeter, and his first wife, Anne Stafford. Henry's grandfather, also named John, was a half-brother of Richard II. He had married Elizabeth of Lancaster, a daughter of John of Gaunt and sister to Henry IV. With these ancestral credentials, Anne and Henry were a good match, and their marriage agreement benefited both parties.

The majority of the Holland estates were in Devon, with the family seat at Dartington Hall. However, a series of land disputes going back many years had left the family cash-poor and Henry's father, John, had become dependent on court favour, spending much of his time either in London or with the English army in France. In 1426, he had married Anne Stafford, a marriage that was concluded without a royal licence and incurred the couple a fine of 1,200 marks which they had to pay the following year. Anne was the widow of Edmund Mortimer, the last Earl of March, and she brought with her into the marriage a good proportion of income from estates in the Welsh Marches. Henry Holland, their only son, was born in 1430. When Anne Stafford died two years after his birth, in September 1432, John went on to marry Beatrice of Portugal, the widowed countess of Arundel. They were married for seven years and she travelled with him on one of his postings to Gascony, dying there in 1439. In 1442 John married his third wife, Anne Montagu, and in recognition of his service to the Crown, he was restored to the dukedom of Exeter on 6 January 1444. The title also brought him a £40 annuity from the county of Devon.[24]

Anne and Henry's wedding ceremony took place on 30 January 1446 at the Bishop of Ely's chapel at Hatfield. Anne was just 6 years old, Henry around 16. As part of the marriage contract, Henry's father, John, was to enfeoff 400 marks worth of lands to go to Henry and Anne and was to retain wardship rights over them until Henry became of age. Provisions were also made if either partner were to die early, or if Anne left the marriage before she was 14. The Duke of York agreed to pay a dowry of £1,500 on the wedding day and 1,000 marks annually thereafter, and he also paid for the wedding itself, although John Holland purchased the wedding outfit for his son.[25] John also agreed to maintain the couple until Henry's twentieth birthday when he would come into his own inheritance.

Marriage at such a young age is so alien to us in the twenty-first century that we can only imagine how Anne would have felt about it. As a mere 6-year-old, was she excited about the new dress she was to wear, nervous about being the centre of attention, resolved to do her duty which no doubt would have been explained to her by her parents? Alliances between families were often sealed by the joining of their children in matrimony and although 6 years old was very young even in those days, it was not extraordinary.

Guests invited to the winter ceremony that day, wrapped up in their finery against the cold January weather, would have watched as Anne and Henry pledged themselves to each other in a service officiated by Richard Caudray. As Anne recited the words, 'Here I take you for my weddyd husbond and alle other forsake and oonly you take terme of my lyfe [*sic*]', perhaps at her tender age she wouldn't quite have appreciated that her union to this man, chosen for her by her parents, would shape the direction of her life as she grew up into a young woman, wife and mother. The reading of the banns provided a small disruption to the formalities when one Thomas Mannyng objected to their marriage on grounds of consanguinity, but the objection was quickly denied as a bull of dispensation had already been obtained and a copy was produced as proof by a man named John de Obizis.[26]

The couple would not, of course, be expected to consummate the marriage until Anne was much older. But it was customary for young brides to live with their husband's family after the wedding and John Holland had agreed to support them until they were old enough to run their own household. Prior to the ceremony, Anne's mother must have sat her down and explained what her marriage would entail and how she would have to leave the family unit. Even though Anne would have understood what was expected of her, it must still have been hard for her to know that she would be leaving her parents and siblings and the life that she had known. Like his father, Henry lived mainly in London, either at the Tower of London, where John Holland was Constable of the Tower, or in their London house at Coldharbour. A beautiful riverside mansion overlooking the Thames, it was originally called Cold Harbrogh. During the reign of Edward III, the house came into the possession of Sir John Poultney, a draper and four times Mayor of London. This led to it becoming known as Poulteney's Inn. Described by Stow as 'a right fair and stately house', it eventually came into the possession of the Holland family.[27] It is most likely that it was to here that the young Anne went to live in 1446, probably into the care of Henry's stepmother, Anne Montagu.

With a decade in age between Anne and her husband, she may not have been much in Henry's company in the early years of their marriage. Henry Holland was already showing signs of the impetuous man he would become and likely had little interest in his 6-year-old bride.

A learned young man who had spent some time studying at King's Hall in Cambridge, between 1439 and 1442,[28] Henry was keen to make his mark in the world and it seems that the king had some regard for him. In February 1446 he was granted the position of Admiral and Constable of the Tower alongside his father; a role that would be reconfirmed the following year. But his own father had seemingly also recognised signs of rashness in his son as, in July 1446, he made detailed instructions, putting his estates into the care of trusted friends and advisors with further instructions issued in February and March 1447 that the estates should only be released to his son when they felt he was responsible enough to run them.

With Anne now living away from the family home, it would be down to 2-year-old Elizabeth to become a playmate for her newborn baby sister, Margaret. Upon their return from France, their father would spend much of 1446 and 1447 administering his estates, and Elizabeth and Margaret would spend those years in the nursery at Fotheringhay, alongside their brothers, Edward and Edmund. A now ever-expanding family, a further son, William, would briefly join them on 17 July 1447, but sadly, like Henry five years before, William did not survive. Then just ten days after his son's birth, York was given the post of Lieutenant of Ireland, news that meant the entire family would soon be packing up and departing England's shores once more.

By 1447, King Henry VI had been married to Margaret of Anjou for two years and she was proving to be a strong-willed and often contentious queen, not afraid of letting her opinions be known. Showing favour to those men she felt she could trust, her closest friends and advisors were William de la Pole, Earl of Suffolk, and Edmund Beaufort, Earl of Somerset. In February 1447, a few months before York's Irish appointment, the council had made a shocking move when it summoned the king's uncle, Humphrey, Duke of Gloucester, before Parliament on charges of treason; a move that many believed was initiated by the queen. Gloucester had held the reins of power in England during Henry's minority. Approaching his fifty-seventh birthday, the summons was in the name of the king, but it was no secret that Margaret did not consider him a friend and many believed she had influenced the king in this matter. Gloucester's arrest was a huge blow to the Duke of York, who, like Gloucester, was one of the old guard and even more so because Gloucester had been a mentor to the duke when he was a young man. Taken into custody, Gloucester unfortunately (or perhaps, fortunately) died before any charges could be brought against him. With Gloucester out of the picture, York himself began to feel pushed more and more out of the king's confidence, and it could be considered that his sudden appointment to Lieutenant of Ireland was, in effect, more of a banishment that a promotion, dispatching him to faraway shores and away from the king's ear. Whether York was of this opinion or not we cannot know, but he accepted the office which came with a remuneration of 4,000 marks for the first year and 2,000 for each succeeding year.[29]

The York family already had connections to Ireland. Lionel, Duke of Clarence, had married Elizabeth de Burgh, daughter of the Earl of Ulster, and Lionel himself had been Governor of Ireland. He also became Earl of Ulster when his father-in-law died, and part of the Mortimer inheritance included estates in Ireland. The Earldom of Ulster and Lordships of Trim and Leith had also passed down to York through the Mortimers. In addition, as a separate part of his inheritance, York had acquired the Earldom of Cork, which was passed down from the 2nd Duke of York.[30]

Having accepted the post, it seems York was in no actual hurry to make the move across the Irish Sea, which may indicate that he also felt this was, in effect, a role designed to take him away from court business. Whilst the family were still preparing for the move, Anne, who had spent the previous eighteen months away from her family, would now find that the move to Ireland would become a reality for her too. For in August 1447, Henry's father, John Holland, died, and Henry's wardship was awarded to the Duke of York, meaning Anne most likely returned home.

John Holland had reportedly been ailing since late 1446, when he began to plan for the future of his estates. He died at Combes in Kent (possibly the parish of Combes in Greenwich?)[31] on 5 August 1447. Upon his father's death, Henry Holland became the Duke of Exeter, and Anne, as his wife, was the new Duchess of Exeter. Aged just 8, she may perhaps have been more delighted to find herself back in the bosom of her family than she was to receive the title of duchess.

For whatever reason, perhaps some clever stalling by York, it would be another twenty-two months before the family actually set sail across the Irish Sea. After losing their son, William, in July 1447, Cecily had fallen pregnant again and, on 7 November 1448, she gave birth to another son, John, at Neyte. Neyte was part of the manor of the Abbot of Westminster, an area extending south towards the Thames, and again we can assume that Cecily was in London with her husband at the time. Once again, though, tragedy struck and their young son, the fifth born to York and Cecily, did not survive.

By May 1449, with York having tied up his administration and the family having no doubt grieved the loss of another York son, they were packed up, ready to move and unable to delay any longer. There are questions as to which of their children travelled with York and Cecily to Ireland, but given their closeness as a family and the fact that York had committed to a ten-year stay, there is a strong likelihood that they would all have gone. Elizabeth, aged 5, and 3-year-old Margaret would almost certainly have accompanied their parents. York's ward, Henry Holland, by then a 19-year-old young man, seemingly remained behind in England. Anne, still not quite 10, may also have stayed behind, but as she was back in the care of her family and she and Henry would not yet have been living as man and wife, it is highly possible that she went too.

As for their male siblings, Edmund and Edward, they would eventually be installed in a separate household at Ludlow but the timing of this transition for the boys is unclear. Older sons from noble families would often be set up in their own household as they grew into adulthood, enabling them to concentrate on their studies and grow into accomplished young men. Different historians have differing views of when Edward and Edmund began their stay at Ludlow, with some indicating they would have gone there from around the age of 5 or 6, and others believing it was later. Edward was 9 years old in 1449, Edmund just 8 and, once again, given the family believed they would be residing in Ireland for the next ten years (the agreed term of York's tenure), and their closeness as a family unit, I think it is highly likely that they would have travelled with their parents.

Leaving Fotheringhay in May with a contingency of around 600 men, the Yorks arrived at Beaumaris Castle on the Isle of Anglesey, a distance of over 200 miles, by 22 June.[32] Here they probably rested for a few days before making their way across the Irish Sea. And whilst they were there, the York girls would almost certainly have learned of the castle's most famous prisoner who was in residence at the time, a lady named Eleanor Cobham.

Eleanor was the second wife of the now deceased Humphrey, Duke of Gloucester. The duke had once been married to Jacqueline, Countess of Hainaut, and Eleanor had become his mistress sometime around 1425. Gloucester arranged an annulment of his marriage in 1428, making way for him to marry Eleanor. For a while the couple lived a dream life, developing their manor at Greenwich into a pleasure garden they called La Pleasaunce (also known as The Palace of Placentia). Eleanor was intelligent and ambitious, the perfect partner for the cultivated and pleasure-loving Humphrey. As a couple they liked to entertain magnificently and their friends were an intellectual group of learned musicians, poets and scholars. But after the death of Gloucester's brother, the Duke of Bedford, Gloucester had become heir to his nephew's throne and Eleanor reportedly became obsessed as to whether her husband would ever become king. Foolishly she decided to commission a horoscope that predicted Henry VI would suffer ill health. Discussing the king's death for any reason was an act of treason and, when her actions were discovered in 1442, Eleanor was arrested on charges of witchcraft. Her loving husband, who had had his first marriage declared unsound so he could marry her, distanced himself from her declaring that their union had been brought about by sorcery.

Eleanor was sentenced, without trial, and was forced to do penance, parading through the streets barefoot and in her undergarments to be shamed in front of the gathered crowds. She was then sent to prison, moving from castle to castle under different custodians until 10 March 1449, just a few months before the Yorks' arrival, she was transferred to Beaumaris under the watchful eye of the king's carver, Sir William Beauchamp, who was constable of the castle.[33] Whilst there, York, once a close friend of her husband's, would surely have paid a visit to her; perhaps Anne, Elizabeth and Margaret were also able to meet the beautiful and unfortunate Eleanor.

After a few days' respite in their journey, the family finally set sail across the Irish Sea, arriving with their retinue in Howth, a small, picturesque village and harbour north-east of Dublin, on 6 July, where the duke was received with great honour. The Earls of Ireland reportedly welcomed him and 'gave him as many beeves for the use of his kitchen as it pleased him to demand'.[34]

Their base whilst in Ireland was to be Trim Castle, although they would also spend time in Dublin, the centre of English rule and where, on 18 October 1449, the Duke of York opened his first parliament. Anne, Elizabeth and Margaret, would, however, have spent much of their time at Trim, an ancient building situated 23 miles from Dublin on the banks of the River Boyne.

The town of Trim was an ancient dwelling, dating back to at least 432 when an abbey was founded there and was once known as Atha Truim (the ford of Trim). During its early history, the town had been a victim of fire several times. The castle that the Yorks would reside in was one of the properties owned by the Duke of York, coming into his possession through the Mortimer inheritance.

The castle itself, surrounded by a large deep ditch, was first built in 1173 by a Hugh de Lacy. Leaving Ireland for a trip to England, de Lacy left it in the hands of a servant, Hugh Tyrell who, after his master had left, suddenly found himself under attack by the King of Connaught. Upon realising he could not defend himself, he fled and burned the castle, determined that their enemies would not be able to take possession. He later returned to repair the remains before de Lacy's return from England. When Hugh de Lacy did return, he continued building and over a thirty-year period he and his son, Walter de Lacy, constructed a magnificent, fortified structure. Most of the castle that is still visible today was completed by 1220.

In 1258, ownership of Trim Castle passed into the de Geneville family through marriage.[35] It was Geoffrey de Geneville who built the great hall beside the keep and founded the Dominican Blackfriary in the north of the town. In 1308 the castle passed into the hands of Roger de Mortimer. The Duke of York also began restoration work to the castle and the parish church during his time in Ireland, eventually restoring it to much of its former glory with the intention of making it a suitable family residence for the next ten years.[36] The castle that the family would call their home was dominated by a monumental three-storey keep. With a massive twenty sides, it was entered by a single door with the lower floor giving access to a staircase and rooms in the side towers. The second floor had a suite of rooms and the third floor had one main room which took up the whole floor and was linked to a gallery. The centrepiece of the castle was the magnificent great hall which looked out over the River Boyne. Built as a defensive structure, the castle was surrounded by curtain walls and the girls may have spent some of their leisure time on the wall walk that linked the towers. Entrance to the castle was through two gate towers, one a west gate that led into the town and the other, the south gate, which led out into the countryside and the road to Dublin. As well as the ditch and the curtain wall, there was a water-filled moat protecting the castle.[37]

Much of the duke's business required him to be in Dublin, and Cecily certainly travelled with her husband when he was there. Whether the York girls went with their parents or remained in Trim is unclear; likely they did both on occasion. If they did travel to Dublin, they would have stayed at the magnificent Dublin Castle, a building that had been in existence since 1204. A year after its construction, a Meiler Fitzhenry was commanded to strengthen the castle, an undertaking that was eventually taken up in 1213 by a Henry de Loundres, who was archbishop and lord justice. He enclosed the fortress with quadrangular walls with four corner towers.[38] The castle needed further restoration in 1415, and again in 1430 when 20 marks per annum were allowed for repairs to the castle hall, building and towers which had been badly damaged by stormy weather and which held the records of the courts of law.[39] Much of the castle that the Yorks would have known was destroyed by fire in 1684.

Whilst Cecily was at Dublin Castle with her husband, she gave birth to another York son. Born on Tuesday, 21 October 1449, he was named George and was surely a most welcome addition to their family after the loss of their last two boys. Baby George was baptised at the Dominican Priory on the other side of the River Liffey to the castle with the Earls of Desmond and Ormond standing as his godfathers.[40] Cecily and York then returned to spend the winter at Trim, perhaps when Anne, Elizabeth and Margaret met their new baby brother for the first time.

As the new year of 1450 dawned bright, the York girls may have been quickly settling into their new homeland. But their parents may not have felt quite so optimistic; back across the sea, at the English court, the queen and her favourites were riding high and York was perhaps already starting to feel that the distance was not working in his favour.

Henry VI was not a strong leader and an undercurrent of discontent had been building for a while amongst the general populace. In April 1450 a full-on rebellion broke out, led by a Kentish man named Jack Cade, an event that the *Croyland Chronicle* believed had been portended a year before by a 'violent and terrible' earthquake that occurred on St George's night 1448, and that some learned teachers had publicly declared was a sign of sinister events to come.[41]

Under the leadership of Cade, some 5,000 men gathered at Blackheath, demanding the end of fighting in France and the end of unpopular taxes. According to the *Croyland Chronicle*, the men fortified their position on the heath with embankments and stakes driven into the ground. They then forced their way into the capital across London Bridge, assaulting the citizens who turned out to defend their city. With all this happening miles away from York and his family in Ireland, it should have been of minor consequence. However, it was to have a huge effect on York's reputation because Jack Cade claimed he was a Mortimer and proudly displayed the York emblems of the falcon and fetterlock on his badge as he made his advance into London.

York immediately wrote to the king to pledge his allegiance, declaring he had nothing to do with the uprising. The king replied, assuring York of his continued trust in him, but the die had been cast and York's enemies were gathering apace.

York had now been in Ireland for just over twelve months and although he was popular with the Irish lords and populace, things were not going as well as they should. He had not been paid any of the stipulated salary, despite writing to the king requesting funds. And now the Cade rebellion highlighted that he was too far away from the court to defend himself against his enemies and the poison they may have been dripping into the king's ear. Realising that the only way to ensure that his loyalty to the king was not in question was to return and defend himself, the York family packed up their belongings. They left Trim on 26 August 1450 and arrived in Dublin two days later.[42] In early September 1450 they set sail, making an unplanned and unannounced return to England. York's sudden return was designed to defend himself and his family, and to pledge his loyalty to the king, but in the end it would have the exact opposite effect.

# Chapter 4

# The duke is dead, long live the king

York's sudden intention to return to England to defend his reputation caused quite a disturbance in London, with the king and court unsure as to whether he was hurrying back as a friend or a foe. As he and his family made shore once again at Beaumaris on Anglesey, attempts were made by members of the royal household to stop him disembarking. They didn't succeed. Whether the family immediately continued their journey or stopped to rest for a day or two is unclear, but if they did stop it would have been the last time York saw Eleanor Cobham as she died on 7 July 1452, still a prisoner on the island. Her remains were interred on Anglesey, most likely in the nearby parish church.

Having landed at Beaumaris in early September, the duke was at his castle at Denbigh by 7 September and arrived at Ludlow Castle shortly after that. It is likely that he left his family within the safety of Ludlow's walls, and by 23 September he had reached Stony Stratford. He arrived in London on 27 September and made his way straight to Westminster.

Seeking an immediate audience with the king, York assured him that he was his true subject. He had returned, he told the king, to defend his good name. He denied he was connected to the rebellion and complained about the unjust accusations of treason. Maintaining that rumours of his involvement had been created by his enemies, he informed the king that now he was back in England, he wished to resume his rightful position as a royal advisor and remove the threat to his lineage: 'the issue that it pleased God to send me of the royal blood' from all who intended 'to have undo me myn issue and corrupt my blode'.[1]

York also complained to the king that he and his family had been hindered from embarking at Beaumaris and that he had been in danger throughout his journey to London, having heard that his enemies had been charged with ensuring he didn't reach the capital. He also told of how some of the king's men had tried to capture and imprison him in Conwy Castle. King Henry heard his complaints and promised to look into them.

Meanwhile, back at Ludlow, the rest of the family must have been waiting on news from their father with some apprehension. Elizabeth and Margaret, aged just 6 and 4 respectively, may not have completely understood the circumstances surrounding their hasty departure from Ireland. Anne, aged 11, would have been more aware of the troubles that her family had been presented with. It is unclear how long they remained in Ludlow or even where the three girls spent the rest of the year; they most likely returned to Fotheringhay with their mother at some point. It was around this time, from around September 1450, however, that their brothers Edward and Edmund were most likely established in their own household at Ludlow, so if the girls did return to Fotheringhay they would have bid farewell to their siblings, with only baby George accompanying them back to Northamptonshire. At Ludlow, Edward and Edmund, by then aged 8 and 7 respectively, were expected to study hard and grow into their roles as the duke's heirs.[2] As Christmas 1450 approached, the Duke of York would spend it at Stratford-le-Bow, perhaps separately from his family.[3] Whether Anne, Elizabeth and Margaret travelled with their mother to be with him, or whether they spent the season with their brothers at Ludlow, or even perhaps alone with their mother at Fotheringhay, the arrival of the new year 1451 would herald the start of an uncertain few years for the whole family.

Assuming Anne had travelled with her family to Ireland, her arrival back into England would have called for a reunion at some point with her husband, Henry. Just a few months before the family's return, on 23 July 1450, Henry Holland had reached the age of 20 and he was granted livery of his lands. In an agreement allowing him to inherit a year earlier than the usual twenty-one years, he now had the means to be financially independent; his wardship to Anne's father also came to an end.

Although Anne and Henry would have been reunited, it is still unlikely that they would yet be spending much time together. Anne was still a child and would have held little interest for the young and ambitious Holland. Later animosities that would show themselves between Holland and his father-in-law may already have been simmering away under the surface. Whilst the Yorks were in Ireland, Henry had almost certainly remained in London mixing in court circles, and he received his first summons to Parliament on 2 September 1450.

When most young men reached their majority, they received their full inheritance but this was not the case for Holland. An intense and headstrong young man, the executors of his father's will had noted John Holland's concerns about his son and paid attention to the clause that stated they were to sell off the lands if Henry contravened any part of the will. As he came of age in 1450, they had not sold any lands but neither would they release them all, recognising that for a young man of his temperament, it would be foolish to allow him such money and power until he was older and hopefully more mature.

Now that the York family were apparently back in England for good, the Duke of York was determined to prove his allegiance to the king. But to do that he had to deal not only with the animosity of Queen Margaret, but also that of her favourite courtier, the Duke of Somerset. Both were clearly keen for York to be out of the picture and not in a position where he could influence the king in any way. For the duke's part, he was keen to maintain a presence so his loyalty could not be called into question. This led to an uneasy atmosphere hanging over all those close to the royal centre of power. Factions were starting to be formed amongst the nobles – those who were in favour with the queen and loyal to the king, and those who also remained loyal to the king but were out of favour and perhaps starting to consider how to best protect their own interests. The unrest was in part due to the actions of the queen herself who was proving to be an unpopular consort. According to the nineteenth-century writer Caroline Halsted, 'The measure of his [the king's] misfortunes was completed by his marriage with Margaret of Anjou, a princess of singular beauty and accomplishments but of so masculine a spirit and so unyielding a disposition that she increased the disaffection that was felt towards her royal consort.'[4]

Whilst their father was navigating the politics of court, life for the three York girls during the 1450s probably fell back fairly quickly into some semblance of normality. Their mother, Cecily, would no doubt have ensured that their daily life was both structured and settled. According to the duke's biographer, Matthew Lewis, York spent the first couple of years of the 1450s in relative isolation at Ludlow, estranged from the king and court, and it is quite possible that Anne, Elizabeth and Margaret also spent some time within the confines of the castle, alongside their brothers.

Ludlow Castle, part of York's Marcher inheritance, was a Norman fortress, built high up on a rocky outcrop overlooking the medieval town and the scenic River Teme. Within these walls the girls would have been sheltered from the political wrangling between their father and his supporters and those of his enemies. Although we know little of their upbringing, we can perhaps get a glimpse into the pattern of their childhood from a set of ordinances left by their mother from later in her life when she lived at Berkhamsted Castle.

By the time Cecily resided in Berkhamsted, she was a widow and her children were all grown and had flown the nest. But her adherence to a strict timetable may give us an insight into her character and perhaps this was how she ran her household even as her children were growing up. The ordinances show that Cecily would rise at 7 am and her chaplain would recite with her the matins of the day and of Our Lady. She would then hear mass in her chamber before going to chapel. After mass, dinner would be served during which she would listen to religious readings. A devout and pious woman, she particularly enjoyed the stories of religious women, stories such as the revelations of St Bridget.

An older Cecily at Berkhamsted would then give an hour to those who wished to discuss matters with her before taking a short nap, after which she would spend time in prayer until evensong. The education of her daughters is generally attributed to Cecily and the girls no doubt spent some of their day in her company, being instructed in all they needed to know to become accomplished gentlewomen. Cecily's household ordinances also reveal she had an extensive library and she appears to have been an especially learned lady with a love of books, all of which she may have passed down to her children. Margaret and Edward especially were later known for their extensive libraries. During their stays at Ludlow, the girls may also have been able to join in with some of their brothers' lessons under the watchful eye of Eleanor Cornwall, who was employed as lady governess to Edward and Edmund. The daughter of Sir Edmund Cornwall, Baron of Burford, Eleanor had married a man named Hugh Mortimer. After his death, she took as a second husband a gentleman named Richard Croft. He was also employed at Ludlow to take care of the duke's sons and was, it appears, not hugely popular with them. In one of two extant letters from the boys to their father, they write that the bearer of the letter was to inform him of 'the odieux rule and demenyng of Richard Crofte, and of his brother'.[5] Whether he was truly odious or whether he was just too strict for the likes of the two young boys, keeping them on a tight leash, is another matter.

As well as learning their academic subjects, the York children would have been raised to know their place in the world. Pride of birth and lineage, particularly in children of noble descent, was encouraged. This was something their mother knew all too well, with Cecily being described as 'queen-like in all her actions, noble and dignified in her conduct and demeanour' … 'neither unduly elevated in days of prosperity, nor was she weakly subdued by calamity and peril: under all her afflictions she carried a steady soul'.[6]

Cecily's ordinances included a set of strict rules of household governance and this presumably also shaped her children's lives as they grew up in both Ludlow and Fotheringhay. Dinner would be served at 11 am (or by 12 pm on fasting days) and supper at 5 pm. On Mondays, Tuesdays and Wednesdays dinner was boiled beef and mutton and one roll, and supper consisted of lechyed beef (sliced beef) and a mutton roll. On fasting days the family would be served fish instead of meat.[7]

During these early years of childhood, studies and routine, it's likely that the York siblings may have grown close. Our trio of York girls were close enough in age to find joy in the same pastimes. Their brothers, Edward and Edmund, would have identical upbringings and although they too were of a similar age to their sisters, their education would have a slightly different focus. Their youngest brother, baby George, born just the year before in Ireland, was still in the nursery, perhaps temporarily joined at some point in 1450–51, when Cecily gave birth to another son, whom they named Thomas. But no details are known of his birth or death, only that he did not live long. Then, in early 1452, Cecily found out she was pregnant again and at some point during that year, the girls likely returned to Fotheringhay with their mother. For it was there, on 2 October 1452, that their brother Richard was born.

The birth of their last son, unbeknownst to them at the time of course, may have been a glimmer of sunshine in what had proved to be a difficult year. A few months before Richard's birth, in March 1452, the Duke of York had been deceived and subsequently arrested; when the news filtered back to the family, still in Ludlow at the time, it must have been highly worrying.

York had written to the king from Ludlow in January, once again having to quash rumours about his loyalty that had been put about by his enemies. He offered to swear on the sacrament that he was, and always had been, the king's true liegeman. Then in February, he had written another letter to the authorities of Shrewsbury, appealing for men to come to his aid. For the first time, he officially named the Duke of Somerset as his enemy who 'laboreth continually about the King's highness for my undoing, and to corrupt my blood, and to disinherit me and my heirs, and such persons as be about me, without any desert or cause done or attempted, on my part of theirs, I make our Lord Judge'.[8] In this letter to the authorities, York announced he was now ready to act against his enemies, making certain to stress that this did not mean the king, only the men surrounding him.

Soon after dispatching these letters, York left Ludlow for London. Upon arrival he was informed that the king was in the Midlands. With the gates of the city closed to him, he set up camp at Dartford with some 23,000 men, made up of men of his own retinue and others in the service of the Earl of Devon and Lord Cobham, both nobles who supported York's cause. Upon hearing of this gathering and potential threat outside the city gates, King Henry, along with the queen and Somerset headed back to London to confront York and his men, sending a delegation ahead to ascertain his demands. York had only one: that the Duke of Somerset be removed from the king's council.

Henry sent back word that this had been done and that Somerset had been arrested. York believed him and disbanded his men, riding to the king's camp to thank him. But as he entered the king's tent, he realised he had been deceived for Somerset and the queen were standing alongside the king, and it was York who was arrested and taken back to London as prisoner. He was escorted to St Paul's where he was made to declare his loyalty to the king, although he had always maintained this had never been in doubt. As part of the oath, York was made to promise that he would never again raise an army without the king's permission.

The news of his apprehension would, of course, have travelled back to Ludlow to reach Cecily's ears; how much she divulged to her young daughters we cannot know. But her sons were seemingly aware of their father's arrest and humiliation, and it is now that we first see the strength of character of both the Duchess Cecily and Edward, Earl of March, if the following account is true.

In 1452, Edward was almost 10 years old. According to the *Grafton Chronicle*, written during the reign of Elizabeth I, a rumour was circulating in London that to avenge his father's arrest, 'Edward Erle of Marche, son and heir apparent to the said Duke, a young prince of great wit and much stomach, accompanied with a strong army of Marchemen [men from the Welsh Marches] was coming toward London, which tidings sore astounded the Queen and the whole council'.[9]

If this were true, this would show extraordinary courage and loyalty from a young boy, not even yet into the second decade of his life, as well as a grit and determination from his mother to allow her young son to do this. Anne, Elizabeth and Margaret, just 13, 8 and 6 themselves, were surely both scared and proud to see their young brother step up to defend their family name.

Whether Edward and his army ever set out towards London or ever intended to is unclear, but the rumour that he was on his way certainly reached London. York was released and allowed to return to Ludlow where the family must have welcomed him back with huge relief.

By the time they all arrived back at Fotheringhay in mid-August, in time for Cecily's confinement, the family surely needed some positive news. So Richard's birth, a fourth living son for York, would have been something to rejoice over. Within the walls of Cecily's birthing chamber at Fotheringhay, Richard most likely entered the world in a normal or even quite unexceptional way, although there is a possibility that he was a breech baby as indicated by some later writers. But given the infamous figure he would one day become, years after his death, chroniclers and writers would portray him as a monster from the moment he was born. Shakespeare, in particular, in his play *Henry VI Part 3*, describes him as breech born and with teeth, and has Richard declare:

> I, that have neither pity, love, nor fear.
> Indeed, tis true that Henry told me of;
> For I have often heard my mother say
> I came into the world with my legs forward:
> Had I not reason, think ye, to make haste,
> And seek their ruin that usurpd our right?
> The midwife wonderd and the women cried
> O, Jesus bless us, he is born with teeth!
> And so I was; which plainly signified
> That I should snarl and bite and play the dog.
> Then, since the heavens have shaped my body so,
> Let hell make crookd my mind to answer it.[10]

Whilst Shakespeare may have written for entertainment, he did not create this story; it had originated much earlier with learned men such as Thomas More who wrote that Cecily had had a difficult birth with

Richard as he was born feet first and with teeth, planting the seeds that Richard was unnatural and monstrous from birth.[11]

That he was born with teeth is probably an invention too far, but he certainly could have been a breech baby, in which case the experience may have been a traumatic one for Cecily and both may have been lucky to survive. But survive they did and once Richard was safely in the cradle, the Yorks could finally rejoice at some good news. Baby Richard would join the nursery with his elder brother George, by then a toddler.

As Christmas 1452 came and went, it may have been Anne's last at Fotheringhay for she was now entering her fourteenth year and would soon be considered old enough to begin married life proper. Exactly when she went to join her husband is unknown, but certainly by the mid-1450s she would have travelled to London to become the wife of Henry Holland in every sense. As Anne left to start married life and fulfil her role as Duchess of Exeter, Elizabeth and Margaret remained with their mother and two brothers at Fotheringhay. As younger sons, neither George nor Richard would join their elder brothers at Ludlow, and it is likely that over the next few years this quartet of York children – Elizabeth and Margaret, Richard and George – formed a close bond. Later in their lives, Margaret and George in particular were said to have a close relationship, as testified by the writer of the *Croyland Chronicle*:

> This piece of foreign history I have here inserted, because it was universally mentioned that after the death of Charles, his widow, the duchess, lady Margaret, whose affections were fixed on her brother Clarence beyond any of the rest of her kindred … [George was later the Duke of Clarence].[12]

Presumably when Anne did leave Fotheringhay for the second time, it was to Henry Holland's Coldharbour Inn in London. She returned there, no longer under the care of her stepmother but as mistress of her own household. The relationship that would develop between Anne and Henry can only be guessed at and, based on later evidence of how he took sides against her family, we have to assume that they were not close. But we only have conjecture for how they felt about each other. As much as Henry was troublesome and headstrong, he may also have been charming and gallant. The young teenage Anne may even have found herself falling for him during the early days of their marriage.

Or maybe she dreaded this life that appeared to be stretching out before her as the wife of a man she disliked intensely. Both are possible, as are all the scenarios in between. Whatever her feelings for him, in 1453 she had to deal with the consequences of his actions when he managed to get himself sent to prison, something that was not, as it turned out, going to be a one-off event.

Coming into his inheritance a year early was not enough for the impetuous Holland, who was determined to increase his wealth and power base as much as he could. In 1453 he became involved in an aggressive land dispute with a man named Ralph, Lord Cromwell. Cromwell owned Millbrook and Ampthill, two estates in the county of Bedfordshire which had once been in the possession of Henry's step-grandfather, John Cornwall. Cornwall had offered Lord Cromwell first refusal of the lands after his death, and Henry had no claim to them at all, a fact he clearly did not accept. The previous year he had sent armed men to attack Millbrook, taking £1,000 of Cromwell's goods in the process. By spring 1453 the manor of Ampthill was also in his sights, and a group of around twenty men attacked and held Ampthill in Henry's name. An angry Lord Cromwell complained to the council and Holland was arrested and sent to prison in Windsor in July 1453. But despite getting into trouble over the attacks, somehow he was allowed to keep hold of the manors, much to the despair of the elderly Lord Cromwell who spent a great deal of money to try and reclaim them, to no avail.[13]

Whilst Anne was awaiting her husband's release in London, a notable event was taking place across the city at the Palace of Westminster when, on 13 October of that year, the queen gave birth to her first child – a boy named Edward. Finally King Henry had an heir to the throne. The arrival of this new baby prince had the potential to calm the tensions between some of those nobles who considered themselves potential claimants if the king had died without an heir. But with a prince in the cradle, they no longer needed to jostle to position themselves as potential successors. But then something terrible and unexpected happened. The king fell ill, entering a strange state of depression that royal physicians were unable to diagnose. It came on suddenly and rendered him into a coma-like state – awake but completely unresponsive. The illness occurred shortly before his son's birth and the unforeseen consequence was that the king was not even able to recognise his own son. Despite repeated attempts by the queen, begging the king to bless the prince, and thereby giving him official recognition, the king would only glance upon the tiny baby boy, before lowering his eyes to the floor, showing no reaction.

Custom dictated that the little boy could not be made an official heir until recognised as such by his father. But worse than that, as the king did not appear to be making any sort of recovery, there was now no-one officially in charge of running the country. Before his illness King Henry may have been deemed quite an ineffectual ruler, but now it seemed he was in no fit state to rule at all.

By January 1454, a worried Queen Margaret realised that she would need to safeguard herself and her baby son, and made a case to the council that she should act as regent until her husband was fully recovered. Her case was rejected. Instead, with the king making no progress in his recovery, the council elected to name a protector, someone who would act as a caretaker of the realm until the king was well again. They needed a man of strong character, and someone who was one of the king's close kin to fill the role. The Duke of York was both of these and, in an unpredictable turn of events that must have proved galling for his enemies, on 3 April 1454, he was officially named as Lord Protector.

This was the moment the duke needed and he took it. With the power to finally confront his enemies, the men that had been trying to blacken his name for the last few years, he acted quickly. He immediately removed those men he considered corrupt advisors from their positions of power. His main target was, of course, Edmund Beaufort, the Duke of Somerset, who was arrested and thrown into prison, much to the chagrin of the queen.

With his fortunes turning, York was supported in his new position of protector by his brother-in-law, the Earl of Salisbury, and his nephew, Salisbury's son, Richard Neville, the Earl of Warwick. The Earl of Salisbury, also named Richard, was Cecily's elder brother. Fifteen years her senior, he was born at Raby Castle in 1400. His son, Warwick, at 24 years old, was already politically astute and a hugely capable soldier and military man.

With the reins of government in his hands, York now needed to spend more time than ever in London. It was around this time that the family took possession of Baynard's Castle, although it would be another couple of years before they took ownership. York and Cecily had maintained a close relationship throughout their marriage, and it is highly likely that she travelled to London to be with her husband, bringing her youngest children – Elizabeth, Margaret, George and Richard – with her.

Assuming that Anne was already resident in London at Coldharbour, she may have been overjoyed to have her family closer to her again.

Baynard's Castle was a large property, situated on the bank of the River Thames. There had been an earlier building also named for its owner (a man called Baynard) which had been located slightly further to the west, just inside the southwest corner of the city walls. Designed to be a counterpart to the Tower of London, this earlier building was built by William the Conqueror and placed in the charge of a man called Baynard, hence the name. In 1275, the building passed into the Archbishop of Canterbury's ownership and he used it as the foundation for the House and Church of the Dominicans (Blackfriars). Robert Fitzwalter, the man who gave Baynard's to the Archbishop, proceeded to build another castle slightly to the east of Blackfriars, on the riverside, retaining the name.[14]

This new Baynard's would eventually make its way into the hands of the Duke of Gloucester, and although it was mostly destroyed by fire in 1428, he rebuilt it back to its original glory. After Gloucester's arrest and death, it came into the possession of the Crown before Henry VI gifted it to his half-brother, Edmund Tudor.

Edmund Tudor was a friend and supporter of the Duke of York, and it is believed that he let the Yorks stay at Baynard's from 1453 onwards. After Edmund's death in 1456, it once again reverted to the Crown and the Yorks eventually took ownership. With four wings, a nursery for the children, several courtyards, a cobbled entrance from Thames Street, a separate river entrance, and a great hall that measured 40 feet by 24 feet, it was a highly suitable base for the Lord Protector of England and his family. Right on the riverbank, it was accessible via a water gate directly from the river which afforded the duke easy access up and down the Thames to Westminster. Sadly this magnificent property disappeared forever when it was completely destroyed in the Great Fire of London in 1666.

Although many of the nobles were supportive of York's new power, he still had his enemies and one of those who proved most dangerous at this time was none other than his son-in-law, Henry Holland, who, after being released from prison, was ready to get himself into even more strife. With York in charge of the country, Henry Holland's enmity towards his wife's family was at an all-time high and during 1454, he allegedly attempted to murder his father-in-law. Caught in the middle, Anne may have appreciated the proximity of her mother at this time, perhaps even turning to her for advice on how to deal with her rebellious husband.

Holland had recently allied himself with the Percy family in the north in a dispute over the king's chamberlain. The Percies were no friends of the Yorks or the Nevilles, and Henry and a group of his men gathered at the Percy manor of Spofforth. Involving himself once again in a land dispute, he now took his rebellious nature one step further by making a play for the Duchy of Lancaster. He declared that he was the king's closest kin and therefore it was he who should be invested with royal authority during the king's illness. This was, in effect, a direct challenge to York's leadership. It must also have been somewhat of an embarrassment to York, given that it was his son-in-law challenging his authority.

As Lord Protector, York was bound to keep the peace and he wrote to his son-in-law from Waltham on Wednesday 8 May asking him to declare what his intentions were in gathering a group of armed men. Addressing the letter 'Right and mighty prince, right worshipful and with all my heart entirely well-beloved cousin and son, I recommend myself to you', he went on to say:

> And however, at your being recently with me at London, I – having consideration of the (nearness) in which we are knit together in nature and alliance, which by reason must drive and guide and so drives me and guides me to will and to desire, of the good zeal and tender affection that, God knows, I have borne to (you, and) your honour rank and prosperity – warned, moved and exhorted you to lay aside the arrogant behaviour and misconduct which has been habitual with you, and to drive from your company those persons accused of riot and violent conduct, as by their behaviour and vexatious actions and provocations have been, and are, so it is believed, causers and instigators of your arrogant behaviour.[15]

Giving Holland the excuse of 'mixing with the wrong crowd', he seemingly didn't believe that this would have much effect. Without waiting for an answer, he followed this up on 11 May with a summons in the king's name for Holland to appear before the king's council at

Westminster on 16 May. Holland didn't attend; instead he set off towards the City of York under the Lancaster standard.

York had little choice but to gather his men and travel to confront the rebels. Arriving in the north, York imposed huge fines on the Percy family for their involvement; so much so that they couldn't possibly pay them and ended up in a debtors' prison. But York's errant son-in-law managed to evade capture, fleeing back to London, and rumours abounded that he had been planning to kill his father-in-law.

This news, when it reached Anne, must have put her in an incredibly difficult position. Either she was married to a man she despised, who had planned to kill her father, or she loved a man who had tried to kill the other man in her life who she loved. It was an impossible situation for a girl of 15 to find herself in. Although Holland eluded capture in the north, he fled back to London and was eventually caught taking sanctuary in Westminster Abbey. York extracted him from the sanctuary confines on 23 July 1454 and he was sentenced to imprisonment in Pontefract Castle, with York escorting him there personally the next day. One can only imagine the conversation that occurred between the two men on the journey. Taking advantage of Henry's disgrace, his cousin Lord Grey of Ruthyn promptly seized Ampthill Castle and Henry would never recover it.

News of the troubles had also reached York's two eldest sons at Ludlow, and in the second of their extant letters, signed by their own hands, they refer to the troubles in the north and send their father 'victorious speed' against his enemies:

> Right high and mighty Prince, our most worshipful and greatly redoubted lord and father – in as lowly wise as any sons can, or may, we recommend us unto your good lordship; and please it your highness to wit, that we have received your worshipful letters yesterday by your servant, William Cleton, bearing date at York the 29 day of May. By the which William, and by the relation of John Milewater, we conceive your worshipful and victorious speed against your enemies; to their great shame, and to us the most comfortable things that we desired to hear. Whereof we thank Almighty God of his gifts; beseeching him heartily to give you that good and cotidian fortune, hereafter, to know your enemies and have the victory of them ...[16]

The letter then continues with details of their studies and is signed:

> Written at your castle of Ludlow the 3d day of June.
>
> Your humble sons,
>
> E. MarchE.
>
> E. RUTLAND.

For the entire family, the disloyalty showed by Henry Holland must have come as a shock. But more than that, if he had actually intended to kill his father-in-law, it demonstrates a ruthlessness in his character that perhaps highlights what sort of a husband he was to Anne. Holland spent the rest of 1454 imprisoned, perhaps allowing Anne some respite from the position she found herself in, with a husband she was bound by law to obey, and her family, to whom she was clearly close.

As the year drew to a close, Christmas Day brought glad tidings to the queen and her young son when the king finally regained his senses after a long period of illness. Able to resume his duties and take back the reins of government, this effectively meant that as 1455 dawned, York's time as Protector was over. It also put him and his family straight back into the line of danger for as soon as the king was back on the throne, the queen persuaded him to drop all charges against Somerset and release him from prison. This he did. At the same time, a review of Henry Holland's case was undertaken. Although the council ordered him to report to Wallingford Prison, he never arrived there because, by March 1455, the king had granted Holland his freedom.

Now that Somerset was effectively back as one of the king's chief's advisors, the duke needed a new plan to prevent him returning to the political wilderness. He retired to his castle at Sandal, and his chief allies, Salisbury and Warwick, also travelled north to their base at Middleham. Elizabeth and Margaret's whereabouts at this time are unknown; Anne, for better or worse, presumably remained at home in London with her husband now a free man.

But as 1455 continued it became clear that King Henry was still not completely well. His mental state wavered between periods of lucidity and periods of depression. Tensions continued to simmer and York and Somerset, sworn enemies, were on a collision course – and there could only be one victor.

On 22 May 1455 all the political wrangling finally boiled over and the first armed battle of the conflict that would eventually become known as the Wars of the Roses took place. York, along with Salisbury and Warwick, had been summoned to a great council meeting in Coventry; gathering their men they left the north and marched to meet the king and Somerset. Although they had been invited, they feared a similar trap that York had previously walked into and that this time they might not leave with their lives. Approaching the king with an army though would, and did, look suspicious, so the duke and his supporters wrote to the king, keen to make it clear once again that they were the king's true subjects but were still unhappy with the behaviour of his advisors. The two groups eventually met at St Albans, York managing to intercept the royal party on the way to Coventry. As the duke and his men set up camp outside the city walls, the king and his men, including Somerset and Henry Holland, were ensconced inside the city.

Initially messengers were sent back and forth between the two camps, with York, Salisbury and Warwick continuing to stress their loyalty to the king. But they had raised an army and marched against the king's standard, a move that looked very much like treason. Eventually, and some would say inevitably, negotiations failed and the fighting began. The poor residents of St Albans barricaded themselves in their houses as the two groups of men battled each other through the town, with fierce fighting in the marketplace and town square. The actual fighting lasted just an hour, during which time Henry VI was wounded and, most importantly, Somerset was killed. According to an old legend, the Duke of Somerset apparently refused to ever enter a castle as it had once been foretold that he would meet his death in one. In the end, although he met his death in the streets of St Albans, he was killed in one of the small streets inside an inn. Bizarrely the name of this inn was 'The Castle'. As the battle came to an end, King Henry was found injured and taking refuge in St Albans church. The Duke of York made it clear he still considered himself a loyal subject and alongside Salisbury and Warwick, they escorted the king back to London. Their aim had been met; with Somerset out of the way, a meeting of Parliament was held and York persuaded the council to promote his supporters into offices of state. A victorious York gained the position of constable of England and the Earl of Warwick was awarded the captaincy of Calais.

Waiting at home, impatient to hear news, Anne, Elizabeth and Margaret must have been relieved to hear that their father had escaped from the battle unharmed. Henry Holland, fighting amongst the king's men, was captured after the battle and promptly dispatched to Wallingford Prison. Was Anne relieved at his incarceration or relieved that he had escaped with his life? Perhaps both?

Their mother too must have been overly worried that the situation had become so tense it had resulted in armed conflict, particularly as at this time she was heavily pregnant. On Sunday 20 July 1455, just two months after Cecily had faced the possibility of losing her husband in battle, she gave birth to another daughter, named Ursula. By then Cecily was 40 years old, reaching the end of her childbearing years and, although she couldn't know it at the time, Ursula was to be her last child. And Ursula may have joined her sisters as the subject of this book had she lived, but sadly it was not to be. Although we do not know how long she lived, the youngest York daughter departed the world before too long and all we have of her is her name.

For the next few years after the Battle of St Albans, there was an uneasy truce. King Henry had remained well enough to continue governance of the realm, and seemingly tried to restore peace between the warring noblemen of the realm, namely the Yorkists – York, Warwick and Salisbury and their supporters – and men such as Henry Beaufort, Somerset's son. Upon the death of his father, Henry Beaufort inherited the dukedom of Somerset and could never forgive the Yorkist lords for their part in his death. He and the Duke of Exeter (Holland), along with their supporters, continued to vie for the king's ear.

For the York sisters, life during the late 1450s was as normal as it could be. By 1456 Elizabeth and Margaret were 12 and 10 respectively and may have spent some of that year at Sandal Castle, where their father chose to base himself for much of the time. In November of that year, perhaps they took a trip to Caister in Norfolk with their mother, who stayed at the house of Sir John Fastolf, and tried to persuade him to sell them the property. Fastolf relayed this in a letter to John Paston on 15 November:

> Sir John Fastolf to John Paston at the Temple Nov 15, 1456
> My Lady of York has been here, and sore moved me for the purchase of Castre. Written the Monday after St. Martin.[17]

As for Anne, she was now 17 years old. Reunited with her husband when he was finally released from Wallingford, in early 1456 she soon found herself pregnant. Was this an indication that there were some sort of feelings between the duke and his duchess? Of course, she was his wife and we cannot assume that their intimacy suggests anything other than she had performed her wifely duty, while they lived together as man and wife. But we also cannot discount any romantic feelings between them, even though they found themselves on opposite sides of the political divide. Back in the Lancastrian fold, Holland resumed his duties to the Crown and in May 1456 he headed a London commission of Oyer and Terminer. Two months later he received the manors of Trematon, Saltish and Calstock. In September that same year, he also received his duchy of Cornwall estates from his inheritance.[18]

As Anne's due date drew near, late in 1456, she would have retired from everyday life into what was known as her confinement. Perhaps her mother hurried back from her visit to Norfolk to be by her side. A few weeks before the birth, her chosen room would have been prepared and she would have entered it and remained there until after the birth. As was custom, the room itself would have been kept in semi-darkness, with tapestries hung over windows, and only a single window left open to provide a small amount of air.

As the eldest York child, Anne had witnessed her mother go through the process of childbirth many times, but for a young girl in her late teens, it must have been a daunting experience as she took to her rooms to prepare for her child's birth. For women in the Middle Ages, there was no guarantee that they or their child would make it through safely, and her mother's delivery record of over ten births did not mean that she, Anne, would even survive her first. But as she waited the onset of her labour pains, her women that accompanied her in the birthing chamber, known as gossips (not at all derogatory, just simply her childbirth companions), would have kept her spirits up during the days and weeks before the birth.

The fear of childbirth would also be tempered by the strong religious beliefs of expectant mothers. Anne's chamber would be filled with crucifixes and religious items that would offer comfort and, in a time where there was no pain relief, women would recite religious prayers and chants during labour, often while clutching holy relics in the hope their devotion would ease the pain and bring forth an easy birth. Birth girdles were also sometimes worn – strips of parchment bearing charms and prayers that women would wear around their stomach. St Margaret, the patron saint of pregnant women and childbirth, would also be called upon to ease the pains of labour.

Whatever methods Anne used to calm and ease her pains, she safely gave birth to a baby girl, who was named after her mother and christened Lady Anne Holland. Custom dictated that Anne remain in her confinement room until approximately a month after the birth, so she would not have attended baby Anne's christening. When Anne did emerge from her chamber, she would have attended a churching ceremony and was then allowed to return to normal life. The churching ceremony was a time for purification when new mothers offered gifts of candles before the altar dedicated to Our Lady. Attended by friends and family, it would have been a joyous occasion, in effect a celebration of the safe arrival into the world of the newborn child and that the mother had made it through the ordeal safely. Anne, Henry and their new baby daughter would have spent Christmas 1456 together as a new family of three.

But would fatherhood tame Henry? Maybe he intended it to, for a while, as in early 1457, Henry Holland paid his first visit to Exeter, the town that represented his dukedom – a move that perhaps showed he was ready to take some responsibility now that he was a family man. Anne and her new daughter likely accompanied him to the Exeter manor at Dartington and they were still there in May of that year when Henry appeared on a peace commission in Devon. Whilst there, Holland also set about cultivating a relationship with the new Earl of Devon.[19]

Dartington Hall was a beautiful location for Anne to spend some time as a new mother. Described as the most spectacular mansion in Devon, it was the largest medieval house built in the west of England and was described in *Pevsner's Buildings of England* as 'one of the most spectacular surviving domestic buildings of late Medieval England', an accolade it still retains today. Granted to John Holland in 1348 by his half-brother, the then king, Richard II, it was John who turned Dartington Hall into a great country house. The extent of the manor formed a huge double quadrangle and covered almost an acre of land. The magnificent great hall, the heart of any medieval mansion, measured 69 feet by 38 feet, and the fireplace itself, which would provide warmth to its occupants, was 17 feet long. The medieval buildings were built around a huge courtyard and forty-eight living chambers were provided by the west and east wings –

plenty of space for the Exeters and their retinue. The hall also boasted a hammer-beam roof, one of the first of its kind in the country, pre-dating the larger and more ornate one at Westminster Hall.[20]

Anne and Henry may have spent much of 1457 and even some of 1458 in the beautiful Devon countryside, especially as Holland's stepmother, Anne Montagu, died in November of that year and her estates were integrated into his inheritance. That they were well received in the locality is illustrated by the neighbouring authorities of Bridgwater who sent gifts to Anne as duchess in both 1457 and 1458; an indication that perhaps they were still residing in Devon in 1458. In 1457 Anne received a gift of wine, and in 1458 the authorities sent oxen.[21]

Whilst Anne was settling into motherhood and running her estates, the time had now come for her younger sister Elizabeth, by this time a young woman of 14, to follow in her footsteps. In 1458 Elizabeth would herself be married. The man chosen for her was John de la Pole, the son of William de la Pole, Earl of Suffolk and his wife, Alice Chaucer. Alice was the granddaughter of the poet Geoffrey Chaucer and his wife, Philippa de Roet.

John de la Pole was an interesting choice of groom for Elizabeth, as his father had been a staunch Lancastrian and his mother, the Duchess of Suffolk, was a close friend of the queen, having held the position of chief lady-in-waiting in the queen's household. Along with the Duke of Somerset, it was William de la Pole who had effectively exiled York to Ireland, and he had also been one of the queen's favourite courtiers until his death in 1450, having been the chief negotiator of her marriage. In the parliament of 1448 King Henry had awarded him the rank of duke and, according to the writer of the *Croyland Chronicle*, 'In consequence of this, his heart was too greatly elated, and became exalted still more and more previously to his downfall'.[22]

The de la Poles were major landholders in Norfolk; their principal residence was Wingfield Castle and they had various other estates dotted around Norfolk and Suffolk, making them neighbours of the Paston family. Elizabeth's betrothed, John de la Pole, was born in 1442, so he was two years older than Elizabeth. He was Alice and William's only child, although it is understood that his father had also produced an illegitimate daughter, a product of a liaison with a nun. She was conceived before William's marriage to Alice and reportedly went on to marry into the Stonor family.

When John was just 8 years old, tragedy blighted his young life when his father was murdered. Although the duke was a favourite of Margaret of Anjou, he was not popular outside of court, particularly in his home county where he was often accused of allowing his retainers to run free. He repeatedly made enemies with his neighbours – the Pastons and the Mowbray Dukes of Norfolk – and neither it seems, was he able to make many friends amongst his fellow peers. In a parliament that convened soon after Christmas 1449, Suffolk was accused of illegally fortifying one of his properties, Wallingford Castle, and of stealing gifts and money from several monasteries in the name of the king. In league with two associates, the Bishop of Salisbury and Lord Saye, the men reportedly swindled sums of money that should have made its way into the treasury and shared it out amongst themselves. Accused by the council, he was promptly committed to the Tower.

Suffolk's arrest and incarceration was hugely unpopular with the queen and it appears she used all her influence to defend her favourite. By March 1450, Suffolk was once again a free man. But even with the queen's favour, his release was unpopular and upon leaving the Tower, he was pursued by a mob of angry Londoners to his home at Westhorpe in Suffolk. Appreciating the dangerous situation he was in, the duke was granted safe conduct to Burgundy, remaining at Westhorpe for the next six weeks until he could arrange his escape.

Once he had a plan in place, Suffolk made his way to Ipswich, arriving there on 30 April and from where he set sail for the continent. But before he reached land, his boat was intercepted by a larger ship. The captain of the ship dispatched a small boat of men, who requested that Suffolk accompany them to meet the captain.[23] Left with little choice the duke had to do as he was commanded. Reportedly on boarding the ship, he was summarily beheaded and his body was later found dumped on the beach near Dover. A devastated king and queen arranged for his body to be collected and returned to Wingfield to be buried, and the identity of his murderers has never been established. His accomplices, the Bishop of Salisbury and Lord Saye, would also both receive retribution for their alleged crimes; so unpopular were they that Salisbury was murdered by a mob in Wiltshire and Lord Saye was caught by the men of Jack Cade's rebellion and beheaded.

During his lifetime, William de la Pole had been no friend to the Duke of York so it would seem, at first, an odd choice to unite the two families in marriage. But the deal was most likely brokered by the formidable Alice Chaucer, who clearly saw a benefit in marrying her son to the daughter of someone as powerful as the Duke of York. At the time of the marriage, he had already completed a stint as Lord Protector. With the king's health as it was, perhaps Alice foresaw that the tide was even then turning in York's favour.

At the time of the couple's marriage, John was 16 years old and Elizabeth was 14. But even though they were still teenagers, Elizabeth was not John's first wife. In 1452 he had been married to his father's ward, the Lancastrian Margaret Beaufort. Margaret, who was born in 1441, was the great-granddaughter of John of Gaunt, through the legitimised Beaufort line; her grandfather was the eldest son of Gaunt and Katherine Swynford. The pair had been betrothed as children and after his father's arrest and imprisonment, Alice Chaucer had hurriedly arranged the marriage of Margaret and John, in the hope it would safeguard the future of her son and perhaps in some way help her husband. Unfortunately it did neither; the duke was attainted in 1450 and although Alice was able to keep hold of the family estates, her son was not officially restored to the dukedom of Suffolk until 1463, although he was popularly known as 'my Lord of Suffolk' after his father's death. His marriage to Margaret Beaufort was later annulled and, by the time of John and Elizabeth's wedding, Margaret was the mother of a year-old toddler, a boy named Henry Tudor who would one day become an integral part of England's royal history.

Elizabeth and John's marriage ceremony took place sometime in early February 1458 – another winter wedding for the Yorks after Anne's January nuptials some twelve years previously. The Duke of York provided Elizabeth with a dowry of 2,300 marks which was payable in instalments.[24]

After the ceremony, like her sister before her, Elizabeth packed her belongings to go and live with her new husband and mother-in-law at Alice's favourite manor of Ewelme in Oxfordshire.

Although Wingfield was the main family seat, Ewelme was very much a favoured family residence, and Alice and her husband had spent much time there before his death. Her influence in the area can still be seen today; in 1437 the couple were licensed to found a set of almshouses at Ewelme. Known as God's House, they were built to accommodate two chaplains and thirteen poor men. The almshouses are situated adjacent to the church and are still there today. By 1448 Alice and William had also built a grammar school in the village. And from January 1440, Alice and her husband, along with her brother-in-law, William Phelip, received the constableship of Wallingford Castle, a position she retained on her own after their deaths. It was Alice that received custody of Anne's husband, Henry Holland, during his incarceration there in 1455.

Arriving at Ewelme Manor in early spring 1458, Elizabeth would have seen a fashionable brick and timber building, framed around two brick and stone courtyards, that had been 'much augmented and beautified' by Alice and her husband.[25] The manor house was described by Leland in 1542: 'the manor-place of Ewelme is in the valley of the village, the base court of it is fair and is builded [*sic*] with brick and timber. The inner part of the house is set within a fair moat and is builded [*sic*] richly of brick and stone. The hall of it is fair and hath great bars of iron overthwart it instead of cross beams. The parlour by is exceeding fair and lightsome, and so be all the lodgings there. The common saying is, that Duke John, son of William the first Duke, made, about the beginning of Henry VIIs time, most of the goodly buildings within the moat. There is a right fair park to the Manor.'[26] Sadly, unlike the almshouses and the grammar school, all that remains of the house today is a single accommodation block.

But through a set of surviving inventories, we can get a glimpse of the house that Elizabeth was to call home after her arrival as a 14-year-old, newly married young woman. The ground floor featured a parlour and a beautiful great hall, spanned by unusual wrought or cast-iron beams. Access to the first-floor apartments was via a set of stairs from the parlour. These consisted of a great chamber, which led onto two further symmetrical apartments, each of which contained a chamber and chapel closet.[27] The manor house buildings were within a moat and, as well as the residential building, ancillary buildings would have perhaps contained a laundry, bakehouse or buttery. Sadly, the buildings and the manor house itself became so run down by the end of the next century that they were demolished in 1612.

With Elizabeth having followed her sister Anne into marriage and hopefully motherhood, 12-year-old Margaret was now the last remaining York daughter still at home, with only her younger brothers, George and Richard, for company. She may have been delighted, suddenly finding herself the only female sibling with her own personal space that she no longer had to share with her elder sisters! But she may also have felt slightly unsettled, with Elizabeth leaving; perhaps she picked up on some of the unease that her parents inevitably must have been feeling as, once again, outside events began to encroach on their happy family life.

York had celebrated his daughter's marriage in 1458, but the following year, the uneasy truce that had been in place since St Albans between him and the royal court was beginning to look fragile. A meeting of the council was held in Coventry in June 1459 and noticeably uninvited were the Duke of York, the Earls of Warwick and Salisbury, and other Yorkist allies. During the meeting, and allegedly at the queen's command, the men were indicted of 'unspecified charges'. York was becoming more and more certain that the queen was planning a coup through an act of attainder that would remove his rights to hold title and property.[28]

Meanwhile Anne may also have been reflecting on how her recent period of stability was coming to an end when her husband, Henry Holland, once again set about getting himself into trouble. In 1459, the feoffees of his father's will delivered several more of his inherited estates to Henry – Fremington, Torrington and Haselbury. But for the ever-ambitious Holland, this still wasn't enough. Despite now having responsibilities as a father as well as a husband, he proceeded to imprison a lawyer named Eyrkham in the Tower for no apparent reason. He also, reportedly, interrupted the proceedings of the King's Bench on more than one occasion. Although mostly in favour at court and one of the king's kin, his irresponsible behaviour could not be allowed to continue and he was promptly ordered back to prison. His place of incarceration this time was to be Berkhamsted Castle, at that time a property that belonged to Queen Margaret. His non-compliance would result in a forfeit of a £10,000 bond. Two months later, he was instructed to appear before the council and again a £10,000 bond was needed to ensure his attendance. The king eventually forgave his recklessness, perhaps not wishing to alienate the support of one of his premier magnates, and Holland continued to misbehave – seizing a property in Southwark on 3 November 1459 which was part of Sir John Fastolf's inheritance and a property that Henry had no claim to.[29]

And while Henry Holland was busy causing trouble, in the wider political landscape, tensions were about to come to a head. The men not invited to the council meeting agreed to convene once again to present a united case to the king. The Earl of Warwick returned from his base in Calais and started towards the agreed meeting place in the Midlands. Although shadowed by the new young Duke of Somerset, he was able to make a peaceful journey. But his father, Salisbury, also en route to meet up with his son and brother-in-law did not fare as well; he and his men were ambushed by the queen's army, under the command of Lord Audley, at Blore Heath on 23 September. With no choice but to engage in battle, they emerged victorious, continuing their march to Ludlow to meet up with York and Warwick. Eventually, by October 1459, all three men were at Ludlow, now under no illusion that their positions were being threatened. York's sons, Edward and Edmund, still resident in Ludlow at the time, were by now 17 and 16 years old and were old enough to be involved in the mini council of war that no doubt took place. In October 1459, their sister Margaret was also at Ludlow with her mother and two younger brothers. On the cusp of being a teenager, she would have been well aware what was at stake and it may have been a scary time for her, hearing the males of her family plotting and planning. Her mother may have been too busy with her own worries to allay any fears Margaret would have had. With neither of her sisters with her for company, Margaret had only her younger brothers, George and Richard, to confide in. No doubt, like most young boys, they would have been thrilled at the idea of a battle and were most likely running around staging mock battles of their own!

Whatever plans were discussed between the men within the walls of Ludlow, it seems that York, Warwick and Salisbury at this stage were still intent on a peaceful solution. The Crown, however, was not. A parliament was summoned, which latterly became known as the Parliament of Devils, and York, Salisbury and Warwick were not invited to attend. This now dramatically changed the positions of the three lords. Believing that they were about to be attainted, when the Bishop of Salisbury arrived in Ludlow with a pardon from the king, he was met with a strong resistance. They were now sure that their exclusion from the parliament was a hostile act and they turned down this later invitation and pardon, believing that if they now attended they would either be arrested or killed. But this act of declining the king's pardon technically made them rebels. There was now no way back.

York, Salisbury and Warwick decided to make a trip to Worcester to the cathedral, just over a day's ride away. Here, before the high altar, they each took an oath that they were still true subjects of the king. They then jointly signed a letter for a herald to take to the king, informing him that they had raised arms ONLY in self-defence. Once again they pointed out their belief that the men surrounding the king were interested only in lands and offices. Returning to Ludlow and hearing news of the king's advancing army, they and their men took up a defensive position at Ludford Bridge on the River Teme in the shadow of the castle. But during the night many of their men defected, fearful of taking on the king's men and committing treason. Knowing they had too few men to defeat the Lancastrian army, they had no option but to flee themselves.

As York's eldest sons and heirs, it was necessary that Edward and Edmund were also taken to a place of safety. The Duke of York, taking Edmund with him, made his escape across the sea to Ireland, a land that once again welcomed him with open arms. And in what was presumably a strategic decision to have York's two heirs in different places, Edward, Earl of March, fled across the channel to Calais with his cousin Warwick and the Earl of Salisbury. Suddenly for young Margaret, alone now with her mother and younger brothers, the castle at Ludlow must have felt like a very scary place.

When the king's army arrived at Ludlow, the town was reportedly ransacked. As the news reached Anne and Elizabeth, they must have been terrified for their younger siblings alone with their mother and worried sick about their father and brothers. Knowing that she had to protect her interests and that of her young children, Cecily gathered Margaret, Richard and George, and they set off to present themselves to the king and council at Coventry. They arrived on 6 December, as testified to in a letter from John Bocking to John Paston, written on 7 December: 'the Duchesse of York come yestereven late'.[30] The letter also listed the names of some twenty-five men who had been attainted alongside the Yorkist Lords, which included: The Duc of York; Therle of Marche (Edward); Therle of Rutland (Edmund); Therle of Warrwyk; Therle of Salusbury; The Lord Powys; The Lord Clynton; The Countesse of Sarr [Salisbury]. The Countess of Salisbury, Cecily's sister-in-law, had fled to Calais with her husband and son which led to her being attainted alongside the men.

On 30 November, the king had made an offer of pardon to anyone in the Yorkist camp who submitted to him within eight days. It is likely Cecily was aware of this, and she had decided the only thing she could do to keep her children safe was to throw herself upon his mercy. On 20 December, Cecily was granted an income of 1,000 marks per year to be drawn from the York estates 'for the relief of her and her infants who had not offended against the King'. Cecily, along with Margaret, George and Richard, was dispatched to Tonbridge Castle, to the home of Cecily's sister, Anne, Duchess of Buckingham, where they were all to remain under house arrest. At the same time, her errant son-in-law, the Duke of Exeter, Anne's husband, was made constable of Fotheringhay Castle.[31]

Born around 1408, the Duchess of Buckingham was Cecily's closest sister in age. She had married Humphrey Stafford, the Duke of Buckingham, in or around 1424 and by the time of the Yorks' arrival in 1459, her children were all grown-up and had flown the nest. For Margaret, arriving at the castle with her two brothers, all very aware of the circumstances that their family had found themselves in, it must have been a very strange time. Cecily, ever resourceful, arranged for Margaret, George and Richard to continue with their lessons to keep life as normal for them as possible.

As 1459 drew to an end, the king and council were well aware that there was every chance the Yorkist men would return and fight. Whilst the men spent Christmas 1459 in exile, the York women were left behind in England, no doubt worried about what the new year would bring. Perhaps Elizabeth and Anne were able to visit their mother and younger siblings at their aunt's home in Tonbridge, to offer each other support and share news?

For the next six months York remained in Dublin, where as a sign of respect for his earlier good leadership he had been offered safe haven. Over in Calais, York's son, Edward, along with his cousin Warwick and uncle, had been planning their revenge. They finally returned to England's shores in the middle of 1460, when an army led by Warwick and Edward met the Lancastrian army at Northampton on 10 July.

Presumably, Cecily and perhaps even her daughters, Anne and Elizabeth, had found a way to stay connected with the men of the family during those six months, both in Ireland and in Calais. They almost certainly would have been aware that Edward, Earl of March, alongside Warwick and Salisbury, was back in the country, and news of the ensuing battle at Northampton, when it reached them, would have brought mixed emotions. For Cecily and her sister Anne in Tonbridge, there was no win in this battle – Anne's husband, the Duke of Buckingham, was the Lancastrian commander. His role pitched him into a situation where he was fighting against his nephew, Edward, Earl of March.

The victory that day belonged to the Yorkists, after Lord Grey of Ruthyn defected. He was involved in a land dispute with none other than Henry Holland, the Duke of Exeter, and Edward and Warwick promised him support against Exeter if he did not fight against them. The messenger riding with the news to Tonbridge Castle would have brought to Margaret and Cecily the glad tidings of the victory of the Yorkist army; for Anne, Duchess of Buckingham, there would be only grief as her husband was killed on the battlefield that day. After the battle, King Henry was captured and held for three days in Delapré Abbey by Warwick, who then returned with him to London, where Henry was placed in relative comfort in the Tower. Queen Margaret, meanwhile, fled to Wales with her young son.

For the young Margaret of York, hearing the news of the death of her uncle, who may have been kind to her during their enforced stay in his house, must have been upsetting, particularly witnessing her aunt in distress. But, of course, she would have welcomed the news that her eldest brother had escaped unharmed. After the battle, Anne, still Cecily's sister, even though they had found themselves on opposite sides, allowed Cecily and her children to leave and they headed straight to London. They sought refuge, firstly at John Paston's law chambers at Temple Inn before moving to the Southwark manor that belonged to Sir John Falstoff.

Anne, at the time of the battle, was residing in the Holland apartments in the Tower, the place the Lancastrian loyalists fled to seeking refuge from her triumphant brother, Edward and their cousin, the Earl of Warwick. It may even have been through the arrival of these bedraggled Lancastrians that she learned the news her husband had fled with the queen after the battle. Perhaps she sought out her mother and siblings upon their return to the capital.

Edward of York, the eldest York son, was growing up into a capable young man and he now demonstrated his sense of responsibility and love for his family, as he stepped up as the man of the household in his father's absence. This is illustrated in a letter from Christopher Hansson to his master John Paston, written in October 1460. Edward had seemingly sent a messenger requesting that his mother and younger siblings could take refuge at Paston's place, Crosby House, upon their arrival into London:

> RIGHT worschipfull Sir and Maister, I recomaund me unto you. Please you to wete, the Monday after oure Lady Day here come hider to my maister ys place, my Maister

Bowser, Sir Harry Ratford, John Clay, and the Harbyger of my Lord of Marche, desyryng that my Lady of York myght lye here untylle the comyng of my Lord of York and hir tw sonnys, my Lorde George and my Lorde Richard and my Lady Margarete hir dawztyr, whiche y graunt hem in youre name to ly here untylle Mychelmas.[32]

Christopher Hannson did agree to give them shelter until Michaelmas (29 September) but it seems that two days after they arrived, hearing news of York's imminent return from Ireland, Cecily set off to meet him, leaving Margaret, Richard and George in London. Reportedly, Edward visited them every day:

She [Cecily] had not lain here two days, but she had tidings of the landing of my Lord at Chester. The Tuesday next after, my Lord sent for her, that she should come to him to Harford and thither she is gone, and in the meantime are left here both the sons, and the daughter, and the Lord March cometh every day to see them.[33]

Another letter from the Paston collection, that treasure trove of contemporary evidence we have for this period, also places Elizabeth in London in October 1460.[34] So it may have been a real family reunion as she too likely paid her younger siblings a visit and was possibly also reunited with her brother Edward. Elizabeth and her husband, John, may have stayed at the 'Mannor of the Rose', in Suffolk Lane, a property which had been in the possession of the de la Pole family since at least 1446 when John's father, William, had stayed there.[35]

Although the family must have been relieved to hear that their father was making his way back from Ireland, Anne also found herself once more in that familiar position of divided loyalties. With her husband fighting on the side of the Lancastrians at Northampton, she must have once more been experiencing a multitude of emotions: anger at his disloyalty, relief he hadn't been killed, perhaps even relief that he had fled and that she may not see him again?

By the middle of October, the whole family could rejoice when the Duke of York arrived back in London accompanied by Cecily, splendid in his livery adorned with his falcon and fetterlocks insignia, alongside the white rose of the Mortimers and bearing the royal arms. He was certainly back in the capital by 16 October when the Yorkist lords called a parliament. York now made it clear that he was no longer declaring allegiance to the king but was ready to take the throne himself. But he had made an early miscalculation; after his declaration he touched the throne and this action was received in silence. Although many were on his side, the right to be king was seen as a divine right, and the gathered men were not yet willing to put aside a living king. The Earl of Warwick advised his uncle to withdraw and speak with the king. This he did and Henry, weak-willed and perhaps still ailing, but in no doubt of HIS divine right to be king, responded 'my father was king, his father was king, I have worn the crown for forty years from my cradle, you have all sworn fealty to me as your sovereign and your fathers have done the same to my fathers. How can my right then be disputed?'[36] A stalemate had been reached.

After much discussion, a middle ground was eventually decided upon that everyone could be happy with. Henry may have been an ineffective king, but he was still king and the council would not depose him. However, an Act of Accord was agreed upon that put York in place as Henry's heir. This seemed to appease everyone – well, almost. The queen, rightly, was furious as this took her son out of the line of succession. Gathering an army, she began marching back towards the capital, intent on defending her husband and her son's right to be his heir. As her men began pillaging Yorkist estates in the north, it was clear that the troubles were not yet at an end. York once more gathered his men and departing London on 9 December, he marched north to face the queen's army. Margaret and her sisters once again had to say goodbye to their father. They could not know that this time they would never see him again. By now, their mother had left the hospitality of Falstoff's manor house and the family had returned to their London home at Baynard's. With York remaining in the north for the Christmas season, perhaps Margaret was joined by her elder sister, Anne, for the Christmas festivities, given that her husband was also in the north with the queen. In which case her daughter, Margaret's 5-year-old niece Anne Holland, would almost certainly have accompanied her mother and it would have been a very female-oriented house that celebrated Christmas 1460, with no doubt thoughts of their menfolk always on their mind.

York and his son Edmund spent Christmas Day at Sandal Castle. Alerted to his whereabouts, Queen Margaret's army surrounded them there. From his position within the castle, the duke could see he was outnumbered. He could, and should, have remained within the safety of the castle walls until further support arrived, but for some reason, he took the decision to emerge from the castle to face the Lancastrian army. Edward, Earl of March, had been in Ludlow for the Christmas period, and hearing the news of his father's predicament, he was hurrying from the Welsh borders with reinforcements. On 1 January 1460, the Duke of York engaged with the Lancastrians in a battle that ended in disaster when both he and Edmund were killed. His ally and brother-in-law, Salisbury, was also executed after the battle. In her victory, Queen Margaret ordered York's head and that of his son and brother-in-law to be displayed upon the Micklegate of York; she mocked York by placing a paper crown upon his head. A letter from the Milanese Ambassador to the French Court reports that some 12,000–16,000 men were killed during the battle.[37] He also reported that Warwick, furious at the death of his father, was on his way to avenge their deaths with some 60,000 combatants.

After what had seemed like reason to celebrate in October 1460, suddenly the House of York was on its knees. The death of the duke would have filtered back to the women in London. Along with their mother, Anne, Margaret and Elizabeth would have been devastated at the loss of their father and brother. Cecily, ever resourceful and astute, realised the danger and immediately arranged for her two youngest sons, George and Richard, to be secretly conveyed out of the country. Enabled by her nephew Warwick, she arranged safe passage for them across the sea to Holland. They were granted a place of safety by Philip, Duke of Burgundy in the city of Utrecht, where they were treated well and were able to carry on with their education.

Things had changed dramatically and suddenly Margaret found herself alone with her mother, who understandably would have been distraught. Whether they remained at Baynard's or whether they went to stay with Anne or even Elizabeth, where the women could all console each other in their grief, is unknown. And alongside that grief must have been a continued sense of fear because they all knew that Edward, York's heir, would take revenge for the deaths of his father and brother. How would this all end?

Edward, of course, intended to do just that. He had been speeding towards York when he heard the news of his father and brother's death. He immediately changed direction and started heading for London.

En route, his army defeated a Lancastrian army led by Jasper Tudor at Mortimer's Cross on 2 February 1461, before continuing their advance towards the capital.

Meanwhile, the Earl of Warwick left London on 12 February and taking the captured king with him, he and his men headed north to meet up with Edward with the aim of defeating Queen Margaret's army once and for all. Elizabeth's husband, the Duke of Suffolk, was with Warwick's party[38] so perhaps Margaret and Cecily had the company of Elizabeth and Anne, once again the four women awaiting news of their menfolk. It was Warwick's men who first encountered the queen's, engaging in a pitched battle at St Albans on 17 February. For the second time, the residents of St Albans woke at dawn to the noise of fighting that started in the town and marketplace before flooding out onto Barnards Heath. This time the Lancastrians had the upper hand, and Warwick and his supporters fled once it was clear they were facing a loss. The king, who they had brought with them from London, was found by the queen sheltering in a tent. Warwick had left the king under a tree about a mile away, and in a demonstration of his state of mind, he reportedly 'laughed and sang as the battle raged.'[39]

Back in the capital, Londoners were hearing the news and terrified of the queen's advancing army reaching the city, an army which they had heard was mainly made up of a band of mercenaries. The Italian ambassador reported on 19 February that: 'In the meantime they [the people of London] keep a good guard at the gates, which they keep practically closed, and so through all the district they maintain a good guard, and those who are here, thank God, feel no harm or lack of governance. Yet the shops keep closed, and nothing is done either by the tradespeople or by the merchants, and men do not stand in the streets or go far away from home. We are all hoping that, as the queen and prince have not descended in fury with their troops, the gates may be opened to them upon a good composition, and they may be allowed to enter peacefully.'[40]

The ambassador also wrote that although Warwick and his men fled the battle and that nobody knew where they were, 'it is thought that they are in this district in secret'. Whilst Warwick was fighting in St Albans, Edward was believed to have been in the Cotswolds. In actual fact Warwick was not hiding in the city; he had made his way to meet up with Edward and his men, and they eventually arrived in London together. In a missive from Nicolo Darabatta to Francesco Coppino,

Bishop of Terni and Papal Legate to England and Flanders, he wrote that the Londoners rejoiced to see the men. Apparently a great crowd gathered and 'with the lords, who were there, they chose the Earl of March as their king and sovereign lord, and that day they celebrated the solemnity, going in procession through the place amid great festivities'. That day was 4 March 1461.

The council and aldermen of London, unwilling just a few months before to install York as king, now seemed to have reached the conclusion that the fighting had to end and that the young, strong man who was Edward, Earl of March, was the man to lead them into a more peaceful and secure future. The House of York had triumphed. Edward, without doubt, would have paid a visit to his mother and Anne, Elizabeth and Margaret as one of the first things he did when arriving back in London. And it was apparently whilst he was at Baynard's that he was visited by the nobles of the realm who asked him to become king. In the midst of their sadness, the girls and Cecily must have found some joy in seeing their brother received so well by the nobles and Londoners.

Edward accepted the invitation to be king, but it was not as straightforward as that. England could not have two kings, and the old king Henry and his queen were still a problem that needed to be dealt with. On 12 March Edward and Warwick took their troops and marched north to face the queen's army once more.

The two armies, the Lancastrians and the Yorkists, met at Towton on Palm Sunday, 29 March 1461, in the bloodiest battle ever fought on English soil. After ten hours of fighting in an almighty snowstorm, an estimated 50,000 men fought for the future of England, their red blood seeping into the very land itself, staining the white snow-covered fields. The Yorkists were victorious. King Henry, Margaret of Anjou, their son Prince Edward and Anne of York's husband, Henry Holland, Duke of Exeter, fled after the battle to the safety of Scotland. For Anne, Elizabeth and Margaret, what a few months this had been. They had reached the depths of despair in January upon hearing of the death of their father and brother. Now just a few short months later, their eldest brother, Edward, Earl of March, was officially king of England.

# Chapter 5

# Our brother, the king

Suddenly everything had changed. The York girls and their brothers may have allowed themselves to consider the possibility that their father might one day be king and what that would be like, but no-one could have predicted that within a few short months not only would their father be dead and gone, but that their 19-year-old brother Edward would be the one to take the throne. What multitude of emotions must they have felt: relief, that Edward had survived the fighting; pride, grief, jubilation? Life had not been easy for the family for a while, but no-one could have predicted how quickly, in the end, things came about.

As the news of Towton and England's new king was reported across the land, Edward did not immediately return to London, but instead he headed for York, his first task to order that the gruesomely displayed heads of his family were taken down from the Micklegate. He arranged for them to be respectfully buried with their bodies at Pontefract. Back in London in his absence, Edward was officially proclaimed king on 4 April at Westminster. Although Edward was in the north, perhaps all three York girls gathered at their mother's house to celebrate. Elizabeth would have her husband, John, to share the occasion with. Anne, however, would be aware that her husband had fled to Scotland along with old king Henry and his son and queen, as reported by William Paston in a letter to his brother John written on 4 April – a letter that also told of Edward's triumph:

> PLEASE you to knowe and wete of suche tydyngs as my Lady of York hath by a lettre of credens, under the signe manuel of oure Soverayn Lord King Edward, whiche lettre cam unto oure sayd Lady this same day, Esterne Evyn, at xj. clok, and was sene and red by me, William Paston.

Item, Kyng Harry, the Qwen, the Prince, Duke of Somerset, Duke of Exeter, Lord Roos, be fledde in to Scotteland, and they be chased and folwed, &c.

Be your Broder,
*W. Paston* [1]

Two other family members were also missing and unable to celebrate along with their sisters – their younger brothers George and Richard were still safely across the sea. It seems that they were being well looked after in Burgundy, and a letter from the Bishop of Elphin to Frances Coppino, the Bishop of Terni, predicted this would bring about a future close relationship between England and the Court of Burgundy: 'It is reported among the English lords that the Duke of Burgundy is treating the brothers of the king with respect. This pleases them wonderfully, and they believe that there will be great friendship between the duke and the English by an indissoluble treaty, and that one of these brothers will marry the daughter of Charles'.[2] Neither George nor Richard would marry a daughter of Charles; it would actually be Margaret for whom this 'close relationship' would have the greatest consequence.

Now that the danger was over, however, it was time for George and Richard to return home. Cecily requested their swift return and by 17 April they were at Sluys. The following day they were to make the journey to Bruges where they would be accompanied home by Master Antonio, the physician to the Bishop of Terni, as a mark of respect on his master's behalf.[3] Even though they were aged just 11 and 9, their brother's position as king of England now afforded them the utmost respect by the foreign nobility.

That they were being looked after would have been a relief to their mother and sisters, all of whom must by now have been anxious to have them home. In a time where there was no instant news, details of the events of the last few weeks and months were spreading like wildfire throughout the country – some true, some distorted by word of mouth, and this included an erroneous report at the time that the old king Henry had been captured. In a letter from the Bishop of Elphin to Coppino, he reported that Edward had sent a great number of men at arms after the fugitive Lancastrians, and that they had all been apprehended. The Bishop of Elphin, a man named Nicholas

O'Flanagan, reported that he was present in the house of the Duchess of York when the Lord Treasurer brought her an authentic letter telling her of the captures. Although the duchess had just been to chapel for Vespers, she immediately returned to the chapel with the bishop and two of her chaplains to say the *Te Deum* in thanks for the capture.[4] That he was with the duchess is undoubtably true, the erroneous part is that the Lancastrians were not captured – they were still on the run and this included Henry Holland.

Straight after the Battle of Towton, Holland had fled north where he was involved in the siege of Carlisle Castle, a bloody episode that saw an army of Scots and Lancastrians take the castle from the Yorkists. When Yorkist re-enforcements arrived in the form of the Nevilles, first John Neville, Lord Montagu, and later the Earl of Warwick, Holland escaped to Wales where he and his men entered into battle with the Yorkist Earl of Pembroke. He then made his way back to Scotland to join the queen and the main Lancastrian party.

Anne, especially, would have been awaiting news of her husband and may even have been with her mother when this came through. Perhaps this was the first time she realised that whatever she had felt towards her husband, that their relationship must now be over. She was just 22 years old with a 6-year-old daughter. And she was also, now, a wife of an exiled traitor. How much did she have to convince her brother, Edward, that she was loyal to him and to her family? That would, one assumes, depend on how close she had been to her husband. Was there ever any question that she would choose her husband over her family? Possibly not. On 1 May 1461, Edward was at Newcastle and here he made a grant, at Anne's request, to transfer some of the Duke of Exeter's estates into the hands of men he trusted so that she could benefit from their income. One of these properties included her home at Coldharbour, a place where she could now reside safely with her daughter, with the other estates paying her an income and a means to live. She may even have travelled to Newcastle to speak with Edward in person, perhaps being the first of the family to congratulate him face to face on his success at Towton.

With Edward on the throne and the old king Henry now in exile, the hope was that the country could now find some peace under its new king. The people of London not only accepted Edward as their new ruler, but the news of his victory brought joy across the land, bringing with it a hope for an end to the wars. A verse prevalent in London in spring 1461 illustrated the mood of the people:

> Lette us walke in a newe wyne yerde, and lette us make us a
> gay garden in the monythe of Marche with thys fayre whyte
> ros and herbe, the Erle of Marche.[5]

Henry VI had not been a bad king, but he was a weak leader and as the news filtered out through the towns and villages and into the countryside, England's hope for a more peaceful reign under the young and strong Edward IV was high. With a coronation date set for June, preparations for the big day began in earnest, a day on which all the York girls would be present in their finery to celebrate their family's success. Their wider family would also be in attendance including their closest kin, the Nevilles, and particularly their cousin, Richard Neville, Earl of Warwick, who would, to history, become known as 'the Kingmaker' for his assistance and loyalty in Edward's journey to the throne. Also present would be Elizabeth's mother-in-law, Alice, Dowager Duchess of Suffolk, whose intention to travel to London to the coronation was recorded in a letter from Richard Calle to John Paston on 5 June 1461.[6]

Edward finally made his triumphant return into London on 13 June when he arrived at the palace of Sheen.[7] At some point he would have undoubtedly made the journey to his mother's house at Baynard's where he certainly would have been welcomed by both his proud and relieved mother and his youngest sister, Margaret.

The date of Edward's coronation was set for Sunday, 28 June 1461. Making his official state entry across the bridge into London on Friday 26 June, he spent that evening at the Tower, where he created twenty-eight Knights of the Bath, two of whom were his younger brothers, George and Richard. The following day, Saturday, George and Richard rode in the coronation procession in front of Edward as he travelled from the Tower to Westminster, dressed in their finery of blue gowns adorned with a token of white silk lace on the left shoulder and with hoods of white silk.[8] Then, on the Sunday morning, Edward was officially anointed England's king, the Archbishops of York and Canterbury placing on his head the crown of Edward the Confessor. The whole family were, of course, in attendance to witness Edward's moment, a success story for the whole House of York. The solemn ceremony was followed by a huge celebrational feast in Westminster Hall, where the gathered guests dined handsomely on swans and pheasants, spiced wine and confectioneries.

The next day, Edward once again returned to Westminster for a service. This second service may well have been due to the superstition that surrounded all Sundays in 1461. During 1460, Holy Innocents Day (or Childermas as it was also known) fell on a Sunday in December. According to superstition, whatever day that feast fell on was considered unlucky for the whole of the following year. Edward, a strong believer in superstition, may have wanted to ensure his reign was blessed by holding a second ceremony on an alternative day.[9] After the Westminster service on the Monday, Edward awarded his brother George the title of Duke of Clarence, at the Bishop of London's Palace. Their younger brother, Richard, would later be created Duke of Gloucester, an honour awarded to him on 1 November 1461.[10]

With the coronation over, Anne, Elizabeth and Margaret could once again focus on their own futures. At some point in 1461 the whole family had become members of the Fraternity of St Nicholas, the brotherhood of parish clerks. They are listed on the Bede (membership) roll for that year. Members of the fraternity included parish clerks and their wives as well as clergy and noblemen, and inclusion in the fraternity would afford its members extra prayers throughout the year. Being part of the brotherhood also meant that when the time came, members would be entitled to a more elaborate funeral ceremony that the parish clerks could provide. Written in Latin in the roll, they are listed as:

> Rex Edwardus Quartus filius et heres illustris principis
>      Ricardi ducis Ebor
> veri Domina Cecilia ducissa Ebor
> Dominus Georgius ducis Clarence
> [Dominus] Ricardus
> Filii dictorum ducis et ducisse
> Domina ducissa Exon
> Domina Elizabeth ducissa Suff
> Domina Margareta ad huc non
> marita filiae eorundem ducis et ducisse Ebor

> King Edward the Fourth, son and heir of the illustrious
>      prince Richard, Duke of York

> The True Lady Cecilia, Duchess of York
> Master George, Duke of Clarence
> [Master] Richard
> The sons of the said Duke and Duchess
> The Lady Duchess of Exeter
> The Lady Elizabeth Duchess of Suffolk
> The Lady Margaret did not come
> The husband of the daughter of the Duke and Duchess of
>     York (presumably John de la Pole)

Margaret was listed but 'did not attend', possibly indicating there was an occasion to celebrate their joining the fraternity that Margaret had, for whatever reason, not been present at?

By July 1461 it seems that Henry Holland may have been considering returning from exile, news that may or may not have been true and which may or may not have reached Anne's ears. Whilst hunting at Windsor, Edward was accompanied by a gentleman named Giovanni Pietro Cagnola. Cagnola, later writing to the Duke of Milan, reported that 'the Duke of Exeter, cousin of the king and a great lord ... now wishes to return and ask pardon'. He also indicated that Edward would grant it.[11] Whether there was any truth in this is unknown, but Holland never did hand himself in and on 4 November 1461, he was included in a bill of attainder against 'Henry, calling himself King Henry the Sixth', Margaret 'late called queen of England', [and the] Dukes of Somerset and Exeter and all his honours were forfeited.[12] The remainder of his lands and estates were granted to Anne in December. She was now an independently wealthy woman.

Meanwhile Elizabeth of York, by now 17 years of age, was settling well into married life and in September 1461 her husband, the Duke of Suffolk, came of age and therefore into his own inheritance. It may have been around this time that the couple chose to fly the nest from Ewelme and spend more time at their seat at Wingfield in Suffolk.

Wingfield Castle in the Suffolk countryside was not a huge castle by any means, but it had ample space and grandeur for the young de la Poles to make their first and main home. Still in existence today, Wingfield is an example of an almost living, breathing dwelling that has constantly changed and evolved over time. When a building first appeared on the current site is unknown, but its ownership came to the de la Pole family through Michael de la Pole in the fourteenth century. Michael had married Katherine Wingfield, the daughter of a local man, Sir John Wingfield, and in 1385 he was granted a licence to crenellate his mansion house there.

The Wingfield family had first owned a manor house on another site in the village near the church, which was known as Old Wingfield Hall. The site that the current Wingfield Castle was built on consisted of 69 acres of land which was ideal for enclosing and making into a deer park. Michael and Katherine chose to do this. Whether Michael began Wingfield from scratch or began developing an existing building on the site is unclear, but the castle that Michael created and lived in in the late 1300s was continued by his son and would later become the primary residence of John and Elizabeth.

The house itself was four-sided but not quite square. Surrounded by a deep moat, it was entered across a bridge and through a three-storey gatehouse guarded by two ancillary towers. A further four towers were joined by a curtain wall and the property contained at least one, and possibly two courtyards. Given the extensive changes the building has gone through, the exact layout of the original castle is unknown, but it is believed that in all probability the residential apartments of the castle lay along the west side.[13]

Within the castle compound, as well as the residential rooms there was a chapel, perhaps with as many as four priests employed there, the obligatory great hall and various service buildings. Outside the curtain walls there were fishponds which would have been both ornamental and functional as a supply of fresh fish.[14]

When the de la Poles lost ownership of the castle in the sixteenth century, much of it was dismantled and in 1544 it was granted to Sir Henry Jerningham. Today all that remains of the castle that Elizabeth and John would have known is the frontage with the gatehouse and supporting towers. Currently in private ownership and obscured from public view, the charm of Wingfield is described in *Wingfield: Suffolk's Forgotten Castle* by Elaine Murphy. Murphy writes that 'the charm of the place lies not in its size but in the combination of medieval fortifications with the pretty, even delicate Tudor house along the west interior wall', referring to the Tudor brick and timber-framed house that was later built to adjoin the frontage of the old castle. Famously represented in *I Capture The Castle* by Dodie Smith as 'Godsend', the house built into the side of a castle, Dodie Smith had visited Wingfield in the 1920s and clearly fell in love with the place, using it as her house in her book set in the 1930s and written during the Second World War.

As for their youngest sister, Margaret of York, in the few months after Edward became king she probably remained at Baynard's with her mother. Now aged 15, she was older than both her sisters had been when they married, but she had not yet been found a husband. It would now be down to her elder brother, Edward, to plan for her future. In the meantime, she and her two brothers, George and Richard, needed suitable living arrangements as members of the royal family and were soon set up in their own household at Greenwich Palace. Edward spent Christmas at Greenwich in 1461[15] and the beautiful palace, on the banks of the River Thames, became an integral branch of the royal household. Richard would remain here until around 1465 when, aged 13, he entered the Earl of Warwick's house at Middleham to receive his military training under the experienced eye of his cousin. It may have been during his time at Middleham that his path first crossed with a young Anne Neville, the youngest daughter of the Earl of Warwick, who would one day play an important role in Richard's life.[16]

George would remain at Greenwich until 1466 when around the age of 17, he relocated to Tutbury Castle to set up his own household. It was from Tutbury that he began his career as a royal duke and, until Edward had children, his life as heir to the throne.[17]

During the early years of Edward's reign, the sisters were able to lead a fairly stable life, each finding their way in this new world where their brother was king. In or around 1462, Elizabeth gave birth to her first child, a son who was named John after his father. In 1463 the whole family may have come together to attend the reinterment of the Earl of Salisbury, Cecily's brother, who had been killed alongside the Duke of York at Wakefield. Elizabeth and John were certainly in attendance as they are mentioned in the funeral proceedings, as is George, Duke of Clarence. Alice, Countess of Salisbury, recently deceased, was to be buried at Bisham Abbey in Berkshire, and the earl's body was taken from its resting place at Pontefract and moved with great pomp and ceremony to be buried alongside her. The earl's chariot was accompanied by his son, Warwick, on its journey from Pontefract and upon its arrival at the abbey, the earl's coffin was brought alongside his wife's, whose hearse was covered in white, and where 'divers ladies and gentlewomen', including Elizabeth, were keeping vigil. The guests attended a funeral service, before the earl and his countess were laid to rest.[18] It is unclear whether the king was present but for Elizabeth and George, their father and brother Edmund must have been very much on their minds that day. A reburial service would also be organised for the Duke of York later into Edward's reign.

By 1464, Edward had been king for three years and was yet to take a wife. To the York sisters, he was just their brother but to the wider world, Edward was a tall, handsome, charismatic youth. He was described by Vergil as 'tall and lofty of stature, so that he towered above everybody else. He had an honest face, happy eyes, a steadfast heart, a great mind, and a memory that retained whatever he had absorbed. He was circumspect in his actions, ready amidst dangers, harsh and fearsome towards his enemies, liberal towards his friends and guests, and very fortunate in fighting his wars'. Edward was charming but had yet to find his queen, perhaps enjoying his freedom as an eligible bachelor. Commynes tells us 'His thoughts were wholly employed upon the ladies (and far more than was reasonable), hunting, and adorning his person. In his summer-hunting, his custom was to have several tents set up for the ladies, where he treated them after a magnificent manner; and indeed his person was as well turned for love intrigues as any man I ever saw in my life: for he was young, and the most handsome man of his time'.[19]

But he could not be this young, carefree youth forever; a king needed to provide heirs, a fact he would have been well aware of. His cousin, Warwick, astutely political and perhaps more aware than Edward about the necessity to secure his throne, had been instrumental in trying to find the woman who would be queen. In Warwick's eyes the best way to do this was to look abroad for a suitable princess who, alongside a bride for Edward, would also bring an alliance with a foreign power. However, on 1 May 1464 in a move that surprised everyone, Edward took matters into his own hands and married in secret, to a woman named Elizabeth Woodville.

Elizabeth Woodville, daughter of Jacquetta and Richard Woodville, was, in the eyes of the nobility, an entirely unsuitable consort. Firstly, she was a widow with two young sons, and secondly, her family had been staunch Lancastrians. Her first husband, Sir John Grey, was killed fighting for the Lancastrians in the second Battle of St Albans and Elizabeth's mother, Jacquetta Woodville, had once been a close friend of Margaret of Anjou. Beautiful and captivating Elizabeth Woodville may have been, but she brought no benefits to the Crown – no sizeable dowry, no alliance – yet Edward fell in love with her and in the words of the chronicler, Edward Hall, who believed that their meeting was written in the stars: 'that if one considers the old proverb to be true then marriage is destiny'.[20]

The date of their first meeting has never been determined. It may even have been as early as 1461 that they first crossed paths, when Edward paid a visit to Stony Stratford, only a few miles away from the Woodville home at Grafton. It is possible he visited Grafton or summoned the family to Stony Stratford where they pledged their allegiance to him, and he officially forgave them for their part in siding with the House of Lancaster. After the death of her first husband, Elizabeth had run into some troubles with her inheritance and had turned to the king's chamberlain, William Hastings, a man she knew of old to ask him for his assistance. He may possibly have been the connection between her and the king.

Events leading up to their marriage are, like most tales, entwined with hearsay, assumption and mystery. The writer of the *Danzig Chronicle* reports that Edward fell in love with Elizabeth when he dined with her frequently.[21] Perhaps Edward was a constant visitor to the manor of Grafton and the more time they spent together, the closer they became.

But the most well-known and accepted version of how they met is that Elizabeth, knowing that the king was due to pass by, waited under an oak tree with her two boys so she could catch his attention and request his help with her boys' inheritance. The oak tree, now known as The Queen's Oak, was situated in a field which is today in the parish of Potterspury, just east of Potterspury Lodge off the A5; it survived all the way to 1994 when it sadly burnt down in a fire. The king, riding by with his men, was said to have stopped when he caught sight of a beautiful young woman on the side of the road, and this was their first encounter.

However they met, the one certainty is that before too long, Elizabeth was Edward's wife and in all but name, the new queen of England. The popular date given for their wedding, which was held in secret, is 1 May 1464. The location for this most secret of royal weddings was believed to have been a small hermitage on the Woodville lands at Grafton.

This marriage would not be revealed until September 1464 at a council meeting in Reading. Purportedly the news was so enormous that Edward took only William Hastings into his confidence, but it is tempting to think that he may have spoken about it with perhaps Anne or

Elizabeth, the sisters closest to him in age. Did they, along with the rest of the country, find out after the council meeting, or had he taken advice from them beforehand as a brother may do from his sisters and sworn them to secrecy? Either way, there was now a new addition to the family and how and when Anne, Elizabeth and Margaret met their new sister-in-law is lost in the annals of time. Edward and his new bride remained in Reading until November 1464, before setting off back towards London, making a short stop at Windsor before arriving at Edward's favourite palace of Eltham in time for Christmas. Perhaps this was the first time the York girls met their new sister-in-law and queen?

1464 had also been an eventful year for Elizabeth of York. If she had attended the Eltham Christmas celebrations, it would have been with two young sons in tow; she had given birth that year to a second son who was named Geoffrey. But a letter in the Paston collection also reports that her husband had been ill in 1464, perhaps seriously, leaving her worried if he would survive. In a letter dated 8 June 1464, Margaret Paston writes to her husband, John, 'It is told that the Duke of Suffolk is come home, and either he is dead, or else right sick, and not likely to escape.'[22] What ailed John is unclear although he thankfully made a full recovery.

The Pastons of Norfolk were close neighbours of the de la Poles at their Wingfield manor, and there was a huge amount of enmity between the families that had carried over from earlier decades over the ownership of land and estates in the area. That they were occasionally on friendly terms is evidenced in an undated letter from Elizabeth, 'unto John Paston in haste' requesting that he please vacate his lodgings for her and she signs it 'Your friend, Elizabeth': 'Master Paston, I pray you that it may please you to leave your lodging for three or four days, till I may be purveyed of another, and I shall do as much to your pleasure. For Gods sake say me not nay; and I pray you recommend me to my lord-chamberlain.'[23] This letter is still extant and is signed in Elizabeth's own hand, making it the earliest signature of any royal lady of England that we have on record.

But the peaceful tones in Elizabeth's letter did not convey the reality, particularly during the following year, 1465, when John de la Pole (no doubt with the encouragement of his mother, Alice) took up his father's mantle in making trouble for the Pastons in what can only be described as a tussle of power and property in the county of Norfolk.

The story of the disputes that occurred between the Norfolk gentry involving the de la Poles, the Pastons, the Duke of Norfolk and, at times, others of the Norfolk nobility can be traced through the extensive collection of letters left by the Paston family. The head of the family at the time was John Paston, who was born in 1421. He had married Margaret Mautby, the daughter of John Mautby of Mautby near Yarmouth.

One of Margaret's relatives was a landed gentleman named Sir John Fastolf who lived in Caister Castle near Yarmouth. Fastolf was an exceedingly rich man and John Paston worked as his legal advisor. When Fastolf died in 1459, John Paston was one of his principal executors and was tasked with founding a college of priests and poor men at Caister. In return he inherited Caister Castle and various other manors in Norfolk and Suffolk, propelling the family up in status. With John Paston often working away in London, Margaret took charge of the estates, and their trials and tribulations have been detailed in the many letters they wrote to each other and to friends and family.

Although there were, at times, friendships between the families, the reputation of the de la Poles in Norfolk was reportedly not good, evidenced in a letter dated 7 January 1462 when Margaret Paston wrote to her husband, stating that George, Duke of Clarence, and the Duke of Suffolk were needed to come and bring about some law and order to troubles that had broken out in the county. She concluded that even though their presence was a necessity in their roles as commissioners of the peace 'they love not in no wise the Duke of Suffolk nor his mother. They say that all traitors and extortioners of this country be maintained by them'.

The inheritance of Caister Castle by the Pastons, which was also disputed by other of Fastolf's heirs, seemed to be one of the main triggers for the tensions amongst the families. In 1465 the Duke of Norfolk seized Caister Castle and took possession of it until well into the next decade, when ownership would eventually be passed back to the Pastons after much legal wrangling. Also that year Elizabeth's husband, the Duke of Suffolk, continued the bad enmity in the area by sending a force of his armed men against the Paston manor at Hellesdon, near Norwich, where they ransacked the manor house, church and village houses.

Rumours of Suffolk's intentions had surfaced in April 1461 when Margaret wrote that she had been given word that the duke was making a claim on Hellesdon and that he was proposing to enter [it] a short time after Easter.[24] Further letters sent in the following weeks confirm Suffolk's claim to the Pastons' manors at Drayton and Hellesdon and, by 27 June, a letter from John Paston to Margaret informed her that he had heard from one of his men, Richard Calle, that Suffolk had sent his bailiff [Philip Lipgate] into the manor of Drayton:

> Item, Calle sendith me word that Master Phylip [the Duke of Suffolk's bailiff] hat entrid in Drayton in my Lord of Suffolk's name, and hat odir purpose to entre in Heylisdon, and he askith my avyse.[25]

By July it seems that the duke had carried out his threats and had indeed sent his men into the manor of Hellesdon. Richard Calle wrote to his master, John Paston, in a letter dated 10 July 1465 that on Monday last past in the afternoon, Philip Lipgate and 300 men had attacked Hellesdon in the name of the duke. It must have been a frightening time for Margaret Paston, who, according to Calle, was resident at the manor at the time. Although she had sixty armed men at her disposal, the fighting must have been terrifying. Margaret herself followed up Calle's news with a letter of her own two days later, dated 12 July, in which she informed her husband that daily her retainers were threatened by the Duke of Suffolk's men. She also wrote: 'The Duk of Suffolk and both the Duchessys shal com to Claxton thys day, as I am informyd, and thys next weke he shal be at Cossey ...' She asked her husband's advice as to whether she should speak with them as she believed that they would be ignorant of what had been done in their names. Sadly we have no detail of what Elizabeth knew of her husband's actions against the Paston properties and, on many occasions, John de la Pole was not personally present, instead sending his 'heavies' in to do the work. As his wife, Elizabeth had a duty to side with her husband. Her mother-in-law, Alice, was known to heavily support and encourage her son in these disputes; perhaps Elizabeth was not so heavily invested?

Whilst all these troubles were taking place in Norfolk, Elizabeth and her husband were busy in London attending the coronation of England's new queen. Elizabeth Woodville's coronation date was set for Sunday 26 May 1465 and she, like Edward before her, made her official entry into the city two days before, on Friday 24 May, across Old London Bridge. Then, on Whit Sunday, 26 May, Elizabeth was anointed Queen of England with great solemnity in Westminster Abbey. Clothed in a mantle of purple (the colour of royalty), with a coronal upon her head, Elizabeth entered the hall walking under a canopy. Ahead of her, the king's brother, George, Duke of Clarence, accompanied by the Earl of Arundel and the Duke of Norfolk, rode around the hall on horseback clearing a path through the gathered crowds. As she neared the lower steps of the abbey, Elizabeth removed her shoes and walked barefoot upon the ray cloth into the building. The two dukes and the earl had now dismounted and proceeded before her into the abbey. Once inside, the Archbishop of Canterbury greeted her.

Following behind Elizabeth Woodville were two of Edward's sisters (most definitely Elizabeth in her position as Duchess of Suffolk, and possibly Anne in her position as Duchess of Exeter) and Elizabeth's mother, Jacquetta. Margaret, aged 19 and still an unmarried lady, would most likely have been amongst the other ladies not thought important enough to mention. Noticeably absent was their mother, Cecily, who reportedly, like Warwick, had been furious at the marriage and perhaps was showing this through her non-attendance, although that she stayed away in protest is only conjecture.

After the formal proceedings, the queen was led to a grand state banquet held in her honour in Westminster Hall, taking her rightful place at the high table. The Archbishop of Canterbury sat to her right and Elizabeth of York had the honour of sitting immediately on her left. The rest of the hall was filled with three other long tables of guests, and Anne and Margaret would have sat amongst them in positions accorded by their status. Each of the courses served to the gathered guests began with elaborate ceremony. Clarence, Norfolk and Arundel, back on their horses, 'richly trapped to the ground' rode into the hall to the sounds of trumpets, and the earls, barons and knights entered on foot. The newly created Knights of the Bath served the first course of seventeen dishes to the hundreds of diners gathered. The queen's brother, Anthony Woodville, had the honour of being cupbearer, serving hippocras (spiced wine) to those gathered. Similar processions followed the second course of nineteen dishes and the third course of fifteen. Throughout the banquet, the king's minstrels and others played music for the entertainment of the guests.

These festivities in May 1465 were followed shortly by another round of family celebrations when George Neville, brother of the Earl of Warwick and therefore cousin to Anne, Elizabeth and Margaret, became Archbishop of York. The festivities took place on 17 June 1465 and at the great banquet that was held, this time John de la Pole had the honour of sitting on the left-hand side of England's new archbishop. For the other guests, the hall was laid out with seven tables, three of which were in the chief chamber. On the first table Elizabeth was seated next to her brother Richard, Duke of Gloucester. Once again Anne and Margaret were likely to have been at this family celebration, seated at one of the tables in the main chamber.[26] After all the excitement of the spring and summer months of 1465, Elizabeth and John's return to Norfolk, most likely Wingfield, in July must have provided a chance for some rest – presuming Elizabeth was not accosted by an angry Margaret Paston upon her arrival back home!

Just a few short weeks after the coronation, some good news reached the royal court on 13 July 1465 that this time was proved to be correct – old king Henry had finally been captured at Waddington Heath. He was brought back to London and housed in some comfort in the Tower. Captured on his own, his wife, son and a few others, including Henry Holland, had escaped across to the continent, where they took up residence in a chateau near St Mighel in Bar, an accommodation provided to them by Queen Margaret's father, the Duke of Anjou. Margaret would remain here, but Holland and the other men around her eventually drifted away. Henry Holland, Duke of Exeter now in name only, eventually made his way to Burgundy where, if reports are to be believed, he arrived in scant state and attached himself to the train of the Duke of Burgundy, barefoot and begging. Philip, Duke of Burgundy, reportedly recognised him and agreed to house him and give him a small pension.

Whether Margaret Paston did visit Elizabeth and Alice on their arrival in Norfolk is unclear, but the feuding continued for the rest of the year. In the middle of October it seems the Duke of Suffolk, alongside 500 of his men, ransacked Hellesdon and took away many of the Pastons' possessions, including bedding, bolsters, pewter bowls, candlesticks and pillows, as well as four great brass pans, a marble pestle and mortar and two dozen pewter vessels from the kitchen. They also stole clothes from the Pastons' steward, Richard Calle, who lost a murrey gown, a doublet of black satin, a pair of hose and other items from his chamber. Margaret Paston also had items taken from her chamber, including a quarter of black velvet, an ounce of silk and an ivory comb. The armed men even ransacked the church, making away with a purse, three gold rings and many other valuable items.

In her reporting of the incident to her husband, Margaret, writing on 17 October, told how the duke then rode to the manors of Cossey and Drayton and how her men had rescued the feather beds and other items from there to keep them safe.[27] Beds were of significant value to families and were often passed down to family members in wills. The de la Poles did not occupy any of the manors that they raided – Hellesdon and Drayton was destroyed and Alice stripped roof tiles off another Paston manor to replace hers at her manor of Westhorpe.[28] The feud would continue to rumble on for the next few years.

As 1465 drew to an end, the country was experiencing a particularly harsh winter, also referenced in the Paston letters, with the cold snap first mentioned in a September letter; by October it seems that heavy snow was falling in Norfolk. This bad weather perhaps put a temporary end to the feuds as people were forced to stay closer to home and preparations for the Christmas festivities began.

As 1466 dawned bright and cold, for Margaret of York back in London, it was going to be a hugely significant year in her life – the year her destiny would be sealed. Now there was a feminine presence at court in the shape of the queen, Elizabeth Woodville, Margaret had been spending much more time at the centre of court life in the company of her sister-in-law. As a young, single woman and the king of England's sister, she was an attractive marriage proposition. Edward had been considering his younger sister's future for a while; as early as 1462 a marriage was being talked about between Margaret and King James III of Scotland. According to the chronicler, Hall, this earlier connection had been discussed as a way to dissuade the Scots from sheltering king Henry and the exiled Lancastrians so that they should be 'destitute of all aid and refuge'.[29] By the end of 1465, discussions were under way for Margaret to be betrothed to Don Pedro of Aragon, and Margaret would have entered the new year, 1466, perhaps believing this to be her future. Edward had already dispatched an ambassador to the court at Barcelona, and Don Pedro had even commissioned a fine diamond ring, set in a band of gold and costing around £200 (around over £120,000 in today's terms).

However, also at the end of 1465, a young suitor named Charles, Count of Charolais, heir to the Duchy of Burgundy, had appeared on the scene. Charles' wife, Isabel of Bourbon, had died on 25 September 1465 and he had since dispatched an ambassador, Guillaume de Clugny, to England to request Margaret's hand. Seemingly keen to explore the Burgundy option, in March 1466, Edward sent the Earl of Warwick to Burgundy to negotiate two marriages: that of Margaret of York to Charles and another for their brother George, Duke of Clarence, to Charles' daughter, the

9-year-old Mary of Burgundy. And when news reached the English court in June 1466 that Don Pedro had died, it seemed that Margaret's fate would lie with Charles and his kingdom of Burgundy after all.[30]

In the fifteenth century, the Europe that we know today looked remarkably different, particularly modern-day France which was segmented and ruled by various houses and noble families. The Dukes of Burgundy ruled an area that encompassed the Low Countries (Belgium, Luxembourg and the Netherlands) and extended into Northern France. A powerful state, they were also often under threat from successive kings of France and a great rivalry existed between the two countries, as well as between the kingdoms of England and Scotland. Relations between France, Burgundy, Scotland and England were changeable, constantly fractious and hugely fragile.

Not wanting to see an alliance between England and Burgundy, the King of France, Louis XI, immediately proposed an alternative marriage for Margaret with Philip of Savoy, Count of Bresse, and Warwick was also sent to Rouen to explore this option. With Burgundy looking the more favourable option to Edward, Louis XI continued to do his upmost to prevent the Anglo-Burgundian alliance, even going as far as to spread rumours abroad that Margaret was not everything a bride ought to be. Some rumours even hinted that she had a son. A gallant Charles, in Burgundy, ordered that anyone repeating these rumours was to be thrown into the nearest river.

In October 1466, Edward allowed Charles' illegitimate brother, Anthony, known as the Bastard of Burgundy, to visit England and during this visit, Edward signed a treaty of friendship with Burgundy.[31] By the summer of 1467 the deal was looking certain, and perhaps Margaret even allowed herself to plan for her future. The court was treated to a jousting event between the visiting Bastard of Burgundy and the queen's brother, Anthony Woodville. According to Hall, around this time Margaret was summoned to Edward's chamber, where she appeared richly dressed and accompanied 'by a great multitude of ladies and gentlewomen'. Hall attributes her with 'so sober of demeanour, so fair of face, with such good countenance and deportment, that she was esteemed for her personage and qualities by the Burgundians'.[32] At this meeting the Bastard of Burgundy presented her with a rich and costly jewel on behalf of his father, Duke Philip, and his brother, Charles, 'which Margaret joyously received and sent words of thanks to her new father-in-law and husband'.[33]

The celebrations ended abruptly, however, when, on Monday 15 June, Philip, Duke of Burgundy died. When news reached the English court, the Bastard of Burgundy immediately set off for home to support his brother Charles, who would now become the Duke of Burgundy in his father's place. Before he left, Edward exchanged promises of friendship for the Bastard to pass onto the new Duke of Burgundy, and by autumn the marriage between Charles and Margaret of York was formally agreed upon. The Bishop of Salisbury was sent to negotiate details on 20 September and on 1 October, Margaret gave her public consent to the union at a meeting of the royal council.

Later that month Charles sent off to Rome for a papal dispensation, which was needed because Isabel of Portugal, Charles' mother, was a granddaughter of John of Gaunt. Although contracts were not signed until the following year, Margaret's future as the new Duchess of Burgundy was sealed. Hall described this match as 'the most measured matrimony in Christendom, to form the greatest alliance and friendship between the realm of England and Burgundy'. He styled Charles as 'a man of high courage, enterprise and audacity', and likening him to the 'son of Mars', depicted him as a hero, inferring that there was no-one else like him in his lifetime. To Margaret, he gave the accolade of 'that fair virgin, a lady of excellent beauty, with gifts of nature, grace and fortune'. Margaret may have been made to wait longer than her sisters for her future husband to be found, but the match was far superior to both Elizabeth's and Anne's, due to their family's now exalted status.

With the marriage agreed upon, it would be several more months before Margaret set off for her new life, but the York family did celebrate one marriage in 1466 when, in another example of an alliance through the joining of families, Anne of York's daughter, Anne Holland, aged just 9 or 10 years old, was married to the queen's eldest son from her first marriage, Thomas Grey. Elizabeth Woodville had borne two sons to her first husband, Sir John Grey: Thomas, who was born in the mid-1450s, and Richard, born towards the end of the decade, so Anne and Thomas were of a similar age. The ceremony between the pair took place in Greenwich in October 1466. With her husband, the Duke of Exeter, still in exile, all the arrangements for the marriage of her daughter must have been down to Anne. The benefits to both families were clear, Thomas Grey would inherit the Duchy of Exeter on behalf of his wife after his mother-in-law's death, and Anne Holland would have a secure future with a man who would one day be half-brother to England's next king, assuming that Elizabeth Woodville would go on to provide Edward with an heir.

Margaret was no doubt present at the family wedding celebrations on that October day to support her sister, Anne, as mother of the bride. Elizabeth, however, may possibly have been absent as she gave birth to her third son, Edward, probably towards the latter end of 1466 so she may have been getting ready to enter her confinement. Certainly if she did attend, she would have been heavily pregnant.

Although the locations and dates of the births of all of Elizabeth's children have not been recorded, we can be fairly certain that she gave birth to her third child in the house of her mother-in-law Alice, at Ewelme, towards the end of 1466 or early 1467. Between August and December 1466, a set of inventories were made of the contents of the main rooms at Ewelme Manor in Oxfordshire, and it is clear from these documents that preparations were afoot for Elizabeth's lying-in and churching ceremony. Alice Chaucer arranged for several items to be transported to Ewelme from her London house, the 'Mannor of the Rose' and from Wingfield in Suffolk.

Keen to make Elizabeth as comfortable as possible for the birth of her child, the inventories detail a variety of textiles brought to Ewelme by Alice, all in a rich blue and red colour scheme. A 'beryng' mantel of crimson cloth of gold, edged with powdered ermine fur, was provided for Elizabeth's use, along with a scarlet mantel, trimmed with miniver and ermine. The items were delivered by a servant, Alison Croxford, to Ewelme. Other items included a pane and 'headshete' of blue velvet cloth of gold, trimmed with miniver and ermine fur for a bed, along with a matching set for a child's cradle in the nursery, several pillows, a swaddling sheet of Rheims cloth and sheets of lawn cloth for both a bed and couch. These items were delivered on 21 December so it is possible that her third child, believed to be their third son, Edward, was actually born in early 1467.[34]

Elizabeth's lying-in room in 1466/67 was decorated with tapestries that possibly adorned Alice's room when she gave birth to John. They are thought to have been commissioned by William de la Pole in 1440 from the London mercer, Robert Worsley. The inventories also show that Alice brought several of her books to Ewelme, perhaps to keep Elizabeth occupied during the weeks she would be closeted within her chamber before the birth.

One of the rooms given over to Elizabeth's use at Ewelme was the Chamber of 'Demi Seyntes', a room situated beyond the great chamber.

A demi-ceint was a type of girdle with a clasp and long chain, worn low on the hips, particularly favoured by pregnant women of the noble classes; its name may come from the French word for pregnant – enceinte. In Ewelme Manor, the great chamber and chamber of the demi seyntes were at the top of a set of stairs accessed from the parlour. Within one of these rooms was a great chair upholstered with purple satin and ermine fur, listed in the inventory as having been transported for the occasion.

Also placed in pride of place within Elizabeth's chambers were a relic of the head of John the Baptist and a crucifix with Mary and Joseph at the foot of the cross. Both would have been the focus of prayer for Elizabeth during her labour pains and were there to bring her comfort. Elizabeth would eventually prove to be the most fertile of all the York girls, going on to give birth at least eleven times during her lifetime.

As Elizabeth was in the middle of her third birthing experience at Ewelme in the cold winter months of 1466/67, her sister Anne may have been wondering exactly how she could extricate herself from a marriage to an exiled traitor. She may even have already begun the affair with the courtier she would later marry. And their younger sister, Margaret, was just on the cusp of her life as wife and mother – a stage of her life that would mean her leaving her country of birth, knowing she would most likely never live in England again. For all three sisters, the years 1466 and 1467 were a shift towards the new; new life, new relationships and new beginnings.

\*\*\*

Marriage contracts between Margaret of York and Charles the Bold were finally signed in early February 1468, and on 17 May 1468 the English Parliament was formally advised of the imminent marriage of the king's sister. Due to her exalted marriage and status, we have many more descriptions of Margaret than either Anne or Elizabeth, and all seem to extol her appearance; hardly surprising given that both Edward and George, Duke of Clarence, were described as handsome and charismatic. This 'lady of excellent beauty, with so many worthy gifts of nature, grace and fortune',[35] now needed to ensure she had all she needed for her new life as a foreign duchess. We also have descriptions of her new husband, Charles, Duke of Burgundy, who was considered stout and not as tall as his father. He was strong in the spine and arms and stooped forward somewhat with rather heavy shoulders. He was also gifted with 'strong legs and large thighs, long hands and elegant feet, neither too much flesh nor too little bone, but his body was light and brisk and well adapted for work and physical force, his complexion was clear and dark his eyes were laughing and expressive and angelically bright, he had thick black hair, a rounded face, and greyish eyes'.[36]

In preparations for her journey to her new home, Margaret was attended by both her sisters and Elizabeth's husband, the Duke of Suffolk; this would be the last time all three sisters were together in the same place. Perhaps they reminisced about their early years, of their hopes and dreams, and of shared experiences that only close family members can relate to. Together they arranged her travelling cases and packed her clothing into trunks. Edward had prepared his sister well and spared no expense; she was awarded £2,450 6s 8d 'to the apparel, costs and expenses of Margaret, our right entirely beloved sister'.[37] Nothing was to be left out and all her needs were met. Amongst her presents from Edward were:

> A couple of gilt pots for our said sister £20;
> Two basins with ewers £20;
> Spoon of gold £4;
> Pair of carving knives £3;
> A dozen garnished silver vessels £120;
> Beddings, carpets and cushions £100.

She was also given £400 'by reason of certain patents and tallies' and £500 'for money to be had by her in her coffers'. The first instalment of her dowry of 50,000 crowns was due fifteen days before the wedding.

By 18 June Margaret was ready to depart. After saying farewell to her sisters and brother-in-law, she set off on the long journey to the coast. The party headed first to St Paul's where Margaret made an offering, before leaving London and heading to the Abbey of Stratford, where she spent the night in the company of her brother, Edward, and Queen Elizabeth. She then continued her journey on through Dartford, Sittingbourne and Canterbury, eventually reaching Margate where she prepared to set sail.[38]

On Friday 24 June, Margaret's ship, *The Ellen of London*, left dock accompanied by thirteen other ships. On board she was attended by two of the queen's brothers, Anthony and John Woodville. The English party arrived in Sluys the next day where Margaret was to meet her mother-in-law for the first time, the intelligent and pious Isabella of Portugal.[39] She then continued onto Bruges, the City of Merchants, arriving in the city on Sunday 26 June, on what turned out to be a dull and soaking wet day. Two days after landing in Sluys, Margaret was visited by the duke, the first time she would meet her new husband. Reportedly Duke Charles then visited every day until their wedding,[40] which took place a week later, on 3 July 'betwixt five and six of the clock' in the morning. Margaret rose that morning, an English princess, and dressed in her finery. She travelled by boat to Damme, a small town which lies between Sluys and Bruges, a distance of 5 miles by water, and there in the beautiful church she became Duchess of Burgundy. One of the gentlemen in Margaret's English contingency that day was John Paston junior who wrote to his mother on 8 July, reporting the good news:

> My lady Margaret was married on Sunday last past at a town that is called The Damme, three mile out of Bruges, at 5 of the clock in the morning.[41]

After the ceremony, the Duke and Duchess of Burgundy returned to Bruges to celebrate and dine. John Paston describes the celebrations and Margaret's welcome by the people of Bruges 'as the best he had ever seen or heard'. All the way from Damme to Bruges, the people lined the streets to witness their processional entry into the city and to greet their new duchess. The city's guilds marched in procession wearing colourful tunics and carrying their standards, and all along the route pageants were performed and songs were sung. The wedding celebrations continued for the next nine days with a great tournament called L'Arbre d'Or (Tree of Gold) held in the marketplace.[42] The sumptuous court of the duke at Bruges was described by Paston as 'again he had seen nothing like it except King Arthur's court',[43] – the legendary court of King Arthur being the epitome of opulence and majesty. The chronicler Hall enthused about the abundant fare served at the feast, about how many cupboards of gold and silver adorned the palace, of the celebrations, the banquets, the tournaments, he 'neither dare nor will write, lest some men might think that I flattered a little' and that he thinks 'they will say a great deal that it can't be true'.[44]

During the wedding celebrations and many times throughout her life, Margaret would spend time at the ducal court in Bruges, the palace that so enamoured John Paston III. The castle dated back at least to the fourteenth century when Philip the Bold married the daughter of Louis of Male, the richest heiress of the period. The palace was extensively refurbished in the years 1445 to 1468. Margaret and Charles' wedding was the last regal event to be held there though, and it was used less and less until the building was eventually sold by Philip II of Spain in 1576. The site of the palace has since been built over, but a reconstruction project in 2018, using the latest digital photography juxtaposed with original sources, has been able to provide an image of how the magnificent castle looked during the time Margaret was there.

The main room of the castle was the great hall which lay above a vaulted basement containing the kitchen quarters and below the duke and duchess' private apartments, which were under the roof. The kitchen basement was sunk partly below ground in relation to the courtyard, and a set of stairs led from the courtyard to the great hall. The kitchen floor contained at least three main rooms, including the space in the adjacent tower.

The private apartments designed for the duke and his duchess were also split into three: the first was a reception room (the grand chambre), which led to the chambre, the private room where successive dukes would sleep. Continuing through that room, one would enter the retrait (withdrawing chamber). The rooms were accessible from a staircase up from the great hall and although situated in the roof, they were well lit by magnificent tall dormer windows.

By 1468 when Margaret arrived from England, the ducal apartments were being used by Charles' mother, Isabella of Portugal, who subsequently retired to her castle at Motte aux Bois, in the forest of Nieppe, presumably vacating them for her new daughter-in-law's use. The duke's residence had already been moved to the nearby Hôtel Vert, the bachelor's residence of Charles the Bold. This was being completely refurbished as Margaret arrived; neighbouring plots to the Hôtel Vert had been purchased and features such as a large two-storey bath house, a beautiful garden and a stunning double gallery were added. The newly enlarged space also boasted a dining hall, an oratory, a spice room and a jewel chamber.[45]

Incidentally, days before the wedding, two guests who had been staying at the court of Bruges were asked to vacate before Margaret's arrival – her brother-in-law, Henry Holland, and the young Duke of Somerset who had been taking refuge there were advised that it would perhaps not be wise to be present during Margaret's stay.

After the wedding celebrations were over, Charles remained in Bruges until Wednesday 13 July, and Margaret until Tuesday 19th. During their marriage, Charles would spend much time away on business. Margaret, however, was not alone. Upon her arrival in Sluys, she was introduced to her stepdaughter, the 11-year-old Mary of Burgundy, Charles' only child from his previous marriage. After her mother's death in 1465, Mary had been brought up primarily by governesses, under the supervision of her aunt, Anne, Duchess of Burgundy. From the moment Mary and Margaret met, they became inseparable. Over the next nine years, they would live together and spend all but a few weeks apart. This was a relationship that could have been so different, as step-relationships often are, but fortunately for Margaret, who was only 22 and suddenly found herself alone in a foreign realm, they really adored each other. Life at the royal court was always a peripatetic one, and more so perhaps in Burgundy than in England. As Margaret set off to travel her realm and meet her people, Mary became her constant companion, the pair travelling together between the royal palaces at Ghent, Brussels, Aire, Hesdin and Bruges.

When Margaret and Mary left Bruges on 19 July, they set out on progress to meet Margaret's new adopted countrymen and women, travelling through Ursel, Ghent, Dendermonde and Asse, and arriving in Brussels on 23 July. They then took a well-deserved rest in the summer heat, remaining in Brussels throughout August, before setting off once again to Aalst, Oudenaarde, Coutrai and on to Aire where they arrived on 7 September. Whilst in Aire, Margaret was quite poorly; what ailed her is unknown, perhaps she was exhausted by all the travelling or perhaps by the change of climate as she adjusted to the warm summer heat. She had recovered by the end September, when she and her stepdaughter set off towards Hesdin where they spent their first Christmas together.[46]

Margaret would not spend her first Christmas with Charles, however; he was in Brussels over Christmas 1468 and it would not be until the following year, 1469, when they celebrated their first Christmas together at the castle of Ghent.[47]

\*\*\*

As Margaret was settling into her new life, back in England her sisters were having to get used to the fact that their youngest sister had moved away, possibly forever. How often the sisters stayed in touch we can never know, but Margaret retained a fierce loyalty to her family throughout her life, so perhaps they remained as close as they could, writing regular letters to stay in touch with each other. With Margaret getting to know all of the ducal castles that she could call her own, Elizabeth and John, Duke and Duchess of Suffolk, were continuing to make additions to the manor house at Ewelme, seemingly with the view to eventually making that a more permanent residence, perhaps away from the troubles in Norfolk and nearer to the court. Elizabeth had given birth to her first daughter sometime around 1468, bringing the Suffolk brood to a total of four, so their need for a comfortable, spacious residence with a nursery was paramount. John continued to bring across furniture from Wingfield and his mother, Alice decided to spend more of her time in her manor house at Westhorpe, vacating Ewelme for her ever-expanding number of grandchildren.

Meanwhile, another matriarch was also on the move for it was around this time that Cecily decided to switch Fotheringhay for Berkhamsted Castle, where she would spend the rest of her widowhood. Fotheringhay, the York family home for so long, was given over for Edward's use.[48] Perhaps the memories of living there with the Duke of York were too strong. Theirs seems to have been a close marriage, one of the lucky couples whose marriage of convenience turned into a real love match. Within the quiet walls of Berkhamsted Castle, Cecily, would find peace, living a life of religious devotion and travelling to London whenever she was required.

Meanwhile, Anne of York was also forging a new path after all the drama of her early married years. A single lady in all but name, it is likely that she frequented the court of her brother whenever she could, eventually crossing paths with a young courtier by the name of Thomas St Leger. St Leger is somewhat of an enigma. The second son of John St Leger of the Manor of Ulcombe in Kent, Thomas was born sometime around 1439/40 and was two years younger than Anne. With his elder brother, Ralph, inheriting the family manor, it was left to Thomas to find his own way in the world and this he did through his association with the York family. Edward clearly favoured him as he would become one of his most loyal retainers, serving in numerous public commissions as required by his king, including Controller of the Mint under William Hastings.

Before joining Edward's court, he may have worked in some capacity for the Duke of York – a pardon was granted to him in 1465 after he assaulted one of the Marshalls of the King's Hall, a wonderfully named Stephen Christmas Esquire, on account of his good service to the king and his late father. It is highly possible that St Leger was on the battlefield at Towton, fighting on behalf of the Yorkists,[49] but other than his public duties, St Leger leaves behind barely any personal footprint of himself. We can only assume that he was charming, perhaps good looking, perhaps he was funny with twinkling eyes and a great sense of humour? And Anne, presumably having reached the conclusion that whatever she had felt about Henry Holland, there was no way back, fell for this young man who was in sufficient favour with her brother, the king, that Edward allowed the relationship to develop. When it started we don't know, but it was very possibly towards the latter end of the 1460s.

By the last year of the decade, things seemed to have fallen into place. In the royal court, with the old king Henry in captivity and his queen Margaret of Anjou in exile, Edward and his wife had been settling into royal family life. With two children already in the nursery, albeit daughters but a certainty sons would follow, Edward should have been secure on his throne. But under the surface an uneasy atmosphere was brewing. For a while now, Edward and his closest cousin, Warwick, the kingmaker, the man who helped him to the throne, had been on a collision course. Edward's choice of bride could be considered as one of the catalysts in the deterioration of their relationship. Alongside this, Warwick had been hugely influential in Edward's path to the throne, but not as influential as he had perhaps imagined he would be during Edward's reign. At the same time, George, Duke of Clarence, now a young man approaching 20, was struggling to find his place in this new world. Heavily under Warwick's influence, a rift was starting to form between George and Edward. As early as 1467, Warwick had broached the idea of a marriage between George and his eldest daughter, Isabel Neville. Sensing that collusion between his wayward brother and the powerful Warwick was a dangerous idea, Edward flatly refused to even consider the notion.

In March 1469, shortly after the birth of their third child, Princess Cecily, the king and queen set out on a planned progress to East Anglia, accompanied by Richard, Duke of Gloucester, and the queen's brothers, Anthony and John Woodville. By the end of June, reports of skirmishes in the north were rife and Edward realised he had little choice but to deal directly with the troubles. As he set off north, issuing a call for Warwick and Clarence to join him, Edward was unaware that on 11 July, in a direct violation of his ruling, the two men had travelled to France and, in a ceremony held in the port of Calais, Clarence wed Isabel Neville. But this was no love match. With Edward having not yet sired a son, if anything happened to him, Clarence was next in line to be king and Warwick's daughter would then be queen. Warwick's motives were clear – he was trying his hand at kingmaking again. Clarence, seeing a route to wealth and power and likely bored of being an underdog to his elder brother, went along with the plan.

As Edward and his men reached his childhood family home of Fotheringhay, he repeated his demand for Warwick and Clarence to join him, still completely unaware that they were in Calais. The men did not heed his call; instead Edward received what could only be described as a rebel manifesto sent by Warwick, which had been signed by himself, Clarence and Archbishop George Neville. The manifesto pledged their support to the northern rebels and accused members of the queen's family, as well as others around the king, of allowing the realm to 'fall in great poverty of misery … Only intending to their own promotion and enriching'. Clarence and Warwick then returned from France and began marching north with the intention of joining the rebels.

Edward was at Newark when he received notification of Warwick and Clarence's treachery, doubtless with shock and disappointment. He sent word out for support and the Earls of Pembroke and Devon answered his call. On Wednesday 26 July, the armies of Pembroke and Devon were ambushed by Warwick's men and in what became known as the Battle of Edgecote, the Yorkist forces were routed. In a horrific turn of events for the Woodville family, the queen's father and brother were captured and beheaded at Kenilworth, on the orders of Clarence and Warwick.

After Edward's defeat at Edgecote, many of his men fled, leaving him in a vulnerable position. Warwick, catching up with the king at Olney, escorted him back to his home at Warwick Castle where he effectively held him as his prisoner.

What a turn of events this was: two cousins, once the best of friends and allies, now one a prisoner and one his captor. As the news reached the ears of Anne and Elizabeth of York (and several days later, Margaret in Burgundy), what must their thoughts have been towards their cousin and brother, George. Surely disbelief? What could possibly be happening?

With Edward and Warwick still shut up in Warwick Castle, it soon became clear to the earl that he could not raise enough supporters to remove Edward from the throne. Without their king, the country was descending into chaos and Warwick found himself without a recognisable authority to regain control. Unable to bring himself to commit cold-blooded murder and kill his king and one-time close ally at this time, embarrassingly he had to let Edward go. Edward returned to London, via York, and was accompanied back into the capital by Elizabeth's husband, the Duke of Suffolk, an indication at least that Elizabeth and her family were firmly in Edward's camp and not her younger brother, George's. John Paston, writing to his mother, described his homecoming:

> The King is come to London, and there came with him, and rode again him [and rode to meet him], the Duke of Gloucester, the Duke of Suffolk, the Earl of Arundel, the Earl of Northumberland, the Earl of Essex, the Lords Harry and John of Buckingham, the Lord Dacre, the Lord Chamberlain, the Lord Montjoy, and many other Knights and Esquires... The King came through Cheap, though it were out of his way, because he would not be seen, and he was accompanied in all people with 1000 horse, some harnessed, and some not... The King himself hath good language of the Lords of Clarence, of Warwick, and of my Lords of York, and of Oxford, saying they be his best friends; but his household men have other language, so what shall hastily fall, I cannot say.[50]

It seems that the benevolent Edward had reached an understanding with his cousin and brother, and had forgiven them. Surely Anne and Elizabeth, along with their mother, must have been trying desperately to smooth the situation over between the warring men of their family. Hopefully it had now been resolved and peace could be resumed. And the drama did seem to be over for a while. Christmas 1469 passed peacefully enough, but it seems that behind the scenes, Warwick and Clarence were not prepared to let things lie. In March 1470 a private feud between two Lincolnshire lords began to spill over, and Edward, riding with his men to control the situation, once again discovered some of the troublemakers were bearing the standards of Clarence and Warwick. By May 1470, the pair, realising that their treachery would not be forgiven so easily this time, fled to France where the men of Calais, remaining loyal to their king, this time refused to allow them to dock. During this sea journey, Clarence's wife, Isabel, gave birth to a son in what must have been horrendous conditions below deck. Eventually making shore further down the coast, Warwick arranged an audience with the Lancastrian Margaret of Anjou. At first she was resistant to him – he was her enemy, one of the main ringleaders in the downfall of the House of Lancaster – but eventually she listened. Together they reached a deal – Warwick would help restore her husband to the throne if she agreed to a marriage between her son, Edward of Lancaster, and his youngest daughter, Anne Neville, who had also travelled with them, making Anne the next potential Queen of England. Margaret agreed and France once again played host to the marriage of one of Warwick's daughters as his youngest child, Anne, married Prince Edward. Warwick then began preparations to sail to England with an army.

This was now serious. The throne that the York family had fought so hard for was now in peril and yet the danger came not from the outside, but from within their own family. Anne, Elizabeth and Margaret must have been incredulous at what was playing out before them. Banding together, they began to exert pressure on their brothers to stop the infighting before it was too late.

As Warwick set sail back to England with an army, Clarence remained in Normandy. Vain and arrogant he may have been, but he was not unintelligent and was beginning to realise that his importance in Warwick's scheme was waning. What he had agreed to had now changed – Warwick was now fighting to put the Lancastrian Henry back on the throne rather than Clarence and Isabel. During his stay in Normandy, it is reported that a secret messenger arrived from England – a mysterious lady reportedly on her way to Isabel, Duchess of Clarence, with letters containing overtures of peace. Who this lady was is a mystery but her real mission was to entreat Clarence not to ruin his own family by being blind to Warwick's plan and helping to restore the House of Lancaster. Meeting discreetly with the Duke of Clarence, she reminded him that it 'was neither natural nor honourable for him to take part against the House of York, from which he was descended, and to set up again the House of Lancaster'.[51]

Was this woman an envoy from either Anne or Elizabeth's household, or even a joint initiative to remind their brother that he was part of the House of York? According to the *Croyland Chronicle*, whilst still appearing to support Warwick on the surface, the duke was 'quietly reconciled to the king by the mediation of [their] sisters, the Duchesses of Burgundy and Exeter. The former, from outside the kingdom, had been encouraging the king, and the latter, from within, the duke, to make peace'. Croyland specifically mentions Anne and Margaret here, but presumably Elizabeth was just as concerned.

Warwick, arriving back on English soil, headed straight for London, his mission to free Henry VI from the Tower of London. By October 1470, Edward found himself trapped, surrounded by rebels in the north and with Warwick's army marching up from the south. He was faced with no choice other than to flee abroad himself with his most loyal supporters, including his youngest brother, Richard, Duke of Gloucester, and William Hastings, his trustworthy friend and Lord Chamberlain.

The Duke of Suffolk was at his house at Wingfield at the time; it is likely that Elizabeth was with him, and an extant letter written by him from Wingfield on 22 October illustrates that he was not with his brother-in-law and king and therefore he did not flee with the men.[52] On 14 November, with the country in disarray, he was commissioned along with the Duke of Norfolk and Lord Rivers to hold the county of Norfolk in order against insurgents.

As the news reached the York sisters in their respective households, it must have been difficult to comprehend. Their elder brother had been forced to flee the country along with their youngest brother, Richard of Gloucester, and although they were doing their best to bring George back into the fold, this was a huge mess. Back in London, when the news of Edward's flight reached Queen Elizabeth Woodville, she was heavily pregnant with their fourth child. Knowing that Warwick was heading towards London, preparing to put the Lancastrian king, Henry, back on the throne, understandably, she feared for her life. Clutching her daughters and with her mother in tow, she took herself to her barge, and fled up the Thames to the sanctuary of Westminster Abbey. Things were looking bleak, and unlike the last time, a decade before, when external influences had been at play, this was a home-grown family-made disaster.

# Chapter 6

# A family at war

By the time Edward and Richard of Gloucester arrived on foreign shores, Margaret had been Duchess of Burgundy for just over two years. Having left in a hurry, the unexpectedness of the situation meant that the brothers and their men did not have a grand plan. According to Commynes, the men made their escape 'by the assistance of a small vessel of his [Edward's] own and two Dutch merchantmen, attended only by 700 or 800 men, without any clothes but what they were to have fought in, no money in their pockets, and not one of them knew whither they were going'.[1] Before they left, his chamberlain, William Hastings, instructed all who remained behind to make peace with Warwick for their own safety but to stay loyal to Edward. It was no surprise though that upon arriving on the continent, it was Burgundy that Edward would head for to call upon the support of the Duke of Burgundy and his younger sister.

But initially, upon reaching shore, the men were rescued by Louis de Gruuthuse, governor of The Hague and spent the winter of 1470 as his honoured guests, regrouping and deciding on their next move. Lord de Gruuthuse dealt honourably with Edward and his men during their stay, and it was an honour that Edward would later repay.

During the 1470s, Margaret had spent a good proportion of time at the castle of Ten Waele in Ghent which was in the process of being renovated, with Margaret overseeing the work. In November 1470, she and Mary of Burgundy left Ten Waele and headed for Hesdin where they joined Charles for Christmas, and news must have soon reached Margaret that her two brothers were recently arrived at The Hague; perhaps she was already making plans to visit them there. On the way to Hesdin, Margaret and Mary took a detour through Mons, where they were welcomed by the townspeople who were so delighted to see them that they gave the two women gifts of wine, enamels and gold plate. Margaret and Mary were escorted on the journey by one of their most trusted advisors, Lord Ravenstein, and as the ladies rode into Mons, dressed in black velvet gowns trimmed with fur as protection against the cold November weather, they were greeted by a long procession of lords, ladies and city representatives.[2]

Meanwhile, back in London, in an illustration of just how bad their relationship had become, Warwick, the king's once-loyal cousin who fought with Edward to gain the throne just a decade before, called on his fellow countrymen to free 'our most dread sovereign Lord, King Henry the Sixth, very true and undoubted king of England and France' from the hands of 'his great rebel and enemy, Edward, late Earl of March, usurper, oppressor, and destroyer of our said sovereign lord and of the noble blood of all the realm of England and of the good, true commons of the same'.[3] In a period that became known as the readeption of Henry VI, Warwick proceeded to free Henry VI from captivity and restored the old king to the throne. For the next six months, the House of Lancaster was back in charge of the country.

In sanctuaries across the city, many of Edward's friends and supporters had taken refuge or were in hiding. Edward's queen and her daughters had sought sanctuary at Westminster, worried for their lives. However, the whereabouts of Anne and Elizabeth of York at this time is uncertain. Perhaps they did not consider themselves in any real danger; Warwick and Clarence were their kin, and although that had not stopped them turning against Edward, Clarence would surely not put his sisters in danger – they were no real threat to him. For Anne the situation was particularly troublesome as the return of the Lancastrians to power heralded the return of one of their biggest champions. Henry Holland, Duke of Exeter, arrived back in the capital in early February 1471. Joining Warwick in London, he was re-established as Justice of the Peace in Bedfordshire, Northamptonshire and Huntingdonshire. All his lands, however, were of course now in Anne's possession and it is highly possible that he attempted to see Anne during this time, if not for her, but for his daughter who he had not seen for almost a decade.

Whilst Edward was staying at the Hague, he received news that Queen Elizabeth had given birth in sanctuary – a much longed for son whom she named Edward after his father. This surely gave him even more of a reason to fight his way back to the kingdom he had ruled over for the last nine years. With Edward a guest at his home, Gruuthuse sent messengers with the news of their arrival to the Duke of Burgundy, who, according to Commynes 'was much surprised when he heard it and would have been much better pleased if it had been news of his death; for he was in great apprehension of the Earl of Warwick, who was his enemy, and at that time absolute in England'.[4] Not perhaps the reaction Edward would have been hoping for.

If Charles was indeed set to ignore the bond of friendship between the two countries and not come to his brother-in-law's aid, this would have been a real blow to Edward. But even if privately Charles was wishing his brother-in-law had not turned up in this situation asking for his help, he did the right thing and agreed to meet him. On 2 January 1471, the two men met at Aire.[5] After their discussions, during which Edward surely reminded his brother-in-law of their family ties, Charles departed and Margaret came to meet her older brother, the first time she had seen him in three years. Together they travelled to Hesdin and from 5 to 31 January, Edward and his men were put up in the castle there. Having not seen either of her brothers for several years, there must have been much to catch up on, although surely all of them wished that they were together again for a different reason. Margaret remained at Hesdin for much of January, making short trips away presumably on court business, but on Wednesday 23 January she departed Hesdin and headed for Lille where she remained for the rest of February.[6] From 12 to 14 February her younger brother, Richard, Duke of Gloucester, came to visit her there.

During their time at the Burgundian court, Edward pleaded with the duke to give him supplies to enable him to recover his kingdom. Margaret no doubt also applied the pressure. Although the duke may not have been entirely willing to help him out, seemingly wary of starting a war with Warwick, it seems that family ties won out and the duke agreed to provide him with 500 golden crowns per month for his support. Attempting to take the middle ground, Charles publicly declared he would not support Edward, but in secret he supplied him with more money and three or four great ships, which he ordered to be fully equipped for the sea crossing home. Edward gladly accepted and on 15 February 1471, the Yorkist men began their journey back across land towards Vlissingen and their passage home, no doubt with Margaret wishing them godspeed.[7]

Commynes reports that the duke later 'received letters from the duchess, his wife, that the king of England was not at all satisfied with him; that the assistance he had given him was not done frankly and willingly, but as if for a very little cause he would have deserted him; and, to speak plainly, there was never great friendship between them afterwards'.[8] Edward, it seems, did personally write and thank the duke himself in a letter sent on 28 May 1471, in which he thanked the duke for 'the valuable and brotherly assistance he had given him in his distress'. Margaret was clearly not impressed that Charles had not immediately jumped to her family's support and had needed some persuading. She would have been even less impressed if the news had reached her ears later that year in November 1471, that Charles had begun to formally set out his own claims to the English throne. His mother, Isabella, was the daughter of Philippa of Lancaster, herself the eldest daughter of John of Gaunt and his first wife, Blanche of Lancaster, and Isabella considered herself the senior surviving representative of the House of Lancaster after Henry VI and his son. It clearly wasn't far from Charles' mind that he, himself, had a claim to the English throne, and in 1471 he was staking his interest.

Edward and his men finally landed back on England's shores six months after they departed. Landing at Ravenspur in the north of England in March 1471, several cities weary of trouble refused to admit him. With only his few loyal supporters with him, Edward knew he was not yet a match for his enemies and declared himself loyal to Henry VI, claiming he was only back in England to reclaim the York title that was rightfully his after the death of his father and brother. He then began a slow march down the country, collecting men in support along the way. His chamberlain, William Hastings, had already ridden ahead to his homelands in the Midlands and by the time Edward had reached Leicester, Hastings had gathered an army of over 3,000 'stirred by his [Hastings] messages sent unto them, and by his servants, friends and lovers, such as were in the country'.[9]

Meanwhile, the Earl of Warwick was in Coventry and refused to engage with Edward, so he bypassed him and continued his march south, meeting up with Clarence in Banbury, where George fell on his knees and begged forgiveness from his brother. Edward hugged him and immediately forgave him. Hearing the news that Edward IV had landed, Henry Holland quickly gathered men from his estates and headed north, accompanied by the Earl of Oxford. He also failed to engage with Edward at Newark and instead joined Warwick at Coventry.

Edward, now in the company of both of his brothers and reconciled to fight together, returned to Coventry where Warwick, who had been expecting Clarence to bring reinforcements to assist him, realised he had lost his son-in-law's support and still refused to engage. Edward's men left him there and began to march on London to reclaim the capital.

This time Margaret of York was probably aware of her brother's plans before Anne and Elizabeth. It was Anne and Elizabeth, waiting in London for their brother's return who would have spent the last six months anxiously worrying about him and their younger brother, Richard. Perhaps they only heard of his return along with the rest of the City of London, who, by Tuesday 9 April 1471, became aware that 'Edward late King of England was hastening towards the city with a powerful army'. As Edward and his men approached the city, Warwick was writing at speed to the city leaders, urging them to remain steadfast in support of Henry VI. With the Aldermen of the City in confusion and unsure of what they were supposed to do, the mayor, John Stockton, allegedly retired to his bed due to the stress and could not be persuaded to leave it.

Archbishop George Neville, who was in London at the time, made a final attempt to persuade the people of London to remain loyal to Henry by parading him through the streets. But the difference between the two kings was striking – the old and fainthearted Henry VI, looking shabby in his old gown was no comparison to the youthful, strong and popular Edward. When Edward finally reached London, the gates were opened to admit him. Commynes believed there were three reasons why the City of London welcomed him in; firstly, because of all Edward's friends in the sanctuaries around the city and the birth of his son; secondly, due to the amount of money he had borrowed from the tradesmen of London, who knew if they did not aid him in his quest he would be unable to pay them back; and thirdly, that all the wives of the city with whom he had previously flirted or charmed persuaded their husbands to declare themselves on his side. Whatever the reason, he was allowed access and upon entering the city, he rode straight to St Paul's to give thanks before heading to the sanctuary to reunite with Queen Elizabeth and meet his son for the very first time.

Without much resistance, Edward IV was back as King of England. In a face-to-face meeting with old King Henry, allegedly the frail and old man greeted him like a friend and cousin, without fear, and Edward dispatched him back into imprisonment in the Tower. But although Edward was back in London and reinstated as king, the danger was still very real and imminent as Warwick was still at large. As much as he was a formidable ally, he had also proved himself to be a dangerous foe. Edward had only one possible choice. Gathering his men, he set off to find his once-loyal cousin. On 14 April 1471, Edward and Warwick finally met on the battlefield at what would become known as the Battle of Barnet. Both men must have been aware that the battle had to be decisive. And it was. Warwick, one of the most powerful and influential men of his time, was killed and Edward, this time with both of his brothers at his side, emerged victorious. Henry Holland was also on the field that day, fighting on Warwick's side, and he emerged badly injured, reportedly managing to lie low on the battlefield until one of his men found him and took him to sanctuary at Westminster.

On the same day that the Battle of Barnet was raging, Margaret of Anjou and her son, Prince Edward, had landed on English shores. Edward, gathering his men once more, headed off to meet her en route to London. The two armies met at Tewkesbury and Edward once more emerged victorious. Margaret's son, Edward of Lancaster, was killed and the defeated queen of Henry VI, broken with grief at the death of her son, was captured and taken to London where she would remain a prisoner for the next few years. Henry Holland was also extricated from sanctuary in May and he too was imprisoned in the Tower.

Not long after Tewkesbury, Henry VI was found dead in his room, apparently of natural causes, although undoubtedly few believed this official version of the story. The death of Henry VI made Henry Holland an even more important and dangerous prisoner as his lineage made him a potential Lancastrian claimant. Given his complete lack of loyalty to their family over the years, it was more important than ever that he be kept where Edward could keep an eye on him.

Having Holland back in London, especially as he was held captive, may have been just what Anne of York needed, for in June 1471 she began divorce proceedings against him. With the full support of her family, she was assisted by her brother-in-law, John de la Pole, who agreed to act as an administrator for her. Proceedings were commenced in her brother Clarence's London house with the appointment of representatives who would act on Anne's behalf. Amongst the witnesses who gave evidence in support of Anne were Agatha Flegge, an old servant of the Duke of York, who had been present at Anne's birth; John Profoot, the king's secretary; and Galfrid Spryng, the clerk of the royal jewels. Others who would speak for her were the king's farrier, and two men from Clarence's household: John Pury, the controller of the household, and Thomas Gryme, the keeper of Clarence's jewels. These were likely people that had known Anne of old, some of whom had served in her parents' household as she grew up.[10]

The divorce proceedings began quickly, and on 19 June Henry Holland was summoned from the Tower to Lambeth. Divorce, as we know it in its modern form, did not exist in the medieval age. Marriage vows were considered sacrosanct and fell under church law which had very strict rules regarding divorce. It was also an expensive process so any cases of divorce that did appear were mainly amongst the nobility who could afford to pay.

There were very few reasons that a marriage could be dissolved, including where one party had a pre-contract of marriage, impotence, clandestine marriages, marrying a minor, or the one that Anne would use: consanguinity, where the couple in question were related by blood. Anne's consanguinity claim was based in the fourth and fifth degree on account of their joint descent from Edward III.

Anne supplied eight witnesses to the proceedings and Henry had four, and all were asked the same questions: How long they had known the couple; what they knew of their consanguinity; what they knew about the dispensation that had allowed their marriage; and what age they had been at the time of marriage. Full details were supplied of the marriage ceremony and the archbishop pronounced the marriage annulled on 5 November.[11]

What did Anne feel about being a free woman again? Relieved? Overjoyed? Did she reflect on what could have been? It was certainly the only thing she could have done in her situation, and it now left her completely free to marry the man she had since fallen in love with, Thomas St Leger. Although they had almost certainly begun a relationship before her divorce, the exact date of their marriage is unknown, but undoubtedly it would have been sometime around 1472. No details remain but it was surely a reason for the whole family to get together and celebrate, her siblings glad that Anne had finally achieved some contentment and happiness in her life. The Exeter estates that she held in her name would pass down to any children they might have together, confirmed in a 1467 grant that had awarded Anne ownership of all the Exeter lands, including the manors of Stevington and Coldharbour 'with remainders to her daughter, Anne and the heirs of her body and to the heirs of the body of the Duchess'.[12]

For the next few years, Anne perhaps found happiness in her daily life. Little is known about her in the early 1470s; perhaps she and Thomas attended the second recrowning ceremony that the king and queen held in the Palace of Westminster at the end of December 1471, when Edward and Queen Elizabeth took part in a second coronation on Christmas Day and Twelfth Night to celebrate Edward's victory over his enemies. That they were based in London is probably a given as Thomas was in constant service at court, and it is likely that they either had rooms at court or continued to live at Coldharbour or the Exeter apartments in the Tower. An ordinance of 1471 lists Thomas as a Squire of the Body, a position he had held since February 1463 and his loyalty to Edward would be rewarded in 1478 when he was knighted by his king.[13]

We can only really get a glimpse of the life of Thomas St Leger, and by association the life he shared with Anne, through the grants he received. On 16 October 1465, a grant for life was made to 'Thomas Seyntleger, one of the esquires of the body for the custody of the park of Guildford, in the County of Surrey', and a second grant was issued on 23 December 1469 when he received the custody of 'all manors, lands, possessions and rents and knights fees', along with another man, Nicholas Gaynes, 'that late belonged to John White, during the minority of Robert White, his son'.[14] On 18 August 1473 he was commissioned along with several other men to look into some unpaid profits from 'certain farms for lands granted and divers other sums of money and yearly profits in the County of Surrey and to report before the king and council at Westminster in the quinzaine of Michaelmas next [the fifteenth day after Michaelmas]'.[15] And on 20 October 1473 he was granted a licence, again with several other gentlemen, to found a perpetual chantry, consisting of one chaplain, in a chapel built by John Champfloure in the church of Alton. The chantry was to pray for the 'good estate of the king, his consort Elizabeth, queen of England, his firstborn son, Edward, prince of Wales, Duke of Cornwall and Earl of Chester and for the founders of the chantry and their souls after death. Also for the soul of John Champfloure'. The chantry was to be called Champfloures Chaunterie. By 7 July 1474, Thomas was also acting as a Justice for the Bench in Middlesex.[16]

After the temporary blip of 1470/71, the York star was on the rise once more. In April 1472, Queen Elizabeth Woodville gave birth to a fourth royal child, a daughter whom they named Margaret, perhaps in honour of Edward's sister, remembering the help she had provided him during his exile. And just twelve days after Princess Margaret's birth, a papal dispensation was issued permitting the marriage of Richard, Duke of Gloucester, to Anne Neville, the youngest daughter of the recently deceased Earl of Warwick. The dispensation was required because of their shared ancestry: Richard's mother, Cecily Neville, was sister to Anne's grandfather, Richard, Duke of Salisbury. The dispensation arrived in England in June, although the marriage may almost certainly have taken place before then.

It is highly probably that Richard of Gloucester knew Warwick's daughters of old, from his time spent as a youth at Middleham under the tutelage of the earl. Warwick had only two children: Isabel, married to George, Duke of Clarence, and Anne, who had, of course, been wed to the Lancastrian Prince Edward in 1470, as part of her father's agreement with Margaret of Anjou. After Prince Edward's death at Tewkesbury, Anne Neville had been brought to London along with his mother, Margaret of Anjou, where she was placed into the care of her sister and brother-in-law.

The motives behind this union between Richard of Gloucester and Anne Neville have always been contentious. Through George's marriage to Isabel, after Warwick's death he held custody of the vast Warwick estates by right of his wife. The earl's widow, the Countess of Warwick, was still living in 1472, and had taken refuge in Beaulieu Abbey during the troubles of the previous year. By rights the Warwick estates should have been hers, but as punishment for the actions of her husband, she was refused her entitlement; a few years later, Parliament, in an appalling move, would have her declared legally dead when they divided up the Warwick estates, even though she did not actually die until the early 1490s.

But once again the York brothers decided to taint their family's success with squabbles. Richard demanded that the Warwick estates, which were worth a considerable amount and represented significant wealth and power, were split between the brothers. George refused to relinquish any, setting both younger brothers on a warring path, with King Edward having to step in to mediate. Upon her arrival in London, Anne Neville had been sent to live with the Clarences at L'Erber, Clarence's London house, which was situated close to his sister Anne's at Coldharbour. Anne Neville was reportedly terribly unhappy living with the Clarences and wrote several letters to the queen and her mother Jacquetta Woodville, as well as Cecily Neville, who all refused to assist her.

At some point in 1471/72, Richard vocalised his intentions to marry his childhood friend. When George became aware of this, he allegedly tried to keep her out of his reach, one account telling of how he sent her to the house of one of his retainers, disguising her as a kitchen maid so Richard was unable to locate her. This story may be fictional, but in truth George may have tried to limit their meetings as much as possible. The pair must have made contact at some point, however, and made plans, as on 16 February 1472, Richard enabled her to escape from L'Erber into sanctuary at the London Collegiate church of St Martin Le Grand. A few short months later they were married.

But were they childhood sweethearts or was Richard attempting to claim some of the Warwick lands through marriage to a Warwick daughter? Whatever the motives behind his actions, the marriage took place sometime between February and July 1472, based on the later birth date of their son. The young couple went to live at Middleham, in the north of England, where they remained for the next ten years, with Richard supporting his brother in the management of the north. The matter of the Warwick estates would rumble on for another two years before Parliament passed an act dividing the lands equally between the two brothers.

Elizabeth and Anne in their households and Margaret in Burgundy may once again have been shaking their heads in despair at the infighting between their younger brothers. Seemingly they remained a neutral stance in court affairs, although, of course, as women their reactions and involvements were not reported. Anne had achieved her happy-ever-after with a new husband and was getting her life back on track. Margaret in Burgundy was a step away from her family troubles, and Elizabeth was presumably busy raising her ever-growing family.

The Suffolks had four children in the 1460s and Elizabeth gave birth to three more children in the early 1470s: Edmund, in 1471, Dorothy in 1472 who sadly did not live long, and Humphrey in around 1474. The Duke of Suffolk had remained in England during Edward's exile, and he and Elizabeth had managed to tread a fine line during the readeption, undoubtedly remaining loyal to Edward whilst living quietly on their estates and avoiding conflict. When Edward returned to London, Suffolk accompanied him on his journey into the capital and was also by his side at the Battles of Tewkesbury and Barnet. He was amongst the group of nobles in attendance on 11 June 1471, when the infant Prince Edward was invested as Prince of Wales at a ceremony in Westminster Abbey. He also attended the great council meeting in early July where the young prince was formally recognised as the heir to the throne, and allegiance was pledged to him by all the great and noble magnates of the land.

They continued to reside primarily at Ewelme and in 1471 Elizabeth's mother-in-law, Alice, had bequeathed them some of her possessions, perhaps those that had been left behind at Ewelme when she herself moved to Westhorpe and which she wanted to formally give them. These included silver- and gold-gilded plates, beds of cloth of gold and silk and tapestries. She also formalised in writing that other items which she could not yet bequeath to them, because they were still in use by her, would eventually come their way after her death.[17]

Around this time, Suffolk was also appointed Constable of Wallingford Castle, the position that his mother had once held. He already held the position of steward of the honours of Wallingford and Saint Valerie and, presumably as a reward for his loyalty, Edward also awarded him the office of Steward for Ewelme, Burford, Pyrton and Lewknor.[18] By May 1474 his was also the first name listed among the Knights of the Order of the Garter.

Whilst her husband was fulfilling his various duties, Elizabeth would have been kept busy running her household. In the early 1470s, a daughter of Jane Stonor was living in the Suffolk household, and she was later joined by a second daughter, who was perhaps placed there on the suggestion of the queen.[19] Jane Stonor's daughters were most likely serving in the Suffolk household, learning their trade as maids and as if the household wasn't full enough, on 11 July 1471 the Suffolks also took on the wardship of a 15-year-old boy named Francis Lovell, who would later go on to be a close associate of Elizabeth's younger brother, Richard of Gloucester.[20] Having a ward was more often than not financially beneficial to the family, bringing with it the income from the ward's family lands until they came of age. Lovell's wardship brought with it 'the custody of all lordships, manors, lands and possessions late of John Lovell, knight, lord of Lovell, deceased, tenant in chief by knight service, during the minority of Francis Lovell his son and heir, with advowsons, knights' fees, courts leet, views of frank-pledge, fairs, markets, warrens and profits and the custody and marriage of the said Francis without disparagement, and so from heir to heir, finding competent sustenance for the heir and supporting all houses, enclosures and buildings, provided that this grant shall not extend to any possessions which may afterwards descend to the heir'.[21]

With Elizabeth contending with a household of children and young people, across the sea in Burgundy, it was a different story altogether and Margaret of York was having little success in producing an heir. As with many relationships today, let alone hundreds of years ago, we cannot possibly even pretend to know what the relationship was like between Margaret and Charles. After her marriage, Margaret lived in her own household; which consisted of around 140 people, with around 90 on duty at any given time, a highly respectable size for a duchess. The majority of the staff were under the command of three maîtres d'hôtel. Her twelve maids of honour and three ladies of the bedchamber were under the charge of Marie, Countess of Charny (an illegitimate sister of Charles). These ladies would have been closest to Margaret and would have been the first to notice if, and when, her courses stopped, heralding the first sign of pregnancy.[22]

Margaret's primary residence was at Ten Waele and perhaps part of the issue was that she spent much of her married life away from her husband. Only the castles of Ghent, Brussels and Hesdin could accommodate both households and therefore Margaret and Charles did not often reside together. Apart from the practical issue of space for both households, another reason that they spent little time together was down to Charles' ambition and work ethic. It was said of Charles that his favourite leisure time was to 'go in the morning from room to room to organise justice, war and finance'. A hugely accomplished man, he was constantly busy, attributes that could also be said of Margaret herself, particularly in her later years of life. But the downside of all of this was that the couple were barely together for much of their marriage.

As for his character, Charles was known to be violent, cruel, moody and temperamental. He was considered immensely vain, egotistic and showy in his appearance and full of self-importance. Allegedly he was heard to claim that there were only three lords in the world: one in heaven that is god, one in hell that is the devil and one on earth who will be he himself.[23] But it was this self-belief and work ethic that made him a great leader.

Another less attractive characteristic attributed to the duke was his apparent low regard for women. It was understood that he purposely stayed in a separate household from his wife as he did not want his household pampered by women. Instead he would visit once or twice a week as he pleased when his household was nearby, and during the first six months of their married life, Margaret and Charles were together for only twenty-one days. The amount of time they spent together did increase over the next few years, perhaps indicating that Margaret did manage to prove to her stubborn husband that she was a woman worth knowing and by 1472, they were regularly residing at short distances from each other. But again in 1473 and 1474 they met only for about ten to fifteen days – perhaps by then it had become clear to Charles that Margaret was not going to be able to provide him with an heir and he had taken to once again focusing his full attention on court business.[24]

By 1474 Margaret and Charles had been married six years and there was no sign of a pregnancy. Given that her mother and sister, Elizabeth, had both shown themselves to be incredibly fertile, perhaps her lack of a child proved to be a great sadness to Margaret? Her stepdaughter, Mary, must have been a blessing and comfort to her, especially if she ever reflected on whether her own chances of motherhood were slipping away. Together, the two women made pilgrimages to shrines associated with health and childbirth, and during the 1470s Margaret made several visits to the statue of the Virgin Mary at Hal. From February to March 1473, Margaret also stayed at the St-Josse-ten-Noode in the forest of Soignes, which was a health resort and spa built by Charles' father, Duke Philip, close to Brussels. This may have been an opportunity for her to rest and pay attention to her health, but some historians have reflected on whether this could, in fact, have been a period of enforced recuperation after a miscarriage?

Wherever she went Margaret was accompanied by Mary; they had clearly developed a very close relationship and Margaret may have to some extent found the mother/daughter relationship she was seeking in the absence of God providing her with any children of her own. Together they resided in the main ducal castles including Maele, where Margaret spent her first Christmas. She returned there again in the summer of 1472 and was there when a huge fire swept through the building, destroying much of her property. She had been entertaining the English ambassadors and thankfully nobody was injured, but the fire rendered the castle uninhabitable and Margaret lost many jewels, tapestries and clothes to the value of 60,000 crowns.[25]

Her primary residence though was at the castle of Ten Waele, a beautiful island residence built between 1349 and 1353 by Count Louis de Male. The building no longer survives, but in its prime it boasted more than 300 rooms, beautiful courtyards and formal gardens, as well as a hexagonal island garden reached by a small boat.[26] But without doubt the most striking residence that Margaret would often call home was the ducal castle at Hesdin, a building that captivated the visiting William Caxton when he stayed there.

Built by Robert Artois between 1293 and 1302, Hesdin can best be described as a mechanical pleasure palace.[27] Philip the Bold made substantial alterations between 1393 and 1396, and it was he that installed all the automations that made the castle so famous. Inside its walls could be found a plethora of unexpected surprises to shock, stun and entrance visiting guests. The highlight of the property was perhaps the long gallery that simulated the weather, dropping snow and rain on unexpected guests and replicating thunder and lightning. Rooms also featured statues that spouted paint and a staircase that tipped people, so its occupants fell onto bags of feathers. Waters from the nearby river were channelled inside the castle to cause amusement to visitors, and several devices sprayed water onto people unexpectedly. There were also more practical jokes such as a book of ballads lying on a table that squirted the unsuspecting reader with soot, and a window that when opened, a figure appeared, sprayed the visitor with water and slammed the window shut again.[28] The mechanics to work all these effects were based on pullied hoists, counterweighted levers and plumbing systems, with the odd bit of clockwork thrown in.

If Margaret was not a fan of the mechanics and waterworks, the castle boasted many other attributes that kept it in favour with Margaret and Mary. Waterfalls and fountains also kept their proper place in the gardens, and in the castle surrounds there was an aviary, a pavilion and a great park. The castle itself also included a lodge, chapel and ducal apartments and the Great Hall at Hesdin, always the centre of any medieval residence, was adorned with expensive tapestries and paintings. However, the main attraction for Margaret, and the thing that perhaps kept Hesdin high on the list of her favoured residences, was the extensive ducal library.

Margaret was well known for her love of books, a passion that may have been borne from her time in Burgundy during the many hours she spent on her own, away from her husband, but more than likely stemmed from a seed that had already been planted in childhood from time spent with her mother and seeing her love of literature. Margaret's own personal collection of books centred around religious writings; within the manuscripts that she commissioned are several images of Margaret herself, often pictured engaging in pious activities.

Margaret's most lavish manuscript was the Apocalypse which contained seventy-nine beautifully detailed miniatures. Also in her collection was a selection of Burgundian manuscripts produced using the naturalistic style of painting in oils that had been perfected earlier in the century by Jan van Eyck and Rogier van der Weyden. Their magnificence and beauty were found not only in the miniatures that decorated the text, but in the borders which were full of minutely detailed flowers, insects, and other flora and fauna painted as if strewn across brightly coloured grounds. But perhaps the most important manuscript in Margaret's collection was the Visions of Tondal, renowned for its importance in the world of historical art. Margaret never did, or could, achieve a collection as big as the Burgundian ducal library, but her collection, despite its small size, is renowned today for being one of the best-known libraries of any medieval woman.[29]

Her passion for books was also shared with her brother, Edward, and several books from Edward's court were produced by David Aubert and his workshop, an artist who had produced manuscripts for Margaret during the 1470s. It is highly probable that Margaret gifted some of these works to her brother, or at the very least arranged their commission. Edward's Wardrobe Accounts, that detail expenses for Margaret's one and only return visit to England in the next decade, lists payments for some of these books.

Throughout the early 1470s all three York sisters seemed to have found their place in life, and perhaps even happiness. Apart from a few petty squabbles, their brothers were reconciled and the future looked positive. But soon everything would change again as the wheel of fortune spun once more.

# Chapter 7

# To love and to lose

As January 1474 dawned, in the depths of a cold English winter, Anne of York, Duchess of Exeter, was to receive the worst possible news – her only daughter, Anne Holland, had died. Had she been ill, perhaps over the Christmas season? Whether she had been ailing for weeks or whether it happened suddenly, sending shockwaves throughout the family, went unreported. Either way, her death at just 18 years old must have devastated Anne. She and her daughter had the shared experience of their early years together with Anne's father Henry Holland, and, perhaps more importantly, the days when it had been just the two of them while Holland was either in exile or in the Tower. It's probably a safe guess that their relationship was as close as any mother and daughter could be and Anne would have been heartbroken.

The exact date of Anne Holland's death is unknown, but it was almost certainly late January because on 2 February 1474, Anne was awarded a grant for 'the next presentation to the perpetual chantry at the altar of St Mary the Virgin in the cathedral church of Chichester, which Master John Nyman now has'.[1] A chantry was a benefice created by the gift of either money or property for the upkeep of one or more priests. The chantry ensured that the assigned priests would sing masses and offer prayers, either for the founder or for their loved ones, or sometimes both. Occasionally a special chapel was set up to be used by the priest, but more often than not the chantry would be founded at an already existing altar within a church. There was also nothing to prevent several chantries being founded at the same altar. There is no evidence that this chantry was requested by Anne for her recently deceased daughter, but the choice of a chantry at the altar of St Mary the Virgin is a good indication that the two events could be connected. Marian worship was of great importance in the Middle Ages, and the Virgin Mary was revered as pure, free of sin and, most importantly, as the perfect mother; women often prayed to her to help them conceive or watch over their children.

That Anne requested a grant for this chantry at this time was very likely her way of ensuring her daughter's soul would be prayed for and guided through Purgatory, safely to heaven.

Anne Holland's husband, Thomas Grey, would marry again just a few months after her death, perhaps illustrating that theirs really had been a marriage of convenience, although given their young ages it would be fair to say that they had barely started married life together. In a marriage contract dated 18 July 1474, Thomas married Cecily Bonville, the stepdaughter of Edward's chamberlain, William Hastings, and the daughter of Katherine Neville, a younger sister of the Earl of Warwick.

This was to be a year of rollercoaster emotions for Anne of York as her grief would have been mixed with joy in the summer of that year when she learned she was pregnant again. It is understood that this pregnancy was her first child with Thomas St Leger and all of the evidence points to that, apart from the occasional brief mention in the genealogical records that references an Anthony St Leger. Anne and Thomas had, by now, been married several years and had been together even longer, so it is possible that Anne had borne Thomas a son, who survived long enough to be named but died at a young age, practically disappearing from the records. There may also have been one or more miscarriages that did not warrant even the briefest of mentions.[2]

But Anne was pregnant in the summer of 1474, and in January 1475 she gave birth to a healthy baby girl, who was also named Anne, no doubt after her mother but also in tribute to her recently deceased sister that baby Anne St Leger would never know. As Margaret and Elizabeth delightedly received news of their new niece, a few days later they received news that would devastate them both. Just a year after her daughter had died, Anne of York also lost her life. She was 37 years old.

Having survived the birth and given her beloved husband a much-loved daughter, just days later she became ill, most likely through complications of childbirth or an infection, and her life could not be saved. Upon her death, Anne's newborn daughter, Anne St Leger, inherited all the Exeter lands.

Not only the eldest daughter of York but the eldest York sibling, Anne had lived a life of duty and rebellion. As the eldest, she was old enough to remember some of their family experiences in Rouen and in Ireland, and her first marriage to a staunch Lancastrian was perhaps, in hindsight, a huge mistake that her parents could, or should, have avoided. Whether she developed any feelings at all for Henry Holland is lost in the annals of time, nor can we know the reaction of Henry Holland when he was delivered the news of Anne's death from his prison room in the Tower. But going against tradition, albeit with the blessing of her family, Anne extricated herself from this difficult period of her life, becoming one of the richest widows in England and finding love later in life to a man seemingly much respected by her family.

In a mark of respect and love for his elder sister, Edward arranged for Anne to be laid to rest in his beloved St George's Chapel, the place he had been rebuilding since the early 1470s as his family mausoleum. It was also designed to be a chapel for the Order of the Garter, an order that was close to Edward's heart. The Order of the Garter, created by Edward III, was of huge importance to Edward IV during his reign and it was a concept that he entirely believed in – a set of chivalrous knights, united in their friendship and loyalty. Inspired by the legends of King Arthur, it originally consisted of twenty-four knights and was reserved as the highest award for loyalty and military prowess.

Anne's final resting place is now known as the Rutland Chapel, situated within St George's Chapel in Windsor amongst a gathering of distinguished persons laid to rest there over the centuries. Her husband, Thomas St Leger, was instrumental in arranging a tribute to her and he would later join her there. In the north wall of the chapel is a copper-plate gilt with engravings of Thomas and Anne; Anne is shown dressed in her robes and wearing a ducal coronet, marking her status as Duchess of Exeter. No details of her funeral service are left to us; in fact it may have been such a quiet affair that it passed by quite unannounced. The Pastons reported her death in a letter almost a year later.[3] Edward's itinerary for early 1475 shows that he was in Coventry for the Christmas period, travelling as far north as Lincoln before returning to London on or around 15 January, which may be when the news of his sister's death reached him. He was at Windsor on 22 and 23 February[4] which may perhaps have been when Anne's funeral took place.

In 1481, Thomas would set up a perpetual chantry for Anne, ensuring that her soul was remembered and regularly prayed for. This required a licence from the king, and the detail within both the letters patent and the setting up of the chantry are worth quoting in detail.

The church of St Andrew's in the village of Wingfield, Suffolk. This was the church of the de la Poles and contains not only the tomb of Elizabeth and John, but also the tomb of Michael de la Pole and his wife Katherine, and the tomb of Sir John Wingfield who founded the church in 1361. (Author image)

Wingfield Castle, the home of the de la Poles and where Elizabeth and John would reside for much of their life. In private ownership today, you can see the remaining front of the old castle, with the later Tudor buildings attached. (Robert Edwards, via Wikimedia Commons)

The memorial in St Andrew's Church, Wingfield, to John and Elizabeth de la Pole, Duke and Duchess of Suffolk. (Author image)

The church and almshouses in the beautiful village of Ewelme, the home of Alice Chaucer and later her son and daughter-in-law, John de la Pole and Elizabeth of York. (Author image)

The one-time palace of Margaret of York in Mechelen (Malines) now houses the city theatre. (Ad Meskens, CC BY-SA 3.0, via Wikimedia Commons)

An artist's impression of the Battle of Bosworth in August 1485 which saw the Lancastrian heir, Henry Tudor, meet the Yorkist Richard III and his men. The decisive battle ended the reign of the Plantagenet kings and heralded the dawn of a new Tudor dynasty. (Georgios Kollidas; Adobe Stock)

**Indenture of The Foundation Of The Chantry Of Anne, Duchess Of Exeter, Sealed With The Seal Of Thomas Saintleger.**

Thomas Saintleger, knight, late husband of the king's sister, Anne, late duchess of Exeter, to all to whom these present letters may come, greeting.

By letters patent dated 30 March 1481, King Edward IV at my humble supplication, gave licence for me or my executors to found perpetual chantry of two chaplains to celebrate divine service daily in the king's free chapel of St. George within the castle of Windsor for the good estate of the king and his wife Elizabeth, queen of England, and his mother Cecily, duchess of York, while they live, and for their souls after death, and for the soul of his father Richard, late duke of York, and for the good estate of me, the said Thomas and of Richard bishop of Salisbury while we live and for our souls after death, and for the soul of the said Anne, late duchess of Exeter, for whom especially the king gave assent for this chantry to be founded.

The chantry is to be called for ever the chantry of Anne, late duchess of Exeter, in the free chapel royal of St. George within the castle royal of Windsor. The chaplains of the chantry and their successors are to be one corporate body in deed and in name, to have perpetual succession and be persons able in law. By the name of chaplains of the chantry of Anne, late duchess of Exeter, they may purchase and receive any properties from any persons whatsoever, and under that name they may plead and be impleaded, sue and defend, answer and be answered as other our lieges are able. Moreover we give licence to the said Thomas and his executors to grant in mortmain the manor of Ham, in the counties of Surrey and Middlesex, the manor of Hartley Westpall and the advowson of the church of Hartley Westpall, in the county of Southampton, 7 messuages in the City of London in Watling Street in the Parish of St. Augustine at the door of St. Paul's, London, between a tenement of the master and brethren of the hospital of St. Bartholomew by West Smithfield on the east, a tenement belonging to the cathedral church of St. Paul on the west, the highway at

Watling Street on the north, and a lane called Distaff Lane on the south and 72 acres of land, 6 acres of meadow, 12 acres of pasture, 20 acres of wood, 9s. 2d. of rent in Chiddingfold and Hambledon in Surrey to the dean and canons of the free chapel of St. George. Also we give licence to the said dean and canons to grant in mortmain to the said chaplains a yearly rent of £23 1s. 8d. from those properties.

I, Thomas, by the strength and authority of the same letters, proceeds in this wise. In the name of the Holy Trinity I found a perpetual chantry of two priests, who are to be masters of arts or at least graduates, to hallow, sing and say divine service daily in the king's free chapel of St. George for the estates and souls aforesaid.

I name William Paynell and Richard Hakforth (Halford) the first chaplains.

I ordain that during my life I shall be patron of the chantry and present a suitable priest to the dean and canons for institution whenever a vacancy occurs. After my death Anne, daughter of the late duchess and myself, is to be patroness, and after her death her heirs. If she have no heirs or if she or her heirs fail to present a suitable person within one month of a vacancy, the dean is to collate within a month. Should he fail to do so, the chancellor is to present a candidate within another month, and if he fail, the archbishop of Canterbury is to make collation.

During the vacancy the dean and canons shall provide a priest to say mass.

Every chaplain at his admission must swear obedience to the dean and to observe the customs of the chapel as far as concerned him and to keep the statutes I have ordained. Chaplains once admitted and sworn are to be perpetual.

Daily when first they enter the chapel the chaplains are to say kneeling the psalms *Miserere mei Deus* and *De profundis* with the collect *Inclina* for their founders quick and dead.

They are to say matins daily together or separately in the duchess' chapel before 8 o'clock, and evensong between the first peal and the end of evensong or compline in the choir 'by note' (with music).

They are to say masses daily by the tomb of the duchess in the north side of the aisle of the new church, one of them at 8 and the other at 10, or at any other hour for a reasonable cause; on Sunday, the mass of the Trinity; on Monday, of the Angels; Tuesday, of the Holy Ghost; Wednesday, of the Wounds of Christ; Thursday, of Corpus Christi; Friday, of Requiem; Saturday, of Our Lady. They are in turn to say the earlier mass for a week.

At the masses they are to say a special collect for the good estate of the king, the queen and the prince while they live and after their deaths, and for the welfare of me and all their founders with the collect *Deus qui justificas impium* while we live, and after our deaths the collect *Deus qui in terra promissionis* which I wish them to say daily for the soul of the late duchess and myself, both expressed by name, after their devotions.

When they go on to the lavabo after the Gospel they are to say the psalm *De profundis* with the collect *Miserere quaesumus domine anime famule tue* with her name and mine.

Daily either together or separately they are to say *Placebo* and *Dirige* with commendations, after the use of Sarum.

Immediately after compline they are to kneel and say the psalm *Deus in nomine tuo* with the collect *Deus qui caritatis* for me and all their benefactors while I live.

Before they leave the chapel after compline one of them is to say in English before the duchess' tomb 'For the soul of the noble Princess Dame Anne late duchess of Exeter' and for me when I am dead and 'for all our founders' souls and all Christians' *De profundis* and the collect *Fidelium*.

If one of the chaplains be too ill to sing mass he is to say a nocturn of David's Psalter, or have it said if he is too ill to say it, or else give a penny to the poor.

If both chaplains be too ill to say mass the dean and canons are to provide a mass daily at the altar at the cost of the chaplains until one of them can say it.

The chaplains are to help each other to say mass or find a substitute so that the mass is not left unsaid.

Every Sunday and holiday after their duties are done, the chaplains are to join in procession and masses in the places in the choir given them by the dean and canons.

They are continually to be resident and dwell in a house which I have built within the precincts of the college. They are to keep their commons there, or at least within the precincts. The house is to be called Exeter Chantry Priests' House, and it is to be repaired at the cost of the chaplains under the dean's supervision.

They are not to be absent from the house for more than 14 days in each quarter except with the dean's permission. The 14 days may be taken either separately or together.

Both chaplains are not to be absent at the same time and neither of them at the great feasts of the year, except for illness.

The dean and canons have full power to warn and remove a chaplain who is a waster and alienates wilfully any goods or jewels belonging to the chapel, who is a common hunter or a tavernhaunter, a dicer, a carder or a tennis player, or if he be excessively unpriestly in his array or his tonsure, or if he be a fornicator, and if he be notoriously foresworn especially in keeping the statutes or found guilty of any other crime wherever it be committed.

I have made a chest for the money, jewels and ornaments of the chantry to be kept under three locks. The dean is to have one key and each of the chaplains another.

In the chest is to be an inventory of the contents, and the muniments are also to be kept in the chest.

A similar inventory is to be in the chaplains' keeping, and my ordinances are to be written in it. The ordinances are to be read out once every quarter. When a chaplain is admitted, he is to see the inventory.

Yearly at Michaelmas or within 4 days after, the chaplains are to present before the dean and chapter their account of the goods they use every day and of all other things that are to be given them.

Whenever a stranger wishes to sing at the chantry altar, the chaplains are to provide bread, wine and wax.

The chaplains are to swear to observe these ordinances, and I may alter them at my discretion during my life. For all this I have given to the dean and chapter the manors of Ham and Hartley Westpall and other lands and tenements as in the king's letters patent. In return the dean and chapter are content to fulfil these conditions:

1. They are to pay the chaplains yearly for their salary, repair of their house, and for bread, wine and wax £20, i.e. £10 each in equal sums at the 4 terms of the year (Midsummer, Michaelmas, Christmas and Easter).

2. They are to put 13s. 4d. yearly in the chest for the upkeep of the ornaments, etc., necessary for mass in number, form and value as I now give them. Besides the yearly repairs, every 10 years the dean and canons and the two chaplains are to see what needs to be repaired or renewed and have it done with the money in the chest. Any residue is to be used to repair the duchess' tomb, or the chapel, or be kept for another time.

3. They are to keep 3 obits yearly.

    (a) An anniversary of the duchess' death, with *Placebo* and *Dirige* on the eve and commendation and mass of Requiem on the day. They are to distribute from their common fund to those who attend: 3s. 4d. to the dean, 20d. to each of the 12 canons, 10d. to each of the king's two chantry priests, 8d. to each of the 13 minor canons, 8d. to each of the 13 vicars, 8d. to the deacon, 8d. to the verger, 6d. to each of the 13 clerks, 4d. to each of the 13 choristers, 6d. to the yeoman sexton, 4d. to the groom sexton and 20d. to the bellringers.
    (b) An obit exactly 13 weeks after the anniversary, and another 13 weeks after that. The distributions at these obits are to be: 2s. to the dean, 12d. to a canon, 6d. to the king's chantry priests, minor canons, vicars, deacon and verger, 4d. to the clerks and yeoman sexton, 3d. to the groom sexton, 2d. to the choristers and 20d. to the bellringers.

4. After my death they are to keep my obit with distributions like those for the duchess' two single obits.
5. For the principal anniversary they are to provide 5 wax tapers to burn about the hearse, each of them weighing 5 lbs, and at each of the three obits 5 tapers, 4 weighing 5 lbs., and 1 weighing 2 lbs. For this they are to have 10s. yearly.
6. They are to give 10s. to the chaplains to buy ½d. loaves to distribute to the poor on the day of the duchess' anniversary, and 6s. 8d. on my obit. The dean is to supervise the distribution.
7. Every Friday the treasurer is to give 5d. to the chaplains to distribute to 5 poor men and women at the tomb of the duchess.

Until my death the money for my obit and 6s. 8d. for alms are to be put yearly in the chest for me to dispose of. The properties which I have given to the dean and canons are to be charged with the payments above.

I have set my seal to this part of the indenture, which the dean and chapter will keep. To the other part which I keep the dean and chapter have set their common seal in the Chapter House 20 April 1482.

In reply the Dean and Canons signed their half of the indenture, agreeing to the terms, dated and sealed with the common seal in the chapter house 26 April 1482.[5]

In time, Anne's family would join her at rest in the chapel and today Anne and Thomas lie alongside their daughter Anne St Leger and her husband, George. A memorial copper plaque on the wall in what is now called the Rutland Chapel reads:

Wythin thys Chappell lyethe beryed Anne Duchess of Exetur suster unto the noble kyng Edward the forte. And also the body of syr Thomas Sellynger knyght her husband which hathe funde within thys College a Chauntre with too prestys sy'gyng for eu'more. On whose soule god haue mercy. The wych Anne duchess dyed in the yere of oure lorde M Thowsande CCCCl xxv.[6]

A 1547 commissioners' report showed that Anne's chantry was still in effect, then alongside five others in St George's Chapel. Eight priests were being paid £78 6s 8d for Edward IV; Anne, Duchess of Exeter; Lord William Hastings; John Plummer (verger); Thomas Passche (canon); and John Oxenbridge (canon).[7]

St George's Chapel today consists of eight chapels: In the Quire aisles is that of Edward IV's at the northeast, the Lincoln Chapel in the southeast, and the Hastings and Oxenbridge chapels in the north and south aisles. In the nave resides the Rutland Chapel in the north section and the Braye Chapel in the south. The Urswick and Beaufort Chapels are at the north and southwest ends of the nave. Although there is only the plaque to Anne and Thomas in the Rutland Chapel and no memorial as such, the tomb to Anne St Leger and her husband George is considered one of the most beautiful monuments within St George's. On top of the tomb, Anne's daughter and her husband George are remembered by their effigies lying side by side. Anne St Leger is clothed in a long gown with fluted sleeves and wearing a richly embroidered belt and mantle; a small dog rests by her feet. She lays forever at rest next to her husband, George, in his full plated knight's armour, in the chantry chapel founded for her mother by her father. The inscription on the upper edge of the tomb reads:

> Here lyethe buryede george Maners knyght lord roos who decesede the xxiii daye of October In the yere of our lorde god Mi Vc xiii and ladye Anne his wyfe dawghter of anne duchesse of exetur Suster unto/ kyng Edward the fourthe and of Thomas Sentlynger knight/ the wyche anne decessed the xxii day of apryll In the yere of our lorde god MiVc xxvi on whose souls god haue mercy amen.[8]

Once the funeral was over and Anne had been laid to rest, King Edward began to focus fully on his preparations to invade France, something he had been planning for a while. In the constant changing world of political allegiance, Edward's close alliance with Burgundy that had come about through Margaret's marriage to Charles had resulted in the two men signing the Treaty of London on 25 July 1471, a formal alliance against France. In the terms of this agreement, it was agreed that Charles would recognise Edward as King of France; in return Charles would have his share of a broken-up France alongside the lands that already made up the estates of Burgundy.[9]

By spring 1475 Edward had amassed a huge number of men, possibly up to 20,000 if some reports are to be believed. Those men accompanying him in his mission included his brothers, Clarence and Gloucester, and Anne's husband, Thomas St Leger. The whereabouts of baby Anne St Leger after her mother's death is unknown; St Leger most likely employed a nurse to take care of his young daughter, or perhaps she was looked after in part by family members, possibly in Elizabeth's household or maybe even in the royal nursery. Another, perhaps surprising addition to Edward's group of men was Henry Holland, the Duke of Exeter. Presumably Edward did not wish to leave the country without his main rival in his sights, but he also perhaps appreciated that Holland had military skills that could be useful to the English army.

Edward left London on 30 May and arrived in Canterbury on 7 June where his army was gathered and waiting for him. The queen's brother, Anthony, Earl Rivers, had already made his way across the Channel as part of the advance party. Arriving in Ghent to meet with Charles, he discovered that Charles was not there but was off on business in the Rhinelands. In the absence of her husband, Margaret had to step in to take charge, dispatching Anthony off to the Rhinelands to bring Charles back whilst personally overseeing the arrangement of Burgundian ships to transport Edward and his men across the sea.

On the same day that Edward arrived in Canterbury, Margaret left Ghent and travelled to St Omer, arriving just two days before her brothers landed in Calais. Upon hearing the news that they had arrived, she rode the 23 miles to Calais to see them, the first time she had seen them since their enforced stay with her four years previously. Taking gifts with her, it must have been a joyous reunion for the four siblings, although perhaps with some sorrow at the recent loss of their sister, Anne. After spending two nights in Calais, Margaret returned to St Omer and would be visited there by her two youngest brothers, Clarence and Gloucester.

Finally, on 11 July, Charles joined them, although frustratingly for Edward he was alone and without an army. Nine days later Charles and Margaret entertained Edward at Fauquemberges Castle near St Omer, and Margaret then said her farewells, returning to Ghent and leaving the men to the business of war. As she embraced them goodbye and wished them well, she could not have known that this would be the last time she would see either her brother, Clarence, or her husband.[10]

But it was not the French invasion that would end their lives. With the English army ready to fight, Charles had seemingly lost the urge to tackle the French. Having come so far, Edward chose to stick to the plan and set off to conquer French lands without the support that Charles had promised to provide. But in the end it seems that Edward's heart wasn't in it either, and the promise of money offered by the French king was tempting enough to sway his desire for French land. Edward met with King Louis in person in late August, and on 29 August the Treaty of Picquigny was signed, heralding a seven-year truce between the two countries. The price Edward received for leaving French territory untouched and returning home was 75,000 crowns upfront with a yearly payment of 50,000 crowns to follow. A marriage contract was also agreed between Edward's eldest daughter, Princess Elizabeth of York, and the French Dauphin. King Louis also bargained for the freedom of his fellow countrywoman, Margaret of Anjou, who would be released from custody in England and allowed to return to France. Some of the men who had travelled with Edward and were ready to fight were disappointed by this turn of events; reportedly Richard, Duke of Gloucester, was furious at his brother's decision to strike a deal. To try and retain their goodwill, many of Edward's men also received handsome pensions, including his chamberlain, William Hastings, and Thomas St Leger.[11]

Much to the relief of wives and mothers all across England, the English army returned without a single drop of blood being shed. But there was to be one casualty on the return journey – Henry Holland, Duke of Exeter, mysteriously ended up 'falling' overboard. His body was later found having washed up near Dover. The Milanese ambassador certainly believed it was no accident, reporting in his dispatches 'When the King of England was returning by sea from London to Calais, he had the Duke of Xestre thrown into the sea'.[12]

Other reports claim it was an accident, while others throw the blame onto Thomas St Leger; both he and the king would have very good motives to want to get rid of Holland. The list of suspects must also include Anne's brothers, Clarence and Gloucester. Much like the death of King Henry, having Holland out of the way removed the danger of any support for him from any remaining staunch Lancastrians. Perhaps whilst their sister was alive, Edward, George and Richard were hesitant to harm Holland; perhaps she may even have forbidden it. But now she was dead, they could take their revenge for all the trouble he had caused their family over the years.

***

Holland's death would have been no loss to the York family, but for Elizabeth of York, 1475 was to be a year peppered with grief. Having mourned Anne in January, she was to experience further loss a few months later when her mother-in-law, Alice Chaucer, died. The Dowager Duchess had possibly been sickening for a while; a letter from Margaret Paston in 1469 reported that 'The Duchess of Suffolk is at Ewelme in Oxfordshire … because of age or sickness'.[13] In March 1475, Alice was at Ewelme again, perhaps being looked after by Elizabeth and John, from where she wrote on 3 March to William Stonor requesting he come to visit her.[14] By May she had died. She was a grand 71 years of age. Buried at the church of St Mary at Ewelme, her tomb is a beautiful memorial to her, beset with angels, atop of which is an effigy of Alice wearing a coronet of a duchess and the order of the garter around her left arm. She left her possessions and property to John and Elizabeth.

The reality of death surely played heavily on all of their minds that year, and across the sea in Burgundy Margaret would receive worrying news in September 1475 that Charles was ill. Margaret and Mary were in Ghent and Charles was travelling when news reached them that he was suffering from what was described as 'an attack of fever and catarrh in the head'. He recovered but it was clearly considered serious enough to be reported. Charles had suffered from three serious illnesses in his reign. On 14 January 1468 it had been reported that the duke had been taken ill the day before, he had more than ten doctors with him and truly he was extremely sick. He was then incapacitated once again by this illness in 1475, from which he recovered, but Margaret once again received reports of her husband ailing in April 1476 when Charles reportedly suffered intense stomach aches and even lost consciousness. He fell ill on 15 April but once again he rallied, and he was fully recovered by 3 May.

With the current spate of sickness and loss in the family, this may have brought their father back into the forefront of their minds, and in 1476 Edward arranged for the reburial of the Duke of York. As the Nevilles had done some thirteen years previously with the Earl of

Salisbury, the Yorks wanted to lay their father to rest with the dignity he deserved. Edward threw both his time and finances into this act of honouring their father and brother, Edmund, Earl of Rutland, who had been killed alongside his father. Both had been hastily buried in Pontefract after their deaths at the Battle of Wakefield and it was time to bring their bodies home to the family mausoleum at Fotheringhay. The choice of Fotheringhay over St George's Chapel was perhaps because Edward knew this, their childhood home, was close to his father's heart, a fact backed up by York's epitaph as recorded by the Chester Herald: 'this good King, to prove his virtue, knowing that his father had decided that his body should rest at Fotheringhay, had him nobly buried here'.[15]

Richard, Duke of Gloucester, arrived in Pontefract in July 1476 to escort the cortège from St John's priory on its journey south to its final resting place. The coffins, covered in rich palls of cloth-of-gold, were placed upon carriages pulled by teams of black horses. Accompanying the solemn procession were 400 'poor men' carrying torches, their black hoods up over their heads. All along the route, nightly vigils were held at each pre-arranged resting place.

The cortège arrived at the churchyard in Fotheringhay at midday on 29 July, to be greeted by Edward dressed in a dark blue hooded robe, furred with miniver, the royal colour of mourning, flanked by his two brothers, Clarence and Gloucester. The latter had ridden ahead for the last part of the journey so he could be there with his brothers to meet the procession. Also amongst the welcoming group of men was Elizabeth's husband, the Duke of Suffolk, and her eldest son, John de la Pole, Earl of Lincoln. Although Margaret of York was not in attendance, she was surely there in spirit and perhaps Elizabeth wrote to her telling her of the occasion. The funeral service was held the following day, a solemn affair with all the usual masses that ended with a stunning piece of theatre. A black warhorse, trapped to the ground in black with the full royal arms, was led to the entrance of the choir. The rider was Lord Ferrers, who, with an axe in his hand that was pointed downwards, dismounted the horse and was escorted by two heralds to offer the harness of the duke at the altar.[16]

The next day a lavish feast was held where up to 2,000 guests dined in canvas pavilions erected especially for the occasion in neighbouring fields. Cooks, bakers, purveyors of spices and servants went back and forth between London and Fotheringhay in the days preceding the festivities, providing over 31 tuns of ale, 2,000 wooden bowls and clay pots, 49 beef cattle, 210 sheep, 90 calves and 200 piglets, as well as large quantities of fish and poultry to feed the assembled guests. Seats for 1,500 people were provided in the tents and pavilions in the grounds of Fotheringhay.[17]

Some years later, Edward paid a considerable amount for a tomb to commemorate his father's final resting place. We have no detail of the original; the tomb and that of his mother, Cecily, who eventually joined her husband at Fotheringhay, was desecrated in the sixteenth century. Queen Elizabeth I, visiting Fotheringhay in 1566, saw the damaged tombs and, as a mark of respect, ordered their removal, erecting newer monuments to York and Cecily around the altar that are still there today.

Although there was much sadness in the late 1470s, as with life there was also much to celebrate too. The family convened for happier events, such as the annual St George's Day ceremony at Windsor, where, in 1476, Elizabeth of York, Duchess of Suffolk, was granted the Livery of the Garter, an honour that saw ladies admitted to the order in ceremonial form. This honour was mostly reserved for wives or ladies connected to the royal family. On the day of the ceremony, which was a Sunday, the king and his knights rode together to Matins, before breakfasting together with the Dean, Bishop Beauchamp. Later they all attended High Mass, Elizabeth travelling on horseback alongside the queen and the Princess Elizabeth, the king's eldest daughter, all dressed in their murrey garter gowns. They were accompanied by the Marchioness of Dorset, Cecily Grey, who was not a garter member and therefore not in livery. Her husband, Thomas Grey, Marquis of Dorset, took up his position as a new Garter knight during the garter ceremony and the ladies watched the proceedings from seats in the rood loft. After the ceremony, the king dined in the great chamber alongside the Bishop of Sarum, Chancellor of the Order, and the Dukes of Clarence and Suffolk, Elizabeth's husband and brother. The following day the king and knights went in procession to the chapter house and the choir where each stood in front of his stool.

Elizabeth was one of the last ladies to be initiated into the Order; the king's daughters, Princess Cecily and Princess Mary, were latterly given the order in the year 1480, and Margaret Beaufort, mother of Henry VII, was admitted in 1488 before the tradition was ended.[18] Future kings and queens did not have quite the same passion for this chivalric order as King Edward IV had, and it was not until 1901 that ladies would once again be invited to join, when King Edward VII invested his wife Queen Alexandra.

By October of that year, Elizabeth of York was at Greenwich along with Elizabeth Stonor, who wrote to tell her husband that she had been waiting upon the Duchess of Suffolk when her mother, Cecily Neville, had come to London. The king was also present and Elizabeth Stonor wrote that 'there I saw the meeting between the king and my lady his mother, and truly I thought it was a very good sight.'[19] Elizabeth of York was reportedly planning a trip to Canterbury, informing Elizabeth Stonor that she would be back the following week.

Meanwhile, across the sea in Burgundy, October 1476 saw the ever-campaigning Charles and his army arrive on the environs of the city of Nancy, the capital city of the region of Lorraine, where they remained for the next few months holding the city under siege. The siege continued throughout the cold winter months and on 5 January 1477, Charles and his army suddenly found themselves surrounded by Swiss infantry and mounted knights under the command of Rene, the Duke of Lorraine. A fierce battle ensued, and in news that was to devastate Margaret of York, Charles' army became overwhelmed and he was killed attempting to escape the battlefield; the consensus is that he probably died when his horse fell whilst trying to jump a frozen stream. He was just 43 years old. His body lay on the battlefield for two days and was reportedly so unrecognisable when he was found that his valet only recognised him by his long fingernails.

As news of his death spread across Europe, Margaret and Mary were at Ten Waele. The news reached them there by 7 January – not a confirmation of his death, only that he was believed dead. Both hoped that he would be found alive and even by 15 January, Margaret was still remaining hopeful that later messengers would bring better news of her husband.

Coupled with the grief that they would naturally feel for the loss of a husband and father, Charles' death, if indeed he was gone, put them and the Duchy of Burgundy in a dangerous position. The news that Charles was unaccounted for would have been received by King Louis of France with something akin to joy; it would now make it easier for him to claim Burgundian territory and bring it back within French borders. In a letter dated 18 January, Margaret and Mary wrote to King Louis expressing their hope that Charles was still alive. They made an early appeal to him to halt his invasion of Burgundian territories and reminded Louis that he was Mary's godfather. Louis, on his part, replied that with no male Burgundian heir, the lands should default to France. As a peace offering, and to sweeten the deal, he proposed a marriage between Mary of Burgundy and his 7-year-old son, the dauphin, an offer that he later withdrew.

As it became clear that Charles was not coming home, on 21 January a memorial service was held in Ghent; by 25 January the court assumed full mourning.

Margaret, in a fine demonstration of her leadership traits, something she had perhaps inherited from her family, now put her own grief aside and became hugely instrumental in taking charge of events and guiding Mary, who now found herself the new Duchess of Burgundy. Margaret dispatched messengers out to the estates general, an assembly of representatives from each of the individual territories across Burgundy, requesting that they assemble at Ghent on 3 February. Things now moved quickly and on 16 February Mary was formally inaugurated as Duchess of Burgundy and Countess of Flanders. Knowing she needed powerful men on her side, the new duchess, just 19 years old, promised to rule with the advice of the Great Council and representatives from the estates.

Margaret, however, somewhat older and wiser, knew that it was not going to be that easy. With France deciding what action they were going to take, Margaret knew that Mary needed a husband, someone who was a strong leader to protect their interests and that of the Burgundian people.

As Mary was reaching the end of her teenage years, possible marriage candidates had already been discussed whilst her father was still alive, including Ferdinand of Aragon (before he had married Isabella of Castille) and even at one time Margaret's own brother, George, Duke of Clarence. But Charles had finally landed upon the Archduke Maximilian as a suitable candidate for his daughter, a son of the House of Habsburg. Born in Austria on 22 March 1459, Maximilian was the son of Frederick III, the Holy Roman Emperor, and his wife, Eleanor of Portugal. Marriage discussions had been initiated in 1463 and formally negotiated in 1476. Margaret understood Charles' reasons for the match and knew that only an imperial alliance could save Burgundy from France. After Charles' sudden death, it was her skilful diplomacy and negotiations that kept the deal on track. Maximilian wrote to Mary on 24 January assuring her of his intention to marry her and in April, the two were married by proxy. Their union won support across the Low Countries, but it would still be several months before Maximilian could arrive in Burgundy, leaving the two women in a precarious position, facing danger both from outside the country in the form of neighbouring France, and from any dissenters within the country.

Both Charles and his father had spent time trying to defend and expand Burgundian territory, and over the years many lives had been lost in pursuit of this cause. Viewing Mary as a weak link without a husband by her side and angry at the loss of their menfolk, some in Burgundy began to rebel. Margaret and Mary also came under fire from the representatives of the estates, who, having arrived in Ghent, saw the letters that the women had written to King Louis and judged it as a betrayal, believing they were making an unpopular deal with France. In the chaos that followed, Margaret was forced to withdraw from Ghent and Mary was placed under house arrest; she was in charge of Burgundy but at the same time a virtual prisoner.

As Margaret packed her belongings, knowing that she had little choice but to obey the council, she made the decision to not go quietly. Along with some of her advisors, also banished and faced with threats if they remained, she made a passionate speech in the town square, outside the castle gates, declaring that although she was a foreigner by birth, in her heart she was a true Burgundian woman. Then to keep both herself and Mary safe, she left her stepdaughter behind, departing from Ghent with a personal bodyguard of 300 archers. Her destination was the city of Oudenaarde, some 16 miles to the south of Ghent and famed for its tapestry production. Upon her arrival, a memorial service was organised in honour of the duke. She may have been strong and determined, but she was also a woman in mourning. Margaret and Charles may have spent much of their marriage apart, but on the surface it seemed to have worked. Both were ambitious, hard-working and dedicated to serving the people of Burgundy, and perhaps they built a relationship based on mutual respect for each other. Whatever the depth of love for her husband, Margaret was grieving, and as the long procession, illuminated by torches, wound its way through the dark streets of the city, which had been draped in black velvet, she must have been wondering what the future now held for her.

As for her family, did Margaret believe that they would send help her way? John Paston certainly thought it was the right thing to do and was sure that Edward would send their brothers, the Dukes of Clarence and Gloucester, to not only help her and Mary restore some sort of order, but also to protect Burgundy from a French invasion and, most importantly, to ensure Margaret's own personal safety. There also seems to have been no mention of Margaret returning home. In the next century, Henry VIII's sister, Mary Tudor, who was also sent abroad to marry a foreign royal, immediately had preparations made for her return after the death of her husband, the French king Louis XII. Of course, for Mary Tudor the timescale was vastly different; Mary had only been in France a few months when her husband died, Margaret had made Burgundy her home after living there for many years. Perhaps the question of her return was raised and discussed privately. But with regard to sending men to support his sister, this did not occur and instead Edward chose to maintain a neutral stance. The Treaty of Picquigny had promised peace between France and England, and Edward was hesitant to appear to take sides. Did Margaret consider this a betrayal, both politically as England and Burgundy were friends of old, but also personally? Presumably so as she wrote to Edward in no uncertain terms, reminding him he had made her 'one of the most important ladies in the world' and that he was now her 'only lord, father, husband and brother'. She told him that she had become 'one of the poorest widows, deserted by everyone, especially you' and begged him to send her protection against the French king, Louis.[20] Edward, in return, made some vague noises of displeasure towards Louis, but that was about the extent of his help. Without any external aid, Margaret and Mary, under virtual house arrest, managed to hold out until 18 August that year when finally Maximilian arrived in Ghent. With a male presence to restore a semblance of authority, Margaret came back to Ghent to celebrate the wedding of her beloved stepdaughter. Maximilian's presence did not immediately calm the waters of dissent, but it certainly gave Margaret and Mary some much-needed support.

Mary, in gratitude for Margaret's support in what had been an extremely difficult time for her, offered her full support in aiding Margaret to receive her full dower payments, which since Charles' death had been under dispute. At the time of Margaret's marriage, Edward had promised a dowry of 200,000 crowns, to be paid in instalments. Eight years later, he still owed 115,000. This put Margaret in a hugely difficult position; the unpaid dowry meant that the Burgundian officials were reluctant to pay her a full dower, funds that Margaret desperately needed to support herself. Mary threw her whole political and personal weight into supporting Margaret to receive full payment, stating that Margaret had always 'held our person and our lands and lordships in such complete and perfect love and goodwill that we can never sufficiently repay and recompense her', a glowing accolade for a woman who had truly learned to love her adopted country.

Now a widow, and with her stepdaughter starting on the path of married life, Margaret had to forge a new life for herself. With regard to the question of her remaining in Burgundy or returning to England, we have no evidence as to what discussions took place. Perhaps she realised that to return to England to be part of her brother's court would mean that any new marriage she wished to make would be in his gift. By remaining in Burgundy she could live as the Dowager Duchess of Burgundy, with her future in her own hands. Whatever discussions did or did not occur, we know that she did stay in her adopted homeland. It was the right choice; with her dower fully paid, Margaret would become one of the richest widows in Europe.

By November 1477, she had set herself up within her own court at Mechelen (also known as Malines). She purchased the largest house, which had once belonged to the Bishop of Cambrai, as well as the seven adjoining houses. She then merged these into a new palace, a home fit for a dower duchess. Built of red bricks with white stripes, Margaret's new home had a long façade, with many windows facing the road that brought natural daylight into the interior. With a hexagonal tower at one corner, the property looked out over a courtyard at the front and onto extensive gardens, containing a tennis court and a bath house at the rear. Margaret's private apartments were on the upper floor where she could survey the surrounding views from a beautiful stone balcony. The property was warmed in the colder months by several large fireplaces, and her private apartments contained a private study and, of course, a library for her beloved book collection.[21]

Although a widow, Margaret was still in her early thirties and she was perhaps ready to live the life of a dowager, but not yet ready to retire from public service. Her residence in Mechelen also contained a vast great council chamber where she could attend visiting dignitaries, as well as state rooms for entertaining. Her household consisted of around 150 people, many of whom lived outside in the town, and arrived at the palace every morning and were checked in by the porter and out again in the evening. Amongst their number were her ladies-of-honour, maids, valets, chaplains, almoner and confessor and, of course, the very busy porter.

Any staff on duty during the day would dine at the palace at noon, and unless she had guests, Margaret would dine alone, concluding each meal by sipping her 'spices of the table'.[22] As well as politics and her books, Margaret developed an interest in preventative medicine; during

1497, when the pestilence was very bad, her doctor advised her not to walk at midday at a fast pace, or when it was hot and cloudy, and never on a full stomach. She took advice to never sleep during the day, and to abstain from eating sweet milk and cheese.

Although they would understandably spend less time together now that Mary was Duchess of Burgundy and a married woman, Margaret nevertheless remained close to her stepdaughter. In the summer of 1477 Margaret returned to Bruges to celebrate the christening of Mary's first son, where she would accept the honour of standing as godmother to the young boy. The christening took place on 28 June, and Margaret, dressed in a black velvet dress, took part in the grand procession to and from the service, walking next to Adolphe de Clèves, Lord of Ravenstein, described by Molinet as a 'very high and powerful prince'. The service was held at the church of St Donat and the new infant, Philip as he was to be named, was dressed in a beautiful christening gown and carried in a very rich blanket of cloth of crimson gold. After the service Philip was returned to his mother and the gathered guests took their repast of wine and spices.[23]

It may even have been whilst staying with Mary and Maximilian that summer that Margaret first heard the shocking news from England that her brother, George, Duke of Clarence, had been arrested. After the fallout between the York brothers in the early 1470s, the death of Warwick and even more so their father's reburial ceremony had brought George well and truly back into the fold. Although there was always an element of sibling rivalry between the three brothers, George had grown, matured and occupied his time with family life; his wife, Isabel, provided him with two living children. Richard of Gloucester, now a young man of 24, had also settled into married life; after his marriage to Anne Neville the pair had retired to the north where they spent their time between Pontefract and Middleham Castles – the first being his state residence as Edward's chief representative in the north and the latter being their family home. The arguments over the Warwick inheritance had rumbled on for several years, until Edward had stepped in and divided the wealth between them, finally settling the infighting. However, harmony was once again shattered when, after giving birth to her fourth child in October 1476, George's wife Isabel died. As much as this would have grieved him, it also, for whatever reason, sent him right back off the rails again.

Immediately after Isabel died, he cited witchcraft, blaming one of his wife's servants, Ankarette Twynyho for her death, and accused her of poisoning his wife. Much to the horror of her family, Clarence had her arrested and summarily executed immediately after a trial, during which he heavily influenced the jurors to pronounce a guilty verdict. Her family complained to the king and Edward attempted to reel his unruly brother in.

Clarence then made a play for the hand of Mary of Burgundy, despite her marriage negotiations to Maximilian at the time. Whether this proposal was ever seriously considered by Mary and Margaret is unclear; Margaret had a soft spot for her beloved older brother, but she knew that an alliance between him and Mary would not safeguard Burgundian lands. Either way, Edward flatly refused to consider it, and according to Vergil, it was due to the obstruction of his marriage plans that 'the ancient hatred between these brothers (nothing stronger) manifested itself'. Clarence took this rebuttal with ill grace and left court, refusing to dine with the king and claiming he feared he would also be poisoned.

His mental state continued to deteriorate over the following months and, in 1477, three men were arrested, accused of plotting Edward's death. One of the accused was a close associate of Clarence's, and all three were found guilty at trial. Two of the three were then executed for treason, the third narrowly escaping with his life. This should have been a warning to George, but he didn't take it. Instead, he elected to align himself with a preacher, who happened to be a notorious Lancastrian, and burst into Parliament to protest the innocence of the condemned men, at the same time taking the opportunity to bad-mouth the king and disrespect the queen and her family. Edward could not let this continue and found himself with little choice but to arrest his troublesome brother in the summer of 1477 and throw him into the Tower. He would remain there for eight long months whilst his brother agonised over what to do with him.

When this news reached both Elizabeth and Margaret, it must have caused them a huge amount of concern. Margaret, so far away from events and having to wait for news, must have been hugely concerned over this new family drama between her brothers. As previously mentioned, Croyland reported that Margaret in particular had a soft spot for her brother Clarence 'beyond any of the rest of her kindred'[24] so she must have been hugely concerned to hear that he was in trouble. Elizabeth, much closer to events, perhaps even having witnessed some of George's unruly behaviour, may have had a better understanding of the king's reasons for arresting their brother. But even so, the situation was ugly and needed resolving.

As Christmas 1477 approached, George was still being held in prison. And by 1478 it seemed that Edward could delay no longer; his brother could not remain in prison indefinitely and Edward would have to act. The trial of George, Duke of Clarence, took place in February when George was accused of treason against his brother, the king. Edward elected to personally question his brother and the *Croyland Chronicle* reported that 'no one spoke against the Duke but the king, and no one answered but the Duke'. In a shocking turn of events for a family that had once been so close, George was convicted and, despite desperate pleas for clemency by their mother, Cecily, for Edward to spare his life, on 18 February 1478, George, Duke of Clarence, was executed. The method used to end his life is unknown, although according to legend, he was given the choice of choosing his own means of execution and elected to be drowned in a barrel of Malmesbury wine. His daughter, Margaret, as an adult, reportedly wore a bracelet with a small barrel attached to it for the rest of her life in memory of her father. A portrait in the National Portrait Gallery of a woman who is yet to be fully identified but traditionally thought to be Margaret Pole, Countess of Salisbury (her later married name), shows a woman with a tiny barrel charm. George, Duke of Clarence, is buried in Tewkesbury Abbey alongside his wife, Isabel.

This was, by far, the worst chapter in their family history thus far. Edward, so close to his mother, ignored her pleas for clemency and although we have no evidence, we can assume that perhaps Elizabeth and/or Margaret also joined their mother in pleading for their brother's life to be spared. Or did they agree with Edward, that George's betrayal over all the years had just simply gone too far? Richard of Gloucester, so loyal to his brother Edward throughout his life, reportedly could not bring himself to agree with Edward's actions, although neither did he argue against them. In his despondency, he set up chantries for George at his northern castles of Middleham and Barnard Castle to pray for his brother's soul. As women, Elizabeth and Margaret's thoughts went unrecorded, but neither could have considered this a happy circumstance whether they agreed with their brother Edward or not. For this once devoted and loyal family, who after the death of their father had banded together in the face of adversity to bring triumph to the House of York, this desperate set of circumstances had proved that blood was not thicker than water. Richard, Duke of York, must have been turning in his grave.

# Chapter 8

# The final act

After George's death in February 1478, the family now had two young Yorks to consider; George and Isabel's now orphan children, 5-year-old Margaret (most likely named after her aunt Margaret) and 3-year-old Edward, Earl of Warwick. Edward was immediately made a royal ward and his care was given over to Thomas and Cecily Grey, the queen's son and daughter-in-law, who would raise him in their household. Margaret's path is less certain – she may have been taken into the royal household; payments in January 1482 from the king's accounts show 40 marks were paid by the Exchequer for her clothing and wages to her household staff, followed by another 50 marks the following November.[1] Perhaps she even spent some time in the household of her aunt, Elizabeth?

If this was the case, the king would certainly have needed to offer financial support, as by the late 1470s the Duke and Duchess of Suffolk were in financial difficulty. Elizabeth had seemingly inherited her mother's track record in bearing children and in 1478 she would give birth to her tenth child, William, with Richard, her last, following in 1480. Their large family, although by no means unusual, must have put a strain on their finances. Their eldest son, John, was by now a teenage lad of 16, with the title of Earl of Lincoln bestowed upon him by his uncle, the king. In 1477 he had also been given a knighthood alongside his royal cousins, Edward, Prince of Wales, and Prince Richard, Duke of York.[2] Related to the king and clearly held in his good favour, the Suffolks were close to the centre of royal power, but even this did not guarantee great wealth. Seemingly John, Duke of Suffolk, was one of the poorest of the dukes, who reportedly at times refused to attend court events as he was unable to financially cover expenses. This is borne out by a letter from John Paston, writing to his brother in January 1478, who reveals that he had been with various people that Christmas who had divulged that the duke needed to make some money, and at speed. Whatever deal John Paston and his brother were planning with the duke, John advises his brother to 'let us not be neglected but with effect applied now while he is in London, and my lady his wife also; for I assure you that 50 marks will do more now in their need than shall perhaps do with 100 marks in time coming'.[3]

The territory disputes also rumbled on throughout the 1470s, and in May 1478 we find that John and Elizabeth were back in the east of England, presumably staying at Wingfield, and on the Wednesday of Whitsun week the Duke of Suffolk was at Hellesdon, playing Herod in the *Corpus Christi* play. As reported in a letter to John Paston, the duke had dined at Hellesdon on stew and had 'taken a great plenty of fish'. The writer of the letter applauded the duke's performance, but also informed Paston that it was after noon, the weather was hot and the duke was so ill that 'his legs would not bear him and two men had great pains to keep him on his feet'. Whether this 'sickness' was actually through the heat or perhaps too much revelling, we can only guess. According to the letter, the plays were enjoyed, but there were calls for the duke to be beaten or put in prison, and it is clear from the letter that the Pastons' servant still considered the duke to be illegally occupying Hellesdon, complaining bitterly that the mayor of Norwich, Richard Ferrer, was refusing to do anything about it.[4]

In early 1479 Elizabeth and John may have travelled to London and Windsor once more to mourn the sad passing of 2-year-old Prince George. There was a serious outbreak of pestilence in the spring of 1479 and George became a tiny victim of the disease. Perhaps an illustration of how close she remained to her family, Margaret of York was written to and informed that her young nephew had succumbed to 'an epidemic', as recorded by a Burgundian chronicler. Prince George was buried on 22 March in St George's Chapel, Windsor, in an elaborate ceremony befitting a prince of the realm and close to his aunt, Anne, who must surely have been in the minds of the Yorks as they buried one of their own, a young boy taken far before his time.

Margaret undoubtedly sent her sympathies to her brother and his queen, but just over a year later she was able to speak to them in person when, in 1480, she made the journey back to her country of birth, the first and last time that she would do so. Having left England at the age of 22, she was now 34 years old, a dowager duchess, and one of the most influential women in Europe. Margaret was visiting Edward partly to discuss the possibility of a marriage between Mary and Maximilian's eldest son, Philip and Edward's daughter, Princess Anne, but she must have also been excited on a personal level to see her family again, in particular her mother and sister Elizabeth. She had seen her brothers since leaving for Burgundy, but had not been in the same room as her mother and sister since she had left England twelve years before. There was a lot to catch up on.

Edward Woodville, the queen's brother, was dispatched to escort Margaret home. Arriving in Calais in his ship named the *Falcon*, he collected Margaret and delivered her safely across the Channel into the port of Gravesend. They then completed the journey into London by barge along the Thames.

The whole family had gathered in London to welcome their youngest sister home, and an elaborate procession was organised to celebrate her arrival. The royal barge that sailed her up the river was rowed by the master and twenty-four oarsmen, all dressed in smart new jackets of murrey and blue, embellished with roses. Once on dry land, Margaret was transported to her teenage home at Greenwich by horses bedecked in harnesses of 'green velvet, garnished with aglets of silver gilt, bordered with spangels'.[5] Waiting for her on the quayside as she left the barge were her brother, the king, and Queen Elizabeth alongside Margaret's mother Cecily, who had travelled from her home at Berkhamsted to welcome her youngest daughter home. Richard, Duke of Gloucester, had also travelled back from his northern home and Elizabeth, Duchess of Suffolk, was there too to give her sister the warmest of welcomes. There was surely sadness that Anne was not alive to greet her but perhaps the ghost in the room during the whole of Margaret's stay must surely have been that of their brother, George.

Prior to her arrival, Edward had given instructions that Greenwich Palace and Coldharbour House were to be prepared for Margaret's stay, two of her favourite childhood residences. As Coldharbour had belonged to her sister Anne whilst she was alive, that is perhaps an indication that Margaret often resided there with her sister, denoting a close relationship between the pair. But Margaret's first stop was to be Greenwich where she was escorted to her opulent chambers, hung with intricately woven tapestries and a feather bed with a valence of velvet. Pieces of woven wool tapestry covered the table containing images of 'roses, sunnes and crowns'.[6] Soon after her arrival a banquet to celebrate her visit was held at Greenwich, hosted in their mother's name. Not only were they celebrating their sister's return, politically they were hosting a visit of a foreign dignitary as Margaret was there as a representative of Burgundy.

Margaret would remain in England until September 1480, during which time she and Edward had much to discuss, including the continuing conversation around England's support for Burgundy against their troublesome neighbour, France. Margaret also wanted to broach the subject of a marriage between Edward's daughter, the 7-year-old Princess Anne of York to the son of Mary and Maximilian, the 4-year-old Prince Philip of Austria, which would cement an even deeper alliance between the two countries. The marriage would never come to fruition.

When her stay ended, Margaret headed back to Flanders, breaking her journey early on to stay for a week at the private estates of Anthony Woodville in Kent (perhaps at The Mote, which was a Woodville family manor). Whilst there she visited the shrine of Thomas à Becket at Canterbury. Margaret and Anthony Woodville seem to have cultivated a friendship, perhaps based on their shared love of books and literature. Arriving back in Brussels in the autumn, she spent Christmas there with Mary who had just had her second child, a daughter, whom she and Maximilian named Margaret in her honour.[7]

Waving goodbye to her sister for the second time, Elizabeth of York once again returned to the business of raising her children. In October 1480, King Edward had been contacted by Oxford University, desiring him to send his nephew 'the Lord Edward Pole' to study at Oxford. Edward Pole was Elizabeth and John's second surviving eldest son, by now a lad of 14 years old. Edward presumably consulted with his sister and brother-in-law and, in March 1481, Edward was escorted to Oxford by the Bishop of Salisbury. He was still studying there a year later when, on 28 March 1482, the university wrote to the king praising his nephew's gifts of intellect and heart.[8]

Whilst Edward was studying in Oxford, his royal uncle, the king, paid a visit there. Accompanied by the college's founder, Bishop Waynflete, Edward travelled from Woodstock, arriving after sunset on 22 September 1481. According to the records, Edward entered the parish of St Giles' with 'a multitude of men, innumerable torches burning before him' and was greeted by the Lord Chancellor of the university, Lionel Woodville, who was the brother of Queen Elizabeth Woodville. Accompanying Edward were the Bishops of Chichester, Ely and Rochester and several other noblemen, including John de la Pole, Earl of Lincoln – Edward de la Pole's elder brother. Travelling amongst the group of ladies who also accompanied the king that day was Elizabeth, perhaps keen to see how her son was faring in his studies. The university honoured the women with gifts of wine and gloves.[9]

Whilst Elizabeth was celebrating her son's scholarly success, across the sea in Burgundy, Margaret had no motherly responsibilities, other than to her beloved stepdaughter, who was now a married woman and forging her own way in life. Their close relationship, however, came to a devastating end in early 1482 when Margaret received the worst possible news that Mary of Burgundy had died. Mary reportedly loved physical exercise, a pastime she had in common with her husband, Maximilian, and she spent much of her leisure time hunting, ice skating, or out in the gardens and fields with her treasured falcons. However, in March 1482, whilst out riding, Mary had been thrown from her horse. Although she had no visible wounds, she most likely had internal injuries and was in great pain. To make matters worse, she was in the early stages of her fourth pregnancy; her third child, Francis, was born in September 1481 but had not survived. After the accident, Mary was taken home to be looked after and to rest, but there was to be no recovery; she died from her injuries on 27 March 1482. A devastated Margaret hurried from her home to attend to Mary before she died. Thankfully she reached her in time, and before her death Mary begged Margaret to look after her two young children. She was buried in the Church of our Lady at Bruges.

Mary's death once again threw the state of Burgundy into disarray. With Mary's son and heir, Philip, still just a child, Maximilian was named as sole regent until Philip came of age. But this was bitterly opposed by many Burgundian nobles who did not want the foreign-born Maximilian to have sole charge of their domains. Margaret herself supported Maximilian; the pair had always shown mutual respect for each other and she clearly believed that he would rule in the best interests of Burgundy and her people.

But not everyone felt the same way and Mary's death triggered a decade-long civil war in Flanders. The three largest cities in the region refused to recognise Maximilian as sole regent for his son, referring to stipulations within his marriage contract of 1477.[10] Even though Mary's will stated that she wished Maximilian to rule until her son was old enough, they considered it void since it was drawn up without their consent. Their opposition also focused on some of the lordships of the

Flemish cities that Mary had granted to Margaret, a number of which exceeded those stipulated in Margaret's marriage contract. This dispute had the potential to have an effect on Margaret's dowry payments.

Maximilian appealed to Edward for help, but at the time he had troubles of his own. In May 1482, Edward and Queen Elizabeth lost their second eldest daughter, Princess Mary, at the age of 15. After a grand funeral, Mary was buried at St George's alongside her aunt, Anne.

With the English unable to support Maximilian, he turned to an unlikely ally, King Louis of France, who offered terms to the Burgundian estates that would at least end the French-Burgundian War, allowing Maximilian to focus on internal disputes. On 23 December 1482, Maximilian signed the Treaty of Arras which, as part of the treaty, required that his daughter with Mary of Burgundy, the 2-year-old Margaret of Austria, would marry the French dauphin, a young lad of 13 at that point. She was to be sent to France almost immediately, and by 24 April she was on her way to her new home, handed over to the French at Hesdin. By June she was betrothed to the 13-year-old dauphin. Meanwhile the City of Ghent refused to hand Philip over to either Maximilian or Margaret, and for the next two years Maximilian fought to regain access to his son.

The Treaty of Arras agreed between France and Burgundy effectively overrode the terms of the Treaty of Picquigny, breaking the marriage agreement between Princess Elizabeth of York and the Dauphin. Back in England, King Edward did not discover this until January 1483; upon hearing the news he was understandably furious. Ending the year 1482 completely oblivious to the dealmaking that was occurring across the sea, the king and his family came together at Eltham Palace to celebrate the Christmas period in festivities that were so opulent, they were thought worthy to be recorded. Edward, in a display of his generosity, reportedly fed over 2,000 people each day during the celebrations. The *Croyland Chronicle* reported 'King Edward kept the following feast of the Nativity at his palace of Westminster, frequently appearing clad in a great variety of most costly garments, of quite a different cut to those which had been usually seen hitherto in our kingdom. The sleeves of the robes were very full and hanging, greatly resembling a monk's frock, and so lined within with most costly furs, and rolled over the shoulders, as to give that prince a new and distinguished air to beholders, he being a person of most elegant appearance, and remarkable beyond all others for the attractions of his person. You might have seen, in those days, the royal court presenting no other appearance than such as fully befits a most mighty kingdom, filled with riches and with people of almost all nations, and (a point in which it excelled all others) boasting of those most sweet and beautiful children, the issue of his marriage, which has been previously mentioned, with queen Elizabeth.'[11]

Whether Elizabeth of York attended her brother's elaborate Christmas festivities is unclear; on 4 December 1482 we can place her at Westhorpe Hall in Suffolk, the residence of her mother-in-law, Alice Chaucer, in her later years. Westhorpe was some 16 miles south of their Wingfield residence in the county of Suffolk, close to Bury St Edmunds. The original Westhorpe Hall was demolished in the eighteenth century and lay on the west side of the moat. Part of the newer hall that was constructed to the east side survives today; now an old people's home, it is a listed building.[12] After the de la Poles left Suffolk, Westhorpe became the home of Mary Tudor and Charles Brandon, Mary dying there in 1533. From here on 4 December 1482, Elizabeth's husband wrote to a tenant of his, Thomas Geffrey/Jeffreys.[13] Perhaps they remained in Suffolk for the Christmas period. If so, there is a chance Elizabeth never saw her brother again.

A few months into 1483, King Edward travelled to Windsor. Returning to Westminster around Tuesday 25 March,[14] just before Easter Sunday, the king was taken so violently ill that he retired to his sickbed. Remaining bedridden for the next few days, he retained a state of consciousness, but presumably realised how ill he was because he called to his bedside those whom he needed to instruct or speak with before he died. He also added several codicils to his will during that time. Then, on 9 April, Edward died. He was not yet 41 and his son, Edward, Prince of Wales, was just 12.

His sudden death sent shockwaves around the country and surely even more so his family. Edward was not the virulent young man he once was and had somewhat indulged himself over his years as king, but he was still in good health. According to the writer of the *Croyland Chronicle*, he was 'neither worn out with old age nor yet seized with any known kind of malady'.[15] His cause of death has never been established but his death ended a twenty-two-year reign that had brought a semblance of peace to England's shores.

The chroniclers lauded Edward in their own words. Croyland described him as 'a worldly prince' and 'a most devout Catholic, a most unsparing enemy to all heretics, and a most loving encourager of wise and learned men, and of the clergy. He was also a most devout reverer of the Sacraments of the Church, and most sincerely repentant for all his sins'.[16] To Edward Hall, he was 'a manne, of a goodly personage, of stature high, and excedyng all other in countenaunce, of courage haute and high, of memorie moste perfecte... against his enemies, fierce and terrible, to his frendes and to straungers bountifuil and liberal'.[17] Thomas More, writing in the next century, describes him as 'a godly personage, and very princely to behold; of heart courageous, politic in counsel; in adversity nothing abashed, in prosperity rather joyful than proud; in peace just and merciful, in war sharp and fierce; in the field bold and hardy, and nevertheless no farther than wisdom would adventurous'.[18]

He was much to many, bountiful and generous to his subjects, but to the remaining members of the family of York – Elizabeth in Suffolk and Margaret in Burgundy, to Cecily Neville in her retirement in Berkhamsted and to Richard of Gloucester in Middleham – he was their brother and son. For the House of York this was not just a shock, it was a personal tragedy.

Edward had fought to avenge their father and he had succeeded, and his family can only have been proud of the strong leader he had become. But in terms of the Crown it was not a disaster. Edward had male heirs and the system of primogeniture could continue. Prince Edward was just 12 years old but princes had become kings at a younger age than this before. The succession was secure. Or so it seemed...

# Chapter 9

# A question of loyalty

On his deathbed, when it became clear that he was not likely to survive, Edward's wish was that his friends and family – his best friend William Hastings; his son-in-law Thomas Grey, Marquis of Dorset; and, of course, his brother, Richard of Gloucester – would watch over his son and guide him in his youthful years. As the prince was still a minor, Edward IV had added a codicil to his will, naming his brother, Gloucester, as Lord Protector until his son came of age.

Whether Elizabeth of York had been able to see her brother in his final days is unknown; perhaps she was already in London or perhaps she made the 100-mile trip from Wingfield to the capital at speed, anxious to see Edward as he lay ill and dying. Margaret, of course, across the sea in Burgundy would have been informed perhaps firstly of his illness and then, by a later messenger, of the death of the king of England, her beloved older brother. Their younger brother, Richard, Duke of Gloucester, was also informed of his brother's death in writing, in a letter written to him by Hastings and dispatched by fast messenger to his home in the north. A letter had also been sent to Prince Edward at his home in Ludlow, that he was to make haste to London. The king was dead, long live the king.

Gloucester replied from his home in Middleham by sending 'loving letters to Elyzabeth the Quene, comforting hir with many woords and promising his allegiance and to increase the credit of his carefulness and natural affection towards his brother's children'.[1] He also commanded all his men to swear obedience to his young nephew, Prince Edward. All that was needed now was for Edward to make the journey to London where he would be crowned England's new king, Edward V.

Edward IV's funeral took place ten days after his death, on Friday 19 April. On Wednesday 17 April, the king's body had been conveyed to Westminster Abbey from St Stephen's Chapel where it had lain since his passing. The coffin was draped with a pall of cloth of gold with a cross of white cloth of gold. Within forty-eight hours of the king's death, letters were sent across the country proclaiming Edward V the new king and announcing a coronation date of 4 May. Prince Edward had begun making his way to London from Ludlow, but he was not expected to arrive in time for the funeral. It went ahead without Gloucester's presence too, as he was also not expected to reach London in time. It was to be the honour of Elizabeth's eldest son, the Earl of Lincoln, to take on the role of chief mourner, walking directly behind the coffin in its procession from St Stephen's to the Abbey. As a king's funeral was primarily a male affair, neither Elizabeth nor their mother would attend the funeral proceedings.

After the service in the abbey, the coffin was loaded upon a chariot for Edward's last journey to Windsor. Six horses were ready to pull the chariot, each in trappings of black velvet. The procession arrived at Windsor on Thursday 18 April and the following day Edward was laid to rest in St George's Chapel with great ceremony, near to his sister Anne and his daughter Mary. Meanwhile his young son, and England's new king, was on his way to the capital and what should have happened next was a simple transition of the crown.

Whilst the queen and councillors waited in London for their new king, Richard of Gloucester had set out on the long journey down from his home in the north of England to London. The new king was being escorted to the capital by his Woodville relatives, his older half-brother Richard Grey, and his uncle, Anthony Woodville, Earl Rivers, both of whom had been with the young prince at Ludlow. Breaking their journey, the two lords met up with Gloucester along his route, and along with the Duke of Buckingham, who had also ridden out to meet the escort, the four men spent the evening in Northampton, sharing a friendly meal together. The new young king did not join them for the meal but remained behind at Stony Stratford. By all accounts all four men enjoyed each other's company that evening. The next day, 30 April, the men continued their journey together to meet up with the new king at Stony Stratford, 18 miles south of Northampton. But before they reached the town, Gloucester and Buckingham pulled up their horses and informed Rivers and Richard Grey that they were under arrest. They then rode on to where the king was staying, informing Edward that they would now take care of him and travel with him to London. Other servants in Edward's company were also imprisoned, and Rivers and Grey were escorted off to one of Gloucester's northern castles as prisoners.[2]

What instigated this unexpected turn of events is unclear. The popular and almost certainly accurate theory is that it was a move designed to separate Edward from his mother's family. The Woodvilles, rightly or wrongly, had never been popular; they were viewed by many of the old nobility as social climbers and there were strong feelings about the king's person being under their control. When news of the arrest of her brother and son reached the queen in London, she realised something was terribly wrong. For the second time in her life, believing herself and her family to be in danger, she gathered her belongings and fled into sanctuary with her daughters and her younger son, Prince Richard.

When Prince Edward arrived in London, he was initially taken to the Bishop of Ely's palace to await his coronation, later being moved to apartments within the Tower. On the surface, things appeared to be proceeding as they should but as the planned coronation date came and went, it became clear that something was amiss. With one of Edward's sons in the Tower, Richard of Gloucester, nominally in charge, decided he needed to obtain custody of the other prince, the 10-year-old Richard of York. Surrounding the sanctuary building with troops, the archbishop was sent in to speak with the queen, warning her that the young prince could be taken by force if she did not willingly hand him over into his care. The official story was that Prince Richard was required as a playmate and companion to his brother, Edward, whilst he awaited his coronation. Knowing they would attempt to take him by force if necessary, the queen had little choice but to hand him over.

Once Gloucester was in possession of both York boys, events then moved surprisingly fast. The council pronounced Gloucester Lord Protector, and on 10 and 11 June he wrote to the City of York and to Lord Neville (his mother's family) asking them to bring troops 'to aid and assist us against the queen, her bloody adherents and affinity; which have intended and daily doth intend to murder and utterly destroy us and our cousin the Duke of Buckingham and the old royal blood of the realm'.[3] Three days later he called a council meeting and, according to Vergil, he invited some of the nobles to a meeting at the Tower, and others to a meeting at Westminster, supposedly to discuss his nephew's coronation. The meeting at the Tower was attended by William Hastings and by all accounts, the meeting began congenially. However, a short while into proceedings, Gloucester allegedly requested that the Bishop of Ely, who was also present, return to his garden at Holborn to pick them some of his excellent strawberries. The bishop agreed to send for some, and Gloucester excused himself and left the room. Returning shortly after, his earlier amiable mood had now turned sour. Demanding of the gathered men what punishment they thought should be meted out to any who threatened his life, it is reported that Hastings replied that anyone who threatened the life of the Protector should be treated as a traitor and punished accordingly. Gloucester then declared that the traitors he spoke of were 'the sorceress, my brother's wife and Jane Shore, the king's mistress, with others, their associates'. Citing witchcraft, he apparently revealed his arm to the group of men, which he claimed had been withered away by sorcery.

Accusing Hastings of colluding with the women, Gloucester gave a cry of treason, causing a retinue of armed men to storm into the room. Hastings was dragged from the room and out onto a patch of grass within the Tower, where immediately, without trial, he was beheaded. The very same day, orders were sent to Pontefract that the queen's other son, Richard Grey, and her brother Anthony should be executed.

This was an extraordinary turn of events. Richard of Gloucester had fought alongside his brother and William Hastings for years, and he knew that Hastings' loyalty to his family was unwavering. Accounts of events throughout Richard's life thus far also point to a man, a brother, who was loyal and honourable; whilst their middle brother, Clarence, was plotting and scheming, Richard had seemingly maintained a level head, supporting his elder brother throughout his reign. Looking back over this period of time, various historians have attempted to make sense of Gloucester's actions over the weeks and months after his brother's death, and although some of his actions can be explained and even understood on occasion, the brutal dispatching of Hastings in that manner is hard to fathom. Perhaps the nearest assumption is that Richard believed that Hastings' loyalty to Edward was so strong that it would only be transferable to his son and that he predicted Hastings would stand in the way of what he was about to do next.

And what he did next was to make two extraordinary announcements. The first was that Edward IV's marriage to Elizabeth Woodville was invalid because prior to marrying her in 1464, he was pre-contracted to a lady named Eleanor Butler. If this were true, then the children of Edward and Elizabeth would be bastards and unable to inherit the throne. The second announcement called into question the circumstances around

Edward's birth and claimed that Edward was a bastard himself, the result of his mother's affair with an archer named Blaybourne during their time in Rouen. Considering their mother was still alive at this point, it was an incredibly bold move. Mancini also alleges that around this time, Gloucester stopped wearing mourning and started wearing purple, an outward show of his connection to royalty.

On Sunday 22 June, a learned doctor, Ralph Shaw (or Shaa) preached a sermon at St Paul's cross, proclaiming to the people of London that Edward's sons were in fact illegitimate. Over the next few days the Duke of Buckingham continued to validate this story to the mayor, aldermen and justices of the city.[4] Then, on Thursday 26 June, a deputation of the city's leaders made its way to Baynard's Castle, which Richard was using as his London base (although he was residing at his London home at Crosby Place) and offered him a parchment roll requesting he accept the position of king.

Was Gloucester acting on his own or was this a plan discussed and agreed upon by the rest of his family? According to Polydore Vergil, their mother, Cecily, 'being falsely accused of adultery, complained afterwards in sundry places to right many noble men, whereof some yet live, of that great injury which her son Richard had done her'.[5] Elizabeth and Margaret's reactions to this slur on their mother went unrecorded. Yet presumably, as formidable as Cecily Neville was, her voice was not strong enough, as was the want of women, to argue publicly against the story. Perhaps she had no inclination to? The general consensus by historians, however, is that the affair did not happen and that it was all part of Richard's plan.

But seemingly this rumour, which worked beautifully in Richard's favour, was not a construct of his imagination; it was an old rumour that had been around for a while. One story holds that it actually sprang from Cecily herself; that upon hearing of Edward's marriage to Elizabeth Woodville, she was so incensed that she had declared Edward to be a bastard son. If this was a throwaway comment by Cecily, she could not have foreseen the damage it would eventually do. The rumour also apparently rose up again and was used by Warwick during the time he was planning to replace Edward on the throne with his brother, Clarence. Perhaps Richard warned his mother and sisters what he was about to do. Perhaps they agreed with him, although it's hard to see that Cecily would have agreed to a stain on her character. Or did the end justify the means?

If his brother, Edward, was actually illegitimate, then his young son had no right to be king of England. But in case the populace was hesitant to believe that – after all Edward IV had been king for twenty-two years and if he were not York's son, why was this information not acted on before – Richard of Gloucester needed to make a watertight case to disinherit Edward's sons. The story of the pre-contract between Edward and another woman then really sealed the deal. News that Edward was already married before he met Elizabeth Woodville was reportedly revealed by Bishop Stillington, the Bishop of Bath and Wells, who had seemingly presented himself before the council on 8 June and volunteered the information.[6] That he was reporting this first-hand was a strong argument for its veracity; Stillington told how he had married them in secret, with just himself, Edward and Elizabeth Talbot present. Elizabeth Talbot had died in 1468 so was unable to either corroborate or deny Stillington's version of events. But was this the truth and did Richard believe it was, or was it again a convenient story and the evidence that Richard needed to take the throne for himself?

This, perhaps more than his mother's supposed affair, was both powerful and plausible. Edward had a reputation with the ladies and his marriage to Elizabeth Woodville had also occurred in secret; was Elizabeth Woodville just lucky in that with her he chose to reveal their union? Alison Weir, in her book *The Princes in the Tower*, points out that there is no formal record that Stillington presented himself to the council on 8 June.[7] All of these little details and pieces of information and misinformation are exactly why nobody over the centuries has ever been able to accurately paint Richard of Gloucester as either a true Yorkist, loyal to his family name and morally correct in his actions, or a tyrant, a schemer and the eventual worst possible accusation, a child murderer.

As the events of May and June were taking place, Edward V's first coronation date passed and although a new coronation day was planned for 22 June, this also came and went. Finally, on 6 July 1483, a coronation did take place. But it was not that of the young prince; instead, Richard, Duke of Gloucester, was crowned King Richard III at Westminster Abbey in a joint coronation with his wife, Anne Neville, just a stone's throw from where the queen and her daughters were confined. Another York son was now king of England.

The reactions of his family to Richard's power grab went unrecorded. That Elizabeth and John attended Richard's coronation along with their son, the Earl of Lincoln, must indicate that they at least had accepted his claim to the throne, perhaps even supported it. Even if they did not believe the claims about their mother's affair, perhaps they too were convinced by claims that Edward had been pre-contracted to another woman. Did they even have prior knowledge of it? Or did they, too, just find it easy to believe that the young, attractive and promiscuous Edward could well have bound himself in marriage to a lady to get what he wanted and then disregarded her afterwards.

Elizabeth of York and her family were rewarded by Richard for their support. Her eldest son, the Earl of Lincoln, carried the ball and cross during the coronation ceremony, walking alongside his father, the Duke of Suffolk, who also took part in the procession, and was given the honour of carrying the sceptre. Both men walked in front of Richard of Gloucester, himself wearing robes of purple velvet denoting his kingship and position as the most powerful man in the land. Elizabeth as Duchess of Suffolk, wearing a circlet of gold on her head, followed in the procession behind Anne Neville, England's new queen. The queen was also dressed in purple robes. Elizabeth's second son, Edmund, was made a Knight of the Bath in honour of the coronation.[8]

Another attendee at the coronation was Sir Francis Lovell, Elizabeth's former ward, who was now a young man of 27 and who had become a close associate of Richard's. He also played a prominent part in the ceremonies, bearing the third sword of state. After the coronation he was promoted to Lord Chamberlain on 14 August 1483, and he became an important part of the Ricardian government, receiving a grant for life of the office of Chief Butler of England, which had become free by the death of Anthony Woodville, Earl Rivers.[9] Along with two other men, Sir William Catesby and Sir Richard Ratcliffe, he remained one of Richard's closest supporters throughout his reign. The three were infamously referred to in a lampoon by a Londoner, William Collingbourne, who posted a rhyme on the door of St Paul's Cathedral that read: 'The Cat, the Rat and Lovell our dog, Rule all England under a Hog'; the hog referring to Richard's emblem of a white boar.

After the formal coronation proceedings, a large and stately banquet was held to celebrate England's new king and queen. Elizabeth was sat on the right of the queen. Hall tells us that it was round 4 pm when the king and queen entered Westminster Hall. King Richard III sat on the middle table, next to the Bishop of Canterbury, and the queen and her ladies sat on the left-hand side of the table. During the second course the king's champion, Sir Robert Dymoke, entered the hall on horseback. Throwing down his gauntlet, he declared in front of the gathered guests that if any man should challenge Richard's right to the crown, he would gladly fight them, to which the whole hall cried 'King Richard'! The feasting and celebrations continued into the night, which given it was June must have been heading towards midnight, after which 'the king returned to his lodgings and sent home all the lords into their counties'.[10]

As well as wearing her circlet of gold, Elizabeth of York in her role as Duchess of Suffolk was supplied with new clothing for the coronation; the Wardrobe Accounts of Richard III record that she received a long gown made of yards of blue velvet finished with six yards of crimson cloth of gold and a long gown of crimson velvet embroidered with white cloth of gold.[11]

From Burgundy, Margaret of York presumably sent support for her brother and her congratulations on his rise to power. But what did Elizabeth and Margaret know or believe about their brother's divine right to the throne? Margaret, in particular, remained loyal to her family and championed the House of York throughout her life so perhaps she and Elizabeth accepted events as they occurred. Their belief in their family's right to rule was not affected; in the end it was a seamless transfer of power with little bloodshed in comparison to the earlier wars that surrounded the throne. Even reaction from Cecily Neville is muted. But if they accepted their brother's arguments for his claim to the throne, the events of the next few months may have been more challenging to their conscience.

*** 

England had its new king, but there was still the question of Edward's sons, Prince Edward and Prince Richard, and their mother and sisters who were still ensconced in the safety of the abbey sanctuary, just yards away from where the coronation festivities had taken place. The fate and subsequent disappearance of the two young princes has become one of England's greatest unsolved mysteries and it is not within the scope of this book to discuss all of the many theories and arguments around what may have happened to them after they entered the Tower. But it is important to look at their story through what their aunts, Elizabeth and

Margaret, may or may not have known about what happened to them after Richard's coronation.

The common and perhaps loudest assertion on the fate of Edward's sons is that they were murdered by Richard III, their uncle. Not long after the young Prince Richard was released from sanctuary by his mother to join his brother, it was reported that the boys were moved into apartments further within the Tower. Mancini, a visiting Italian to London in the summer of 1483, wrote about events as he saw them and tells of how they were seen less frequently through bars and windows, and that all their servants were soon dismissed until eventually they were never seen again. One of the last attendants to see the boys was reportedly their physician, John Argentine, who, according to Mancini, reported that Prince Edward daily sought remission of his sins because he believed that death was facing him. Mancini was reporting this second- or third-hand so we cannot be sure that the statement that Edward was aware of his impending death is fact or embellishment. Whether the young king considered himself captive or just believed he was awaiting his coronation is unknown and may have changed as time went on. It is likely that in the first instance, he trusted his uncle and did believe he would be king. How quickly that changed would depend on what their fate actually was and how soon he became aware of it, and is part of the integral mystery of their disappearance.

The idea that Richard murdered them is possible but like all suppositions, it has its flaws. He had already proved them to be illegitimate and he had now been sworn in as king so it was already a fait accompli. Of course, whilst his nephews were alive they would be a magnet for any dissenters who might use them to try and overthrow him; to many, his brother's eldest son was still the rightful king. Was this a good enough reason to kill two young children? Perhaps. And was Richard capable of murdering his nephews? He certainly had proved his ruthlessness with the murder of William Hastings, but prior to this he had also showed family loyalty in bounds. He must have known his nephews since they were young boys; was he that brutal? Even though he would not have committed the act himself, would he really have given the order to murder his young relations?

According to the *Croyland Chronicle*, whilst queen Elizabeth Woodville and her daughters remained in sanctuary, plans were being made for the princesses to escape and flee overseas: 'There was also a report that it had been recommended by those men who had taken refuge in the sanctuaries, that some of the king's daughters should leave Westminster, and go in disguise to the parts beyond the sea; in order that, if any fatal mishap should befall the said male children of the late king in the Tower, the kingdom might still, in consequence of the safety of his daughters, someday fall again into the hands of the rightful heirs'.[12] Richard, reportedly aware of this, surrounded the sanctuary precincts with his troops so that 'not one of the persons there shut up could go forth, and no one could enter, without his permission.[13]

King Richard's first activity as England's new king was to go on progress, to show himself off to the people. His first destination was the north, an area where his popularity was already guaranteed, having acted as his brother's caretaker in the region for much of his reign. He supposedly left London with the two princes remaining behind in the Tower. But it was during his absence from the capital that rumours first began to spread that the princes had died 'a violent death'. But with a lack of evidence, no one could report how.

A failed rescue attempt to free the two boys reportedly took place at the end of July, after which time another plan began to be formed between two women who were unlikely bedfellows – one a Yorkist and one a Lancastrian – but with the common goal of removing King Richard from the throne.

These two women were Elizabeth Woodville, Edward's queen, and Margaret Beaufort, the young girl who had once been betrothed to Elizabeth of York's husband, John de la Pole. The great granddaughter of John of Gaunt and Katherine Swynford, she had come a long way since her union with John de la Pole had been broken off in the early 1450s. In 1455, aged just 12 years old, Margaret had been married to a man named Edmund Tudor, the half-brother of Henry VI, and by the age of 13 she was pregnant with his child. Giving birth at such a young age proved a traumatic experience for Margaret although the end result was a healthy baby boy. She would never, though, have any further children. Margaret named her son Henry Tudor, and due to her lineage from Edward III, the young boy was considered to have a potential claim to the throne.

Staunchly Lancastrian, Edmund Tudor died in 1456 and his brother, Jasper Tudor, swore to take care of his widow, Margaret, and her young son. He arranged a second marriage for Margaret to Sir Henry Stafford and took Henry Tudor into his care. Sir Henry Stafford died in 1471 and a year later, in a marriage of her own choosing, Margaret Beaufort married Thomas Stanley.

When Edward IV became king, Jasper Tudor went into exile with other Lancastrians and the young Henry Tudor was placed as a ward into the household of Sir William Herbert, a Yorkist supporter. In 1470, Henry briefly attended court during the readeption of Henry VI, but in 1471, when Edward re-took the throne, Henry fled abroad into exile with his uncle, Jasper, and they had been living in France under the care of the Duke of Brittany ever since.

By 1483, Henry Tudor was a young man of 26 and after the death of men like Henry Holland, he was considered the last Lancastrian claimant to the throne. At some point after Richard's coronation, a plot began to be formed through messages that were smuggled into the sanctuary precincts, from Margaret Beaufort to Elizabeth Woodville, of an alliance between the Houses of York and Lancaster, through the marriage of Henry with the 17-year-old Princess Elizabeth, Edward IV's eldest daughter. The messages were conveyed by Margaret's physician, Lewis Caerleon.

This plan, forged by two mothers, leads to the question as to what Elizabeth Woodville knew or didn't know about the fate of her sons. The answer, of course, is that we can't possibly know, but perhaps at this stage she too had heard the news that they were considered dead and felt she had nothing to lose but to take her chances with Margaret and attempt to remove her brother-in-law from the throne.

By 24 September 1483, Richard's reign was already under threat. Whilst the king was mid-progress around his new kingdom, the Duke of Buckingham, who had been hugely supportive of Richard since Edward's death, suddenly defected. What caused him to distance himself from the king is unknown, but he left the king during his progress and returned to his home in Brecon. Whilst there, it is thought that he was persuaded by John Morton, Bishop of Ely, to turn coat and join those who were supporting an invasion by Henry Tudor. John Morton had been an important part of Edward IV's court and was an executor of his will; he had been held in custody at the duke's home in Brecon since the infamous council meeting that led to Hastings' death. He was also a close friend of Margaret Beaufort and it is thought that it was through her that Buckingham also began to communicate with Elizabeth Woodville. From his home in Brecon, Buckingham also wrote to the exiled Henry Tudor asking him to bring an army to assist in overthrowing the king. He then began to do the same himself, assembling men and arms at Brecon Castle.

In October and November 1483, the king issued several commissions to Francis Lovell and a man named James Tyrell to deal with Buckingham and others in Kent, Sussex, Devon and Cornwall who had risen up in support of the rebels.[14] Meanwhile, by Saturday 18 October, Buckingham was ready to move and he and his men began their journey towards England, ready to form a rebellion. But nature itself was to prove the first valiant enemy and in a flood of torrential rain, Buckingham reached the River Severn to discover the banks had burst and he had to turn back. Many of his men, who had never been that keen to fight in the first place, turned around and returned to their homes.

Having to quickly revise his plans, the duke decided to make his way to Weobley, in Herefordshire, to the home of Lord Ferrers. From Weobley, Buckingham continued to attempt to raise an army, but the men of Herefordshire would not rise, hearing reports that the king and his army were on their way. By this time, Buckingham was a wanted man with a reward on his head. His castle in Wales had been raided and seized by members of the Vaughan family, loyal to the king, who looted the building and took his daughters into their custody. Realising he was in trouble, he disguised his eldest son, who had travelled with him, as a girl and had him smuggled away by loyal retainers. Buckingham and his wife Katherine Woodville, a sister of Elizabeth Woodville, went into hiding in Shropshire in the house of a servant, Ralph Bannister. But Bannister sold them out and on 1 November, the duke was captured and taken to the king at Salisbury, where the following day he was beheaded in the marketplace, without trial. His wife and younger son were taken to London and into custody.

Other men who had been intensely loyal to King Edward IV, and by association the House of York, also joined Buckingham's revolt, in what can only have been an indication that they felt Richard's claim to the throne was unlawful. These men included Elizabeth Woodville's son, Thomas Grey, Marquis of Dorset, who had made his way to Exeter and raised the standard of rebellion there. Upon hearing the news of Buckingham's capture and execution, he fled across the Channel to join Henry Tudor. Although Richard's sister Elizabeth and her husband had seemingly accepted without question Richard's rise to power, another of

Edward IV's closest allies, Thomas St Leger, also allied himself with the rebels. Alongside Elizabeth Woodville's brothers, Lionel and Richard Woodville, Thomas St Leger, Anne of York's second husband, took up arms against his brother-in-law, the king.

Whether he would have made the same decision if Anne was still alive is an interesting question. Would she, like Elizabeth, have chosen to support her brother, Richard, in his actions? But Thomas, without Anne to influence his decision, clearly took the stance that his unwavering loyalty to Edward IV should transfer to his son, not Richard of Gloucester. St Leger had travelled to Exeter along with the Marquis of Dorset but unlike Dorset, St Leger had been captured before he could flee abroad. According to reports, very large sums of money were offered to save his life, although it is uncertain by whom, but it was all in vain and he was executed in Exeter alongside some of the other rebels. Did Elizabeth and the de la Poles attempt to save her brother-in-law? There is no evidence that she did plead for him, but if she was at all involved in trying to save his life, she was ignored by her brother as no clemency was shown towards St Leger. At the same time as ordering the execution of the rebels, Richard called a parliament and attainted Henry Tudor and all the men who had recently fled the country, stripping them of their lands and titles.[15]

Unaware of Buckingham's capture and subsequent death, rebels in the Cornish town of Bodmin had declared Henry Tudor as king. Tudor did set sail from France as requested, but as he neared the English coast, he sensed luck was not on his side and his small fleet turned and sailed back to Brittany. The rebellion may have failed in the short term, but at dawn on Christmas Day 1483 in Rennes Cathedral, in the presence of 500 supporters, Henry Tudor made a public promise to marry the Yorkist Princess Elizabeth as soon as he was king. He then began, once more, to plan his invasion.

As 1483 turned into 1484, Elizabeth Woodville and her daughters remained in sanctuary. Although she had agreed to the plans involving Henry Tudor, she had no power to bring them to fruition and there was always the possibility that they would fail. She and her girls could not remain in the Westminster sanctuary indefinitely so she had to give some thought to their next move. Eventually she chose to leave, a decision that she has been heavily criticised for over the centuries, because she made a deal with the supposed murderer of her sons. But in reality, she had little choice, and of course, we once again cannot know what information she had about her sons. Before she left the confines of Westminster, she took steps to ensure her girls were going to be safe by exacting a solemn oath from the king, guaranteeing the safety of her daughters. The terms of her surrender were tough; she had to acknowledge that she and the princesses now had no royal status, and that they were merely gentlewomen. She also had to allow herself to be placed under house arrest.

Matthew Lewis, in his book *The Survival of the Princes in the Tower*, makes a hugely plausible argument that by the time the queen and her daughters left sanctuary, she had been informed by Richard that the princes were safe. This theory also focuses on a place named Gipping Hall in Suffolk, and the family home of James Tyrell, one of Richard's loyal henchmen. A Tyrell family legend, passed down through the centuries, tells of Gipping Hall being used to host the stay of Elizabeth Woodville and her children around this time; and by children, it infers that it was both her daughters and her sons.[16]

Gipping Hall's location is paramount to the theory that the princes were not murdered. It is near to the coast but also, more interestingly, it is close to Wingfield, the home of Elizabeth and John de la Pole. The idea that the dowager queen was allowed to spend some time there with her sons before they were spirited away, not only to safety but out of the way of any who may use them to challenge Richard's rule, is a hugely plausible theory. Elizabeth Woodville may not have been happy about her son's right to rule being snatched away, but relief that they were alive may have been enough – for then.

Lewis surmises that at Gipping the boys may have been permitted to see their mother and sisters briefly before being separated. One train of thought is that perhaps Edward, the eldest, was then taken into the north of England by Elizabeth's son, the Earl of Lincoln.

Elizabeth's eldest son, John de la Pole, had been created Earl of Lincoln on 13 March 1467 with a grant of £20 a year from the issues of the county of Lincoln.[17] Richard III reconfirmed the patent on 14 February 1484. According to the writer of the *Croyland Chronicle*, Elizabeth of York was very much in favour with Richard, who was 'always looking for ways to advance her', which may throw doubt as to whether she made a personal or monetary plea for the life of St Leger. Or perhaps, even from his beloved sister, that was a request too far?

But Richard did bestow gifts and trust in Elizabeth's eldest son and on 13 April 1484, Lincoln had another grant from the king to him and 'and the heirs male of his body, of the manor of Wodehey in Berkshire, and other manors which are specified, in the counties of York, Wilts, Northampton, Essex, and Southampton'. On the same day an annuity of £176 13s 4d was settled on him out of the issues of the Duchy of Cornwall,[18] and on 18 April he was awarded a grant for his good service against the rebels, indicating that he had played no part in trying to oust his uncle from the throne. In addition to these grants, on 21 August Richard appointed his 'most dear nephew', John, Earl of Lincoln, as Lieutenant of Ireland.

Lincoln was not the only member of Elizabeth's family to be rewarded. Richard was also reportedly looking into arranging a prospective marriage for his niece, Lady Anne de la Pole, with the Duke of Rothsay, the eldest son of the King of Scots.[19] This never came to fruition but would have been a real source of pride to the Suffolks to see one of their daughters become the potential queen of Scots.

Also in February 1484, the king granted a licence for Elizabeth's husband, John, Duke of Suffolk, and their ex-ward, Francis Lovell, to found a fraternity of twelve masters within the church of St Helen, Abendon (Abingdon). It was to be known as The Fraternity of the Holy Cross of Abingdon. As well as paying for the sustenance of thirteen poor men and women and two chaplains, it was to celebrate divine service daily for the good estate of the king, queen Anne, their son Edward, Prince of Wales and for their souls after their death and for the souls of Richard, late Duke of York, William, late Duke of Suffolk and William Lovell, late Lord Lovell.[20]

Just over a month later, however, the king and queen were plunged into grief when on 31 March 1484, Edward, Prince of Wales, died; he was 11 years old. He was their only child and both the king and queen mourned his loss deeply. After his death, Elizabeth's son, Lincoln, succeeded Prince Edward as president of the council of the north, and although nothing was ever formalised, it was widely believed that after the death of the prince, Richard considered his nephew, Lincoln, to be his heir until such time as he and queen Anne had more sons.

After the coronation festivities, Elizabeth and John had returned to Wingfield. They had taken to spending more and more time in their Suffolk home, whilst Lincoln, who was by then 24 and married, made his base at Ewelme. From Wingfield, on 1 May 1484, the Duke of Suffolk wrote again to his tenant Thomas Geffrey/Jeffreys, demanding he pay the money that he owed the duke, with the threat that non-payment might mean he would lose his farm, perhaps giving an indication that Elizabeth's family were still financially insecure.[21] In 1484 the Suffolks had nine of their eleven known children still alive, many still financially dependent on them and their two youngest, William and Richard, were just 6 and 4 years old.

***

Across the sea, in Burgundy, little is known of Margaret of York's support towards her brother and his sudden rise to kingship. Presumably she took the same view that her sister and their mother had taken. Civil war was still raging throughout Burgundy, which was likely keeping Margaret's focus on internal affairs. Perhaps in some indication that she and her younger brother were on friendly terms, Richard agreed to send Margaret 6,000 archers to assist her and Maximilian to regain control of their domain, something that Edward IV had not done himself after Mary of Burgundy's death.

In the summer of 1483, as King Richard was on progress around England, King Louis XI of France died, news that Margaret and Maximilian would receive with joy. Coming so soon after Edward IV's death, this would herald a real climate change. France was now much weakened, and along with it, its threat to Burgundy. Louis' young son and heir, Charles, was still a young boy so France would enter a regency under Louis' daughter Anne. The French threat was now removed, but it would still take until 1484 for the Burgundian rebels to be put down and before Maximilian could be reunited with his son, Philip.

That Margaret kept in touch with her brother Richard during the years 1483–85 is highly likely. Returning to the supposition that Richard had not murdered his nephews and that at least one of them had been sent to Richard's stronghold in the north of England under the care of the Earl of Lincoln, the idea that the other, perhaps the youngest Richard, was dispatched to Margaret's court in Burgundy is an interesting one, further borne out by events a decade later. A grant on 23 April 1484 to Philip Goguet, 'Chapelyn to the Duchesse of Burgoyne and for III persons with him. Given at Nottingham the xxiii day of April' plus a later entry in December 1484 that 'Clement Goguet hath a like letter to passe & repasse to my lady Burgoyn with a servant with him…' illustrates that messengers were going between Margaret and Richard. The addition to the entry that the message was sent 'without any serche' (given an exemption from being searched) could point to the fact that the letter contained sensitive information.[22] We do not know what the messages contained, of course; it may just have been regular court business, but as with all good mysteries, anything is possible.

As 1485 dawned, Richard had been king for nearly two years and, so far, the expected invasion by Henry Tudor had not taken place. The year began badly for the king when, on 16 March 1485, during an eclipse of the sun, Queen Anne died. She had grieved enormously after the death of her only child and her health had been in a gradual decline ever since. The king had also had to field off rumours that he had planned to marry his niece, the Princess Elizabeth, himself, some say to thwart Henry Tudor's plans. There was even talk that the queen's death was convenient in this scheme of his to marry his niece, hinting at foul play. This sounds like tittle-tattle, gossip that spread through the London streets and taverns like a city-wide game of Chinese whispers, but it was actually taken so seriously at the time that Richard was forced to make a public denial. Rumours were so rife that the majority of Richard's council felt the need to discuss it and were horrified at the idea, including his closest friends and advisors, Sir Richard Ratcliffe and William Catesby. Vergil certainly believed that an attraction did exist, but only one way: 'The King, thus lowysd from the bond of matrimony, began to cast an eye upon Elyzabeth his nece, and to desire hir in maryage; but because both the yowng lady hirself, and all others, did abhorre the wickednes so detestable, he determyned therefor to do everything by leisure'.[23]

Whatever the truth of the matter, the council made it clear to the king in no uncertain terms that the public would never accept such an act, even presenting to him more than twelve Doctors of Divinity, who asserted that the Pope could grant no dispensation in the case of such a degree of consanguinity, and Richard was eventually forced to make a public statement in front of the mayor and citizens of London denying that he had ever considered taking Princess Elizabeth as his wife. Princess Elizabeth herself, who had been at court since leaving sanctuary, was dispatched north into the care of her cousin, the Earl of Lincoln.

With that rumour put to bed, Richard now had to focus on Henry Tudor's planned invasion, which his informants were reporting was now imminent, advising the king that Tudor had set sail from France, determined this time to complete his mission. Aware that he would need to face his rival on the battlefield if Tudor made land, Richard went to Berkhamsted to see his mother,[24] perhaps to seek advice, perhaps because he feared he may never see her again. Sadly, but not surprisingly, Cecily and the voices of Elizabeth and Margaret of York are once again silent over the Princess Elizabeth rumours and over the trouble that was inevitably coming. What advice would they have given him, and how worried were they for his safety? These were women who lived in an era that was so different to today; where knights fought hand to hand combat for causes they may not even have believed in, but their band of brothers did. Richard's prowess as a military man had been proven time and again; perhaps they accepted what was to come and believed that right was on his side. Margaret, of course, was far across the sea, but perhaps Elizabeth saw her brother at their mother's house in early 1485. If she did, it would be for the last time.

With operations under way, Sir Francis Lovell was reportedly dispatched to the south coast to guard against Henry's landing. But in the end Henry Tudor made shore at Milford Haven, off the coast of Wales, on 7 August 1485. The king gathered his men and set off to meet him. Both men knew what was at stake. The Lancastrians and the Yorkists would once again meet each other on the battlefield, in a battle that had to be decisive. The two parties came together at Bosworth field and after fierce fighting, Richard, who fought valiantly, was defeated. Even his detractors agree that he fought bravely, but it wasn't enough. Vergil tells us that he had realised he was in danger and could have saved himself by fleeing the field, but he was determined that this battle be the final word, 'that very day he wold make end ether of warre or lyfe'.[25]

There is no evidence that any of the Suffolk family fought alongside Richard at Bosworth; that may mean nothing other than the fact that the Earl of Lincoln remained in his post in the north and Elizabeth's husband, John de la Pole, had never really been a military man.

If Richard had defeated Henry Tudor, he could, in time, have brought peace to the realm. Whatever his reasons for taking the throne and the rights and wrongs of whether it was his to take, firstly as a son of the Duke of York, and secondly with a better claim than Edward's 'illegitimate son', had he managed to suppress those who still fought for the princes, perhaps in time he would have made a great king. The historian, George Buck, writing his *History of King Richard the Third* in 1619, concluded that:

> Although this prince was not so superlative as to assume the name of holy or best, you see him a wise, magnificent and a valiant man and a just, bountiful and temperate; and an eloquent and magnanimous and pious prince; and a benefactor to the holy church and to the realm. Yet for all this it hath been his fortune to be aspersed and fouled and to fall into this malice of those who have been ill-affected towards him...

But with the Lancastrian Henry Tudor arriving back in England to claim the throne, the battle at Bosworth had to end with a death, and it was Richard who had fought so valiantly many times before alongside his brother Edward who met his fate that day.

The dead king's body was thrown naked upon a horse and taken to be buried at the Grey Friars in Leicester, a nearby Franciscan priory. After his victory, Henry Tudor knelt and gave thanks to Almighty God, before his father-in-law, Sir Thomas Stanley, took Richard's crown and placed it upon his head. Henry and his men also proceeded to Leicester, where they stayed for two days, making plans for his journey to London, where he would be officially recognised as England's new king.

The death of Richard was a disaster; the House of York fell from power spectacularly. Not only was it a personal tragedy in the loss of a brother and a son, but his death heralded not just the end of the House of York but also the end of the great Plantagenet reign. The men of the family were all gone; Elizabeth, Margaret and their mother Cecily alone would be witnesses to the new dawn and it would be down to their niece, Princess Elizabeth, to represent the House of York in this new era of Tudor kings and queens.

# Chapter 10

# The Tudors

There is no record of how the news of Richard's death reached his sisters and mother or their reaction, although undoubtedly they received it with great sadness. As the new Tudor king approached his capital, the writer, Francis Bacon, who penned a history of Henry's reign in the seventeenth century, tells us that he was met with applause and acclamations in all the towns and villages that he travelled through. This may have been true of the common people, who once again welcomed a new king to the throne in the hope that peace and prosperity would be restored to the kingdom, but for the supporters of the House of York, Henry was surely not such a welcome prospect. Making his first entry into London on a Saturday, England's new king was received by the mayor and livery company representatives at Shoreditch, who accompanied him into the city. He then made his way to St Paul's, where the *Te Deum* was sung before finally heading to his lodgings at the Bishop of London's Palace.[1]

Before leaving Leicester, Henry Tudor had sent messengers north to escort the Princess Elizabeth to London. Alongside her came the two children of Clarence, Margaret and Edward, Earl of Warwick, who had also been based in the north, all under the care of the Earl of Lincoln. The two girls were brought to Coldharbour House, Anne of York's former home which was now in the possession of Margaret Beaufort. The young Earl of Warwick, as a living male of the House of York, would be sent to a set of comfortable rooms in the Tower where he could be kept an eye on, under guard and out of the way of any rebel Yorkists who might want to restore one of their own to the throne.

But perhaps a bigger problem for Henry than the Earl of Warwick, who was only 10 in 1485, was the fate and location of Edward IV's sons who would have been a real threat to his kingship. It seems that Henry Tudor, like many others, had no idea of their whereabouts, or indeed whether they were alive or dead, something that would perhaps haunt him throughout his reign. According to the chronicler Molinet, upon his arrival in the capital Henry issued a challenge that if there was anyone in Edward's family who felt they had a right to the Crown, they should show themselves and challenge him for it.[2] Was this a test to see if either of the princes would show themselves, or if someone would offer up information as to their fate? Presumably it was also a warning to men like the Earl of Lincoln; Henry was in effect making use of the famous phrase, 'speak now or forever hold thy peace'. The real threat to Henry this early on though were Edward's sons, if they were alive. Not only would a living son of Edward IV have a stronger claim to the throne than Henry himself, the danger was also compounded by the fact that before Henry could marry Princess Elizabeth, something he had sworn to do in exchange for the support his invasion would receive, he had to make her legitimate again. But the very act of reinstating Princess Elizabeth as her father's rightful heir would mean that he would also be reinstating Edward's sons.

When Richard III had taken the throne in 1483, he had drawn up a document entitled *Titulus Regius* (Royal Title), establishing his right to the crown of England. This had been legally enshrined as an Act of Parliament in January/February 1484 and had consequently rendered the York children bastards in the eyes of the law. One of Henry's first official acts had to be to repeal this act and this he did, ordering that all copies be destroyed, although a copy survived in the parliament roll, allowing us sight of the act today. In his bill annulling the act, Henry ordered that: 'for its false and seditious contrivance and untruth, [the bill] be void, annulled, repealed, cancelled and of no effect or force. And that it be ordained by the said authority that the said bill be cancelled and destroyed, and that the said act, record and enrolment be taken and removed from the roll and records of the said parliament of the said late king and burnt and entirely destroyed'.[3] Henry Tudor must have taken this action with bated breath, hoping that Edward's sons did not reappear. We can only assume that Henry, like most people, had no idea what had happened to the two princes; he never made an announcement on their whereabouts, but nor did he ever directly accuse Richard of murdering them.

Dating his reign to the day before Bosworth, Henry effectively and cleverly made traitors of all who had fought on Richard's side. In the days and weeks after the battle, some of Richard's supporters were arrested and executed; many more fled across the sea to Flanders to

Margaret of York's court, and others had to resign themselves to the new regime to continue living their lives. With Margaret welcoming Yorkist exiles to Burgundy, in England, Elizabeth of York and her husband, on the surface at least, had to take the latter option and defer to England's new king.

Another of Richard's most trusted supporters and a close friend of the Suffolks, Francis Lovell, had been on the run since Bosworth. There is some uncertainty as to whether he was on the battlefield that day; originally listed among the early dead, he showed up in Colchester some four to five days after the battle.[4] Hearing the news that Henry Tudor had in fact landed in Wales, he returned from the south coast and had plenty enough time to reach Bosworth to fight alongside his friend and king. He may well have been there and escaped with his life, but Matthew Lewis offers a train of thought that perhaps Richard had not wanted him at Bosworth, but instead had sent him elsewhere, namely, to secure either one or both of Edward's sons if Richard did not survive.[5] Arriving in Colchester in mid-August, Lovell, along with two of the Stafford brothers, took refuge in sanctuary in the church of St John's in Colchester. He would remain there for the next six months.

With men like Lovell in hiding, things could have been tricky for the Duke and Duchess of Suffolk, who clearly as family of Richard III would have been suspected enemies of the new Tudor king. But it appears they had decided that at least for now, their best option was to live under the new regime. During August and September 1485 they and their son, Lincoln, managed to persuade Henry that they were of no danger to him. Not only was Lincoln made welcome at court, but they, in their roles of Duke and Duchess of Suffolk, were also invited to take part in the coronation festivities.

Henry Tudor's coronation took place on 30 October 1485 and Elizabeth's husband, John de la Pole, took part in the king's procession from the Tower to Westminster, walking behind the king and alongside the Duke of Bedford, Henry's uncle, Jasper Tudor. The Duke of Bedford bore the king's crown and the Duke of Suffolk carried the king's sceptre.[6]

Then eight days after, in Henry's first parliament, the king 'in consideration of the good and faithful service which his faithful subject, John, Duke of Suffolk, had performed, and intended to perform, granted to him the office of Constable of the Castle of Wallingford, to hold for life by himself or deputy'.[7]

That the Suffolks would have been prepared to accept the rule of Richard III over their nephew was understandable, but why did they bend so easily to this new Tudor king? Equally, why did Henry welcome them so easily when other obvious Yorkists like Lovell and the Earl of Warwick were in captivity or in hiding? Most likely, in those early days, both parties were dancing around each other, politely avoiding any trouble. The grant to the duke was probably a ploy by Henry to keep the Suffolks onside and prevent them becoming involved with any rebellion. From their side, Elizabeth and her family were no doubt deploying their survival instinct, perhaps even dissembling whilst assessing their new situation.

Margaret of York, however, with the benefit of distance, was not so easily coming round to an England ruled by a Lancastrian, and her court began to fill up with Yorkist exiles, a haven for those escaping the new regime. By the end of 1485, Margaret was still living in Mechelen (Malines) and her young step-grandson, Philip, now 7 years old, was living with her under her care. The hostilities that had been raging in Burgundy had seen the defeat of the rebels in Ghent in late 1484, allowing Maximilian to be reunited with his son. The young Duke of Burgundy had been taken into custody by a council appointed by the estates and in July 1485, Margaret had been allowed to travel to Ghent to take him into her household.[8]

Having lived in her house since the death of Mary of Burgundy, in the summer of 1485 Margaret sold the building to the city corporation for 12,000 crowns, who then gave it over to Maximilian and Philip, ensuring Burgundy's future ruler lived in his own property. Margaret continued to live there too, overseeing Philip's education and training to enable him to successfully govern his domains when he came of age.

As 1485 ended, Henry Tudor may have been made to feel welcome by the general populace, but he would have been aware that he needed to keep his side of the deal that had been struck, which was to take the eldest daughter of Edward IV as his wife and queen. He had been accepted as the victor of Bosworth but Princess Elizabeth was popular across the realm and Henry needed her to properly secure the future of his kingship; to bring the two warring factions together once and for all.

The marriage of Henry Tudor and Princess Elizabeth finally took place on 18 January 1486. The bridegroom was 29, his bride a mere 20 years old. The marriage ceremony took place in Westminster Abbey, and Princess Elizabeth wore a wedding dress of silk damask and crimson satin with a kirtle of white cloth of gold damask and a mantle furred with ermine to protect her from the winter weather. Her loose blonde hair was threaded with jewels. The king was attired in cloth of gold.[9] All across the land, the people celebrated to see the popular York princess take her rightful place beside England's new king. Bernard Andre, a contemporary of Henry Tudor who wrote his biography, witnessed the event and recorded that feasts, dances and tournaments were held throughout the country and great gladness filled the kingdom. When people heard that Henry and Elizabeth were joined in happy marriage, they built fires for joy far and wide, finally hoping that this union would bring peace and prosperity to England. But despite the agreement to make her queen, Princess Elizabeth's coronation would not take place for almost two years.

Given that their marriage was arranged between their respective mothers, Henry and Elizabeth would go on to have a good marital relationship, although he would always remain wary of her Yorkist roots. According to Francis Bacon, Henry would prove to be a good husband to Elizabeth and an affection was borne, although Bacon reflects 'And it is true, that all his lifetime, while the lady Elizabeth lived with him, for she died before him, he shewed himself no very indulgent husband towards her, though she was beautiful, gentle, and fruitful. But his aversion towards the House of York was so predominant in him, as it found place not only in his wars and councils, but in his chamber and bed'.[10]

After their January wedding, the king, like his predecessor Richard III, set off on progress to the north. But unlike Richard, he was not as sure of a good reception. Aware that the people in the north in particular had held a real affection for Richard III, the progress was an opportunity for Henry to present himself as their new king and to try and unite the kingdom.

Sometime in early 1486, Francis Lovell had also escaped from his Colchester sanctuary and headed north. Why he remained so long in Colchester, when Yorkist supporters chose to either flee abroad or disappear into the woodwork, is a mystery. Again in his excellent book that looks at what may have happened to the princes other than their deaths, Matthew Lewis surmises that Lovell may have been waiting there to receive a young charge, perhaps someone who would be brought south by the Earl of Lincoln after Bosworth. Colchester was just down the road from Gipping Hall and there is evidence that

Colchester became a focal point in Henry's reign for many reasons, often without explanation.[11]

But immediately after Bosworth, Lincoln had been summoned to London with the Princess Elizabeth. One theory is that, in early 1486, Lovell headed north himself, perhaps to take over from Lincoln in his charge of at least one of the princes. As with the whole narrative around the fate of the princes, nothing is conclusive, and it's a tale filled with red herrings and dead ends, and perhaps by 1485 both had already been dead for over two years.

But with Lovell and Henry VII in the north, it's no surprise that an assassination attempt was made. The men struck on St George's Day, 23 April, and the attempt was made either whilst Henry was at High Mass or at the celebrations just after. Reportedly the Earl of Northumberland saved Henry's life that day, and he latterly caught and hung several of those involved in the attempt on the king's life.[12] There is no definitive proof that Lovell was involved, although his presence in the north makes it highly likely and it was certainly reported as Lovell's revolt. Perhaps the assassination attempt was the reason he travelled north in the first place. His close friend, Elizabeth's son, the Earl of Lincoln, immediately went to join the king and remained with him throughout the progress. Was he in complete ignorance of Lovell's plans, or was this another example of Elizabeth's family dissembling?

After the attempt on Henry's life, Lovell made his escape, heading back south. On 19 May 1486, Margaret, Countess of Oxford, writing to John Paston, reported that Lovell had fled into Suffolk (into the Yle of Ely).[13] Did he head for Westhorpe and the safety of the Suffolk family? Did Elizabeth help shelter her former ward, or even perhaps Lovell and one of her nephews? By January 1487, Lovell managed to get on board a ship to Burgundy; his destination, of course, was Margaret's court at Mechelen.

There is no proof that Elizabeth and her husband were helping Francis Lovell. If they were, they were certainly playing the game well for, on 24 September 1486, the Earl of Lincoln was still trusted enough to represent the family at the baptism of Prince Arthur. Born on 21 September, Prince Arthur was baptised on the following Sunday in the cathedral at Winchester. Queen Elizabeth's sister, Princess Anne of York, carried the chrisom whilst another of the queen's sisters, Princess Cecily of York, was given the honour of carrying baby Arthur.[14] The baby prince, completely oblivious to the importance of the occasion, was wrapped in a mantle of crimson cloth of gold, furred with ermine, with a train which was supported by Cecily Dorset, wife to Thomas Grey, Marquis of Dorset. Dorset, as the queen's half-brother, had also been welcomed into the new Tudor court, as was Elizabeth Woodville; no doubt Henry Tudor had little choice as they were close relatives of his wife. Dorset and the Earl of Lincoln both accompanied the ladies in the procession. After the baptism, Dorset, Lincoln and the Lord Strange served the Dowager Queen Elizabeth Woodville with the towel and water.[15]

Lincoln remained a trusted member of the court throughout 1486 and attended a privy council meeting at Sheen on 2 February 1487. But then, departing from Sheen on 9 March, he returned to Suffolk, most likely to see his parents, before immediately boarding a boat for Flanders. Henry learned of his treachery when his secret agents began to suspect something was amiss and reported that Lincoln's servants were on secret business in the north. Did Lincoln himself perhaps escort a precious cargo out of England? By 19 March, Lincoln had reached his aunt Margaret's court. Upon his arrival in Mechelen, a meeting was held between Lincoln, Lovell, Margaret and Maximilian to discuss ways that Henry Tudor could be eliminated. Was Lincoln travelling with his mother's blessing, perhaps taking a message from Elizabeth to Margaret, or did she advise him against rebellion? Whatever conversation was had between mother and son, with Lincoln's escape the die was cast. Elizabeth and John were now going to have to navigate some choppy waters if they wanted to prove their allegiance lay with the king and not their family.

***

Since coming to the throne two years earlier, Henry had, by and large, not really invested his time and focus into the Anglo-Burgundian alliance that had been so prominent during the years of Edward IV and Richard III – an alliance that had centred around both a friendship and mutually beneficial trade deals agreed between the two countries. In hindsight this may have been an error of judgement on his part, because Flanders, in the presence of Margaret of York, was fast becoming a Yorkist safe haven, full of men who wanted to topple the fledgling Tudor dynasty. Margaret is often considered to have been the sole instigator of Burgundian support for the English enemies of Henry Tudor, but she did not act alone. Maximilian was just as determined to restore the Anglo-Burgundian alliance. Through his lineage back to John of Gaunt, the young Philip of Burgundy also had a claim to the English throne, as did Maximilian independently, and this was surely discussed amongst the rebels in early 1487 during conversations about how to oust the new Tudor king from his throne.

The first major threat stemming from Burgundy that Henry Tudor had to deal with arose in the spring of 1487 in the shape of a pretender, eventually revealed to be a young man by the name of Lambert Simnel. News reached Henry's ears shortly after Lincoln's flight to Burgundy that a young man had surfaced in Ireland proclaiming his right to the English throne. Accompanying him was the Earl of Lincoln, Francis Lovell and some 2,000 of Margaret's troops.

Ireland still held a strong affiliation towards the House of York, and the Earl of Kildare, a Yorkist supporter himself, received Lambert Simnel and his party when they landed on Irish shores on 5 May. Convincing the Earl of Kildare and others of his claim, Simnel had himself crowned Edward, King of England, on 27 May 1487 in Christ Church, Dublin. But he was not claiming to be one of the missing York princes as some may have thought; his supporters insisted that the man they had crowned king was Edward, Earl of Warwick, Clarence's son, whom they argued had a stronger right to the throne than Henry Tudor.

The calculations behind this plot are somewhat of a mystery. Lincoln and Lovell certainly knew that the man they were claiming was Warwick was an imposter; Lincoln had been in charge of the real Earl of Warwick during Richard III's reign and knew him well. He also knew he was in the Tower of London. Perhaps they were using Simnel to gain support in the hope that once Henry Tudor was removed, they would replace him with the real Earl of Warwick. Or perhaps Lincoln even coveted the throne for himself? Hall certainly believed that the plan was to put the Earl of Warwick on the throne:

> So that if their doynges had good and prosperous successe, then the forsayde Lambert (mysnamed the Erie) shoulde by the consent of the counsaill be deposed, and Edwarde the true Erie of Warwyke to be delyuered oute of pryson, and after by the aucthoritie and aide of his frendes of the nobilitie, should be published, proclaymed, and anoynted kynge.[16]

175

Even though he had been barred from the accession due to the attainder and execution of his father, as the son of George of Clarence, he had a strong claim. But in 1487, Warwick was just 11 or 12 years old and was rumoured to be a weak lad, perhaps even with some form of mental instability. As a man in his mid-twenties and the son of Elizabeth of York, the Earl of Lincoln would have been a much stronger and capable candidate.

Departing from Ireland, the rebels first made land in England on the Cumbrian coast. When they reached Masham in north Yorkshire, the Earl of Lincoln sent a letter to the mayor of York in the name of King Edward VI, saying that his army was weary and asking for food and lodging.

Hearing that the rebels were heading south, Henry Tudor, as a precaution against the arrival of more of Margaret's men, made the decision to fortify the whole east coast. He set off to Bury St Edmunds, leaving Queen Elizabeth and Prince Arthur in the safety of Kenilworth Castle, to personally see this was done. He also had the real Earl of Warwick brought from the Tower and paraded through the streets of London, to show to the people that the man accompanying the rebels was not Clarence's son.

To add another dose of intrigue to the pot of suspicion, Thomas Grey, Marquis of Dorset, was also arrested at this time, as he too was making his way to the east coast. He protested coincidence; that he was journeying there to visit the Shrine of St Edmund in the Abbey Church of Bury St Edmunds. Henry, ever wary of Dorset's loyalty, had him apprehended by the Earl of Oxford and taken to the Tower. According to Francis Bacon, 'He sent the Earl of Oxford to meet [Dorset] to accompany him back to London and forthwith to carry him to the Tower; with a fair message nevertheless that he should bear that disgrace with patience, for that the king meant not his hurt, but only to preserve him from doing hurt either to the king's service or to himself'.

By 16 June, the two armies – that of the king and that of Lincoln and Lovell – eventually met at Stoke Field in Nottinghamshire. The king's men were nearly twice the number of the rebel army and it was a decisive victory for Henry. The Earl of Lincoln was killed in the fighting and Lovell fled when it became clear they were defeated. That is the last that was heard of Francis Lovell and where he escaped to remains a mystery, although legend tells that he eventually ended up in his house at Minster Lovell, where he was hidden by a servant in a secret underground chamber. It is said that in the early eighteenth century, during building work at the hall, an underground room was discovered. In this room, a skeleton was found, sitting upright at a table, surrounded by books, paper and pens. According to the tale, the loyal servant died before Lovell, and with no one else knowing he was there, Lovell was unable to escape the room from the inside and starved to death.

The imposter 'Warwick' was captured and Simnel's real identity was revealed. Once it was established who he actually was, it came to light that he was a baker's son, and a pupil of a priest called Richard Simon, who lived in Oxford. It is said that Henry took pity on the young lad and he was taken to London and given a job in the royal kitchens.

For Margaret of York in Burgundy, this attempt at overthrowing Henry had ended in disappointment; for Elizabeth of York in England, it had ended in tragedy. Henry Tudor was seemingly annoyed that Lincoln had died in the battle as, according to Polydore Vergil, Henry had wanted him taken alive so that he might learn more about the conspiracy. For Elizabeth, receiving the news of her beloved eldest son's death must have been one of the worst days of her life; reportedly she was unable to even bury him as his body was buried in an unmarked grave on the battlefield. How and when she heard of the rebels' defeat and her son's death we don't know, but it is tempting to wonder whether the news was delivered by Lovell, perhaps fleeing to somewhere he knew was a place of safety after the battle. If he did head to Wingfield or Westhorpe, he knew he must avoid painting the duke and duchess with the stain of rebellion and could not remain with them for long as they would undoubtedly already be under suspicion. Elizabeth and John, who had always remained loyal to the throne, were now in real trouble.

\*\*\*

In the parliament of November 1487, the Earl of Lincoln was posthumously attainted and the Duke of Suffolk was made to attend to witness proceedings. Reportedly heartbroken at the death of his boy, he had to listen to a catalogue of treachery and attainders pronounced against his dead son. Lincoln was stripped of his lands and his title, and the attainder went even further and included lands that he was due to inherit upon the death of his father. The consequence of this for the Duke and Duchess of Suffolk was that they were allowed to keep their own lands but only for the remainder of the duke's lifetime; on his death manors like Ewelme, Westhorpe and Wingfield would revert to the Crown.[17] This was more, perhaps, than they could have hoped for with a rebel for a son, and it is possible the queen played a small part in speaking up for her aunt and pleading her case. They had a temporary reprieve but whichever way you look at it, the de la Poles were completely ruined.

The Earl of Lincoln's wife, the daughter of Thomas Fitzalan and Margaret Woodville (a sister of Edward IV's queen), never remarried after her husband's death; she was still living in October 1524 when her father bequeathed her a great ring with a turquoise stone. She and Lincoln had no children together.[18]

With the troubles of the last few months over, the coronation of Princess Elizabeth finally took place in late 1487; Henry perhaps realised that by officially crowning his wife, this would hopefully appease those who wanted to see a Yorkist on the throne. Coming just a few weeks after the act of attainder was passed, somehow the Duke and Duchess of Suffolk had managed to convince the king and queen of their continuing loyalty and they too were in attendance.

On Friday 23 November 1487, Princess Elizabeth, soon to be queen, left Greenwich by water, wearing her royal robes and was escorted by the Lord Mayor, sheriffs and aldermen of London in a grand procession of barges down the great River Thames. She spent that night at Greenwich with Henry, who created eleven new Knights of the Bath in her honour. Then the next day, 24 November, her sisters helped her dress for her state entry into London and there was a grand procession through the streets of the city. The Duke of Suffolk rode in the procession alongside other leading nobles and the ladies travelled by carriage; the queen's litter at the head of the procession was followed by a chariot covered in rich cloth of gold containing the Duchess of Bedford (Katherine Woodville, one-time wife of the Duke of Buckingham and now married to Jasper Tudor) and the queen's sister, Princess Cecily. Elizabeth of York, Duchess of Suffolk, travelled in another carriage accompanied by the Duchess of Norfolk and the Countess of Oxford. The coronation party spent the night at Westminster, and the following morning, 25 November, Princess Elizabeth proceeded to Westminster Abbey accompanied by her ladies, including Elizabeth, Duchess of Suffolk; the duchess's husband bore the sceptre.

The coronation ceremony was followed by a state banquet in Westminster Hall and the festivities eventually came to an end the next evening when a grand dinner and ball was held with much dancing by the queen and her ladies. The royal party all returned to Greenwich the next day.

Why did Elizabeth and John ingratiate themselves with the court again? Was it because they believed in the total authority of kingship? Perhaps they were protecting their other children and attempting to restore their name somewhat; maybe they even hoped that by demonstrating their loyalty, it might earn them back some much-needed favours. Or were they, in effect, pretenders themselves, continuing to present a face to the court that they were the king's true subjects when, behind their masks, they were wishing for his downfall as much as many other Yorkists? For those of the old Yorkist regime who did remain in England, figures such as Elizabeth Woodville, the Dorsets (the Marquis of Dorset had been released from prison after the Battle of Stoke) and others who had played prominent roles in or around the Yorkist court, there was, of course, a very good reason to keep the peace in the shape of England's new queen. As the eldest daughter of Edward IV, she was not only part of the old regime and therefore deserved their loyalty, but she was also family. To remove Henry from the throne would also remove Queen Elizabeth and as time went on, her children too. So without doubt, some of the Yorkists who did remain in the country would have wanted to be loyal to Elizabeth, and perhaps the Suffolks fell into this category too.

But with Margaret of York clearly making her feelings known about the new Tudor regime, did this, perhaps for the first time, become a contentious issue between the two sisters? Did Margaret feel her sister was too compliant? Did Elizabeth believe her sister should accept this new Tudor king because of their niece, Queen Elizabeth? That the Suffolks chose to remain part of court life to some extent is further illustrated by the duke's attendance on the king at Christmas that year with the royal court at Greenwich. He was also at Windsor with the king the following Easter. Elizabeth may well have been with him.

The new year, 1488, brought with it preparations for the future of England when, in March, the king and queen began negotiations for the betrothal of the 2-year-old Prince Arthur to Katherine of Aragon, one of the daughters of Ferdinand of Aragon and Isabella of Castile. With Arthur destined to be the next Tudor king, he needed a suitable bride and none could be better than a daughter of the two great Spanish leaders. After the reverberations from the Battle of Stoke had settled, life returned to normal for the new royal family. The king and queen welcomed a daughter, Princess Margaret, on 29 November 1489, and eighteen months later their second son, Prince Henry, was born at Greenwich Palace on St Peter's Eve, 28 June 1491.

In the late 1480s and early 1490s, Elizabeth and John began to spend less and less time at court, instead preferring to live quietly at Wingfield. The duke was noticeably absent at an election of Knights of the Garter on 16 November 1488, although no reason is recorded for why he did not attend. That he would have mourned his eldest son was understandable, but perhaps his depth of grief proved overwhelming. He was to live out his last few years mired in sadness and William Camden certainly believed that it was grief that eventually killed him.[19] The last record we have of John de la Pole, Duke of Suffolk, is on 14 May 1492 when he sat as a Justice for the Peace; six days later he died.[20] He was 50 years old.

For Elizabeth, his death brought even more grief to add to that she was already feeling for her son. She had been married to the duke for over thirty years and it appeared they certainly held a mutual affection for each other, which may or may not have developed into love. They had many children together and seemingly spent much time in each other's company. Elizabeth was aged 48 at the time of his death, and her youngest child was still only 12. Coupled with her sadness must have been the fear that now her husband was dead, the terms surrounding the attainder of her eldest son might mean she now risked losing her home. The Duke of Suffolk was laid to rest in St Andrew's Church, Wingfield, just a stone's throw from the castle that he and Elizabeth had made their primary residence in their later years after handing over Ewelme to their eldest son some years previously.

Whilst Elizabeth was mourning her husband, another threat to Henry Tudor's throne was brewing, one that had been rumbling away since the summer of 1491. Once again it proved that the threat from the old Yorkist regime was ever-present. Two months after the birth of Prince Henry, in August 1491, a young man of considerable refinement had sailed into the Irish town of Cork. He was 16 years old and he claimed he was Prince Richard of York, the younger of the missing York princes. When news of his appearance reached the English court, it unquestionably caused a certain amount of worry to the king and his advisors.

King Henry had not been idle since the young man's appearance in Ireland; he had sent his spymasters far and wide to out to find out the youth's 'true' identity and the officials had seemingly managed to identify him as a young man called Perkin Warbeck, the son of a peasant couple from Tournai (in modern-day Belgium). But even with his supposed identity revealed, he was still very much a magnet for any disaffected Yorkists and therefore a worry to this still very fledgling Tudor court.

In 1492 the royal court was informed that 'Richard of York' had left Ireland and had arrived at Margaret's court in Burgundy. The involvement of Margaret of York with this new and even more dangerous threat to the English throne is intricately tied up in the mystery of the missing princes. Reportedly, when he presented himself to his 'aunt', news that filtered back to England was that Margaret had indeed recognised him as her long-lost nephew and had bestowed upon him the title of 'The White Rose of England'. If this was the first time she had seen this young man, it would disprove the theory that he had been escorted to Flanders some years before, either in the company of Lincoln or Lovell. But perhaps he had been with her a while, waiting for the right time to make a move? Assuming reports of events are true at this stage, did she recognise him as her long-lost nephew or was this just another attempt to remove Henry from the throne and put the governance of England back into the hands of the Yorkists?

The youth whom Henry Tudor identified as the son of a boatman and not the son of a king remained at Margaret's court for nearly two years. Philip of Burgundy was also still at Mechelen, and although four or five years younger he became friends with the young lad, the two of them reportedly riding and hunting together.[21] And when, in March 1494, Philip came of age and stepped into his role as Duke of Burgundy, he went on a tour of the Low Countries and was accompanied by the young man purporting to be Richard, Duke of York.[22]

Margaret treated both young men as her family and in a letter to Queen Isabella of Spain, she informed the Spanish queen that the young man was without doubt her nephew, saying she recognised certain characteristics in him, and she could be doubly sure of his identity by the way he had answered questions about his family and his childhood.[23] Some credit Margaret with 'training' the youth so he knew about his supposed Yorkist roots, knowing full well he was an imposter.

An existing letter from the young man himself, written shortly after Margaret's in 1493 and also to Queen Isabella of Spain, attempts to explain his back story in his own words.

In the letter, he writes that his elder brother, Edward, Prince of Wales, had been assassinated. He, Richard, had been delivered to a gentleman who had meant to kill him but took pity on him, sparing his life on the condition that he did not divulge his name, birth or lineage for many years. He had been taken abroad under the care of two gentlemen and had spent nearly eight years of his life moving around Europe in hiding, spending some time in Portugal before arriving in Ireland and being 'recognised' and welcomed by the Earls of Ormond and Kildare.

He went on to tell of his welcome from his aunt in Burgundy, as well as his support from Maximilian and the Dukes of Austria and Saxony, and the Kings of Denmark and Scotland. He also wrote that 'many of the chief personages in England, whose indignation had been roused by the iniquitous conduct of the usurper, Henry Richmond, had done the same in secret', seemingly inferring he had Yorkist support back in England. The letter ends with the wish that Queen Isabella would also offer her support and entreat her husband to do the same and is signed: 'From the town of Andermund, 8th Sept. 1493. Richard Plantagenet, second son of the late King Edward and Duke of York'.[24]

Could this story be true? That the eldest York son, Prince Edward, never publicly re-appeared generally leads many to believe that he did in fact die, either through natural causes or perhaps through murder – either accidental (i.e. manslaughter), or through intention. But the fate of Prince Richard is less clear. The story of the younger prince being smuggled away does have an air of truth to it, coupled with other pieces of evidence presented by contemporaries and historians over the years. But then, in 1674, workmen digging below the stairs of the White Tower at the Tower of London, discovered an urn containing bones of two children, believed to have been around the same age as the missing princes. Four years later, these bones were reburied in Westminster Abbey. There was, of course, no scientific way in the seventeenth century of identifying the bones, but their existence led many to believe that the bones of the princes has been found and seemingly confirmed the theory that both of the princes had died in the summer of 1483. As of 2023, permission has not been granted for an exhumation of the bones to allow further investigation and modern DNA testing to attempt to prove if these could be the remains of the two princes. Later in Henry Tudor's reign, a supposed confession by Sir James Tyrell, one of Richard III's henchmen, made shortly before his death that he had murdered the princes at Richard's request also points to their death in 1483. Henry Tudor proclaimed Tyrell's confession publicly, but the confession has never been seen nor proven and Tyrell was unable to tell his confessors the location of the bodies, which throws doubt on whether this was just a story concocted by the Tudor king to discredit any other Yorkist pretenders. Over half a millennia later, the story of the lost princes is as intriguing as ever.

***

Margaret in Burgundy was certainly kept busy in 1493; as well as having Philip and 'her nephew' at court, her step-granddaughter, Margaret of Austria, also returned from France and came into her care. Having resided at the French court since her betrothal to the French dauphin in 1483, when she was just 3 years old, the marriage had since been broken off. In a tale akin to a modern-day soap opera, the dauphin, Charles, by then a young man of 21, had invaded Rennes (an area of Brittany) in November 1491 and married, possibly against her will, the heiress Anne of Brittany. To complicate matters even further, Anne had been engaged to Margaret of Austria's father, Maximilian, since December 1490. The French, not wishing to see an alliance between Brittany and the Holy Roman Empire, decided the only way to prevent this was for Charles to marry the 14-year-old Anne of Brittany himself. When Maximilian heard that Anne had become the wife of Charles VIII, and that his daughter Margaret was about to be returned to him and denied her future as queen of France, he was furious. The ensuing war lasted from 1491 to 1493 until peace was restored by the Treaty of Senlis.

Margaret of Austria remained in France, the only real place she knew as home, for two years after Charles' marriage but was handed back to the Burgundians in 1493. Returning as a young woman of 13, she was escorted first to St Quentin, then on to Cambray and Valenciennes, before finally arriving at Mechelen. She was welcomed back with open arms by Margaret and her brother, Philip, although she would barely have remembered either of them from her first three years in Burgundy. Reportedly, when she exited her litter near a mill by a small stream, she 'thanked the said lords and ladies who had brought and accompanied her, begging them all to recommend her very humbly to the king their master, bearing no ill-will because of his separation from her, believing that marriages ought to be voluntary'.[25]

Despite his marriage problems, Maximilian and Margaret of York, in her role as Dowager Duchess of Burgundy, continued to have a remarkably close relationship, based on mutual respect; he clearly trusted her to bring up his children in her care and later, when speaking of Margaret, he claimed that it was she who had taught him to listen.[26]

Both Maximilian and Philip supported 'Richard' in his claim that he was the son of Edward IV and together they wrote to the Pope, basing their argument on moral grounds, that only certain individuals have a God-given right to the throne. Their letter, dated 8 May 1495, argued that 'Rightful heirs should be allowed to hold their kingdoms in peace' and called Henry a tyrant if he continued to rule without sufficient title.[27]

Prior to this letter, in December 1494, they had also drawn up deeds for a planned invasion of England. Within these deeds, 'King Richard IV of England' gifted the castle and town of Scarborough to his 'very dear and well beloved lady' [Margaret] and promised to repay 8,000 gold ecus that he owed her once he was in his rightful place as king of England. Why he selected Scarborough as a gift is unknown; perhaps it was a place that Margaret held dear from her younger years, maybe staying at Scarborough Castle or visiting the famous Scarborough Fair. He also promised to pay the rest of her dowry, that her brother, Edward IV, had never finished paying.[28]

A further document was then drawn up at Mechelen on 24 January 1495 that granted England to Maximilian and Philip if he, Richard, died without heirs. He signed this document 'Richard, King of England'. At the same time Holy Scriptures were laid open for Richard to touch and kiss and seal his pledge before witnesses.[29]

Would a real heir to the English throne sign over his beloved country to another realm? A later queen, Elizabeth I, would seemingly deny foreign suitors for the very reason that England would be under the power of another country, much as many feared her sister, Mary Tudor's marriage to Philip of Spain for that same reason. Perhaps if he were truly Richard of York, he believed he would have heirs if he succeeded in his invasion. Perhaps he was dissembling. Perhaps he was a pretender after all.

By the spring of 1495, a fleet of ships was ready to leave Zeeland to take this young man back to his claimed homeland. Yorkist supporters back in England were waiting for him. As far back as June 1493 a Yorkist envoy, Sir Robert Clifford, had travelled to Burgundy to report to Margaret what the Yorkists in England were planning. Upon meeting the young lad that Margaret called her nephew, he sent word back to the English Yorkists that he really was Richard, Duke of York.

But did this young man's Yorkist supporters in England include Elizabeth of York and her mother, Cecily? Sadly, Elizabeth's knowledge and awareness of Margaret's plans is lost to us now; if she were involved it is unlikely she would have broadcast it even then. It is reasonable to believe she would have had contact with her sister during the years 1493–95, but whether she too believed that her young nephew had survived would, of course, depend on what she already knew to be true and how much she had been involved in his fate prior to then. This could range from knowing nothing at all, to knowing categorically that both her nephews were dead, to having assisted her son and Francis Lovell in their escape. And all and anything in between.

As for their mother, Cecily Neville, she had spent many of the latter years of her life living in solitude at her castle in Berkhamsted. Sadly, before she had a chance to come face to face with the man who claimed to be her grandson, Cecily died on 31 May 1495, and Elizabeth and Margaret, her only two surviving children, had to deal with the loss of their mother. Being closer in distance, Elizabeth of York presumably saw her mother often throughout her life and must have been heartbroken at the death of the strong, proud and resilient woman who had kept their family together throughout their darkest days. Margaret, from afar, perhaps mourned at how little time she had been able to spend in her mother's company over the years. How much mother and daughter kept in touch is impossible to tell, as is how often Margaret and Elizabeth communicated. There are some indications, perhaps, in Cecily's will, that Cecily supported Margaret in her cause to keep the York flame burning. Generous bequests to a man named Richard Lessey, the Dean of Cecily's chapel, and his wife Jane, as well as to Richard Boyvile and his wife Gresild suggest that Cecily maintained an involvement in Margaret's schemes. These four individuals, serving in Cecily's household, were strong Yorkist supporters and also close allies of Margaret of York, which perhaps proves that the women shared their lives and perhaps their schemes when required.[30]

Elizabeth of York was also remembered in her mother's will, as was Anne of York's daughter, Anne St Leger. To Anne, Cecily left 'her largest bed of baudekyn, with a counterpane of the same' and to Elizabeth, 'her chair with the covering, and all the cushions, horses, and harnesses for the same, with all her palfreys'.[31] In an indication that she might have written her will several years earlier, she also left 'to my son of Suffolk, a cloth of estate'. John de la Pole, her son-in-law, was, of course, already three years dead himself, although there is the possibility that she used this term for one of her grandsons, perhaps Edmund? There was also a bond ratified by Parliament that same year in favour of Elizabeth, Duchess of Suffolk, that she 'be not prejudiced, nor interrupted of any manors, lands, and tenements, which she hath, or ought to have, for her jointure and dower'.[32] Margaret in Burgundy was not left anything by her mother, but that was most likely just a question of practicalities and the unlikelihood that Margaret would return to claim a bed or a chair. Cecily Neville, the grand dame of the York family, was laid to rest next to her beloved husband, Richard, Duke of York, at Fotheringhay.

*** 

Having dispatched her 'nephew' on his mission to England in mid-1495 and mourned the death of her mother, Margaret of York turned her attention to the marriages of her beloved Philip and Margaret. Her relationship with Isabella of Castille was enhanced when a double marriage deal was reached that would see Philip of Burgundy marry the second daughter of the Spanish king and queen, Juana of Castille. The same agreement would see Margaret of Austria's betrothal to Prince John of Asturias, the heir to the Spanish monarchies. A proxy wedding was held in August 1496 and Juana then departed her homeland to travel to Burgundy and her new life as Duchess of Burgundy alongside Philip. Margaret of York and Margaret of Austria went to Antwerp in September of that year to greet Juana and welcome her to their home.

The Spanish princess arrived with a glittering retinue and a fleet of over 120 ships. When she docked, she became ill and was taken to the Abbey of St Michael at Bergen Op Zoom, where she was greeted and cared for by the two Margarets. When she had recovered, they escorted her back to Mechelen and on 20 October two marriage ceremonies were held at the Church of St Gommaire in Lier,[33] with a proxy standing in for Prince John. The double weddings were celebrated with the usual banquets and tournaments.

The following January, Margaret of York said goodbye to her step-granddaughter when she in turn departed for her new life in Spain.

Margaret of York also vacated the palace of Mechelen for Philip and his new Archduchess to begin their married life together. Moving across the street into a suite of rooms in the building opposite, Margaret remained on hand to guide Philip and Juana when they needed it. Margaret's new house was next to the Church of St Peter and St Paul, separated only by a narrow street. In order for Margaret to access the church without venturing outside, the authorities built her a gallery at first-floor level adjoining her apartments directly to the church.[34]

Whilst Margaret was busy arranging royal marriages, she surely kept abreast of news involving her 'nephew'. Having set off from Flanders, he and his supporters had landed in Deal in the summer of 1495. The men of Kent, however, remained loyal to their king and chased him away. He had subsequently made his way to Scotland where he was received with honours by King James IV, who not only allowed him to live at the Scottish court and treated him as he would a son of Edward IV, but also arranged a suitable marriage for him with a respectable lady named Katherine Gordon, the daughter of the Earl of Huntly. He was still at the Scottish court on 18 March 1496 when Queen Elizabeth gave birth to her third daughter, Princess Mary, at Sheen. After a further failed attempt to enter England from the north that same year, he eventually set sail from Scotland in late 1497, making his way to the south coast. Here he found that the men of Cornwall were not as loyal to their king as their Kentish counterparts had been. Disillusioned with Henry VII and his exorbitant taxes, they allowed him to land and march northwards through their county. Collecting supporters along the way, he had himself declared Richard IV at Bodmin.

The distant threat to Henry Tudor's throne had now become very real and he had no choice but to set off to meet his challenger with an army. As the king drew near, many Cornishmen began to desert – a charge of treason was too serious a penalty for them to risk for a man whose identity was so uncertain. With his supporters fading away and knowing his cause was lost, the young man went into hiding in Beaulieu Abbey, where he was finally captured. He was taken to Taunton and it was there on 3 October 1497 that the Tudor king and the alleged York king came face to face for the very first time. Official records tell us he admitted his deception at this meeting when he was put face to face with men he should know. One of these men was the Marquis of Dorset, his half-brother. It is understood that he failed to recognise Dorset and that none of the men present were able to recognise him. Or perhaps they would not admit that they recognised him, for some might argue that no good could have come of it if they had admitted to knowing him, and he them? He and his wife Katherine were taken back to London; Lady Katherine Gordon was made one of the queen's ladies and the pretender was allegedly kept close to Henry, not exactly a prisoner but also not at liberty.

No reaction came from Margaret of York on his capture, nor, less surprisingly from Elizabeth of York, Duchess of Suffolk. Interestingly, only the Marquis of Dorset seems to have met him and denied him; would Elizabeth have recognised her nephew if she'd met him again? Surely his sister, the queen, could refute his identity or confirm he was her brother. Or any of the other surviving daughters of Edward IV. What would Cecily Neville have made of him had she survived a little longer to identify, or not, her grandson? But as with the princes' disappearance back in the early 1480s, the silence was deafening.

Margaret of York did, it seems, send out a delegation to sort out trade agreements with the English king, who at the same time was tasked with discovering the wellbeing of the man she believed was her nephew. This delegation was headed by the Bishop of Cambrai who, upon his arrival in London, asked to see how the prisoner was. On 30 July King Henry escorted the Bishop to the Tower where Perkin was allegedly made to swear his true identity in front of him. It was reported that 'he swore solemnly to God that the Duchess Madame Margaret knew as well as he himself did that he was not the son of who he said he was'.[35] He was also, reportedly, battered and bruised.

Margaret of York was later advised to write to Henry apologising, to which Henry was reported to have replied that if she desisted in supporting the pretender, he wouldn't kill him.[36] She did withdraw her support, as her step-grandson Philip had also done much earlier. If this was a ploy to save his life, it didn't work. If King Henry did indeed make Margaret that promise, he perhaps had no intention of keeping it. Reportedly after an attempted escape, the man Henry Tudor insisted was called Perkin Warbeck was recaptured and thrown into the Tower alongside the Earl of Warwick. In a further escape pact between the two men, which was highly likely to have been at least a partial set-up, both Warbeck and Warwick were caught and executed in November 1498. In one fell swoop, the imminent threat from any active male Yorkists was over.

Neither Margaret's withdrawal of her support nor his public confessions that he wasn't Richard, Duke of York, have ever put to bed the question of who he was. Did he confess under duress? Why did none of Richard of York's family in England make a public statement that he was an imposter? Would Queen Elizabeth allow her brother to be killed by her husband, if that was who he was? There are many great books discussing the theories and counter-theories around Perkin Warbeck, some of which are listed in the bibliography. But for Margaret, in 1497, the game, if that's what it was, was now over. She returned to the family life she had built in Burgundy and it was around this time that she left Mechelen and retired to Binche, in modern-day Belgium. She took up residence at the Ducal Château de la Salles, reportedly ill and restlessly unhappy. In 1498 she attended the christening of Philip and Juana's first child, Eleanor, in Brussels at the Church of St Gudule, where she stood as godmother. Maximilian was baby Eleanor's godfather, although he didn't attend in person. The christening took place on a chilly November evening, and perhaps in a sign of Margaret's deteriorating health and advancing years (by now she was 52 years old), she managed the hilly walk from the palace to the church but travelled back in a litter alongside the torch-lit procession.[37]

Back in England, Elizabeth of York, two years older than Margaret, was not, perhaps, finding as much peace in her widowed years as her sister was able to in her chateau at Binche. With surviving sons who were healthy Yorkist males, although none of them had followed their elder brother into rebellion, their lineage and their very existence still posed a threat to the Tudor regime.

After the death of her husband, his title of Duke of Suffolk passed to her son, Edmund. Edmund was her fourth son, the third to survive to adulthood; his elder brothers, Edward and, of course, John, Earl of Lincoln, had both pre-deceased their father so Edmund, aged around 21 when his father died, was now the head of the family. In 1492, after the death of his father, he became the king's ward.

Seemingly close to his cousin Queen Elizabeth, there are many records of him attending ceremonial events and court festivities in the early years of Henry's reign, including his cousin Elizabeth's coronation in 1487. But Edmund's love for his cousin didn't soften the resentment he felt towards Henry VII after the death of his father. Due to the attainder of his elder brother, the Earl of Lincoln, many of the estates and properties that should have come to Edmund on his father's death instead reverted to the Crown. On top of that, when he came of age in 1493, he was forced to accept the lesser title of Earl of Suffolk, rather than Duke of Suffolk, in exchange for a licence by indenture to enter some of Lincoln's estates. But the price was steeper than that still. He also had to agree to pay £5,000 (over £3 million in today's terms), paid in yearly instalments of £200 (over £135,000 today) during the life of his mother, and of £400 after her death.[38] Thankfully, in what must have been some relief for Elizabeth, part of the indenture that Edmund made allowed him to maintain Ewelme for himself and Wingfield for his mother to live out her retirement years. Edmund would use Ewelme as his base, living there with his wife, Margaret Scrope, who he married in 1495/6.[39]

Little is known of Elizabeth during her years of widowhood. She remained primarily at Wingfield and although most of her other children flew the nest, her son William and later his wife, Katherine Stourton, lived there with her. Details of payments in the Tudor Chancery records show that from 1496 to 1499, they were also obliged to pay Henry £100 a year at Michaelmas (around £67,000 in today's terms) over a four-year period. The entries read:

> 1496
> My lady of Suffolk Dam Kateryn Grey & William Pole are bound by obligation to pay at Michaelmas during 4 years, £100
>
> 1497
> My lady Suffolk dam Kateryn Grey & William Pole are bound by obligation to pay
> £100 at Michaelmas yearly during 3 years, £100
>
> And by 1499:
> My lady of Suffolk Dam Kateryn Gray & William Pole owe by obligation £100[40]

William was Katherine's third husband; her second husband was Henry Grey, Baron Grey of Codnor, hence the use of Dame Kateryn

Grey in the records. She was around twenty years older than William, having been born around 1455.

On the surface, Elizabeth and her family continued to maintain their loyalty to the Crown. And perhaps their loyalty did extend deeper than surface level; although they undoubtedly would have preferred a Yorkist king on the throne, things were what they were. Like her son Edmund, Elizabeth also maintained a good relationship with her niece, Queen Elizabeth, and her presence in the royal palaces perhaps was enough to maintain that connection between the Yorks and the utmost seat of power. In the set of extant accounts that survive for the queen between 1502/3, there are several items that illustrate their continued relationship:

> May 1502. Item. To John Williams, Thomas Nelmes, Hugh Dolbyn, Edward Davy, and John Fitzwilliams, to every of them 3s. 4d., in reward for giving attendance at the house of the Duchess of Suffolk at Stepney.

> January 1503. Item. For a pair of buskins for the Duchess of Suffolk; Item. To William Gentilman, page of the queens chamber, for carrying of two bucks from Windsor to London, the 24th day of the said month, one to the Duchess of Suffolk, &c., 5s. 4d.[41]

As the senior male of the family, the Earl of Suffolk was very much present at court; he took part in the jousting when Prince Henry was created Duke of York at Westminster in November 1494 and he even entertained Henry VII at Ewelme during Michaelmas 1495. However, perhaps like his elder brother, there was always an undercurrent of rebellion running through his veins, which eventually spilled over during Michaelmas 1498. He got into a fight and was subsequently charged with the murder of a gentleman named Thomas Crue.[42] Three other men were also involved in the attack on Crue – Lord William Courtenay, Thomas Neville and William Brandon. Rather than face punishment, Edmund decided to flee the country and on 1 July 1499 he travelled to St Omer in Picardy, heading for the court of his aunt Margaret in Burgundy.

The king was furious; perhaps less so about the murder than about the fact that another son of York was at the court of Margaret in Burgundy, and what that would mean for the safety of England. On 20 August 1499 he issued a proclamation against leaving the kingdom without licence, presumably to stop any more disaffected Yorkists following Edmund abroad. The writs were directed to the Sheriffs of Norfolk, Suffolk, Kent, Essex and the warden of the Cinque Ports.[43]

He then dispatched two men, Sir Richard Guildford and Richard Hatton, to negotiate with Philip of Burgundy for Suffolk's return. Their method of persuasion was to threaten a trade embargo, a move that would affect Burgundy financially, and it worked. Philip agreed to co-operate in returning Edmund back to England, and it was made clear to Edmund that his only hope of escaping severe punishment was to submit to Henry. Whether Margaret of York ever saw Edmund during his time in Mechelen, and what advice she may have given him, is unknown. But Philip was now in charge of Burgundy, and he did not want to start another trade war with England so Edmund was politely requested to return to his homeland. Upon his return, he was fined £1,000 and had to place land in feoffment until the money had been paid.

Elizabeth must have been relieved to have her son back; whatever her internal beliefs, memory of how rebellion had ended for her eldest son must have been at the forefront of her mind. Back in his home country, Edmund was seemingly welcomed back to court; Henry VII perhaps taking the stance that it was better to keep his enemies close. On 15 May 1500 Edmund witnessed the treaty for the agreed marriage between Prince Arthur and Katherine of Aragon, and a few days later he attended the king at Calais at a meeting with Philip of Burgundy. But anger and rebellion were still in his mind and just over a year later, in August 1501, he fled the country again, once more without royal licence, and this time he was accompanied by his younger brother, Richard, a 21-year-old youth. Their destination this time was Maximilian's court.[44]

Was this news devastating to Elizabeth of York or did she fully support the actions of her two sons? There are indications that around this time, as their mother, a close eye was being kept on her by the Tudor regime. A letter written by the king to the Earl of Oxford and John Paston in 1499, just after Edmund's first flight across the sea, requested that they 'enquire as well of such persons as to be departed over with the said Earl as of them that accompanied him in his journey to the sea and returned again, or in any ways were privy to the same...'. It also instructs that if they suspected any person in future of being of the same affinity as the Earl they should also put them into surety (under a financial bond) and keep them safely (keep their eye on them). It is highly likely that Elizabeth herself was questioned as to her sons' intentions and whereabouts.[45]

And even more indication that she was being kept under surveillance can be seen in another entry in the Tudor Chancery records for the year 1500 for a payment to a number of men who were 'paid for watching my lady Suffolk at Colchester'. The payment was most likely made in 1500 but may have been for an incident in 1499 when Elizabeth presumably had business in Colchester and was being carefully watched, either in case she was meeting with her son or other Yorkist sympathisers, or perhaps they may even have suspected she was heading for the coast herself.[46]

When Edmund and Richard de la Pole reached the continent, they were stranded at Imst until the earl's steward, Thomas Killingworth, could arrange financial support from Maximilian. They then travelled to Aachen, where Edmund began to plan an invasion of England. In what was clearly designed to be a threat to Henry, he began calling himself the 'White Rose'. In response to this threat, the king declared him and his brother, Richard, outlaws and, in February 1502, many of his close associates who had remained in England were arrested. Sir James Tyrell was among these men detained for lending his support to Edmund and he was subsequently executed, after, according to Thomas More writing several years later, confessing to murdering the princes. A few months prior to this, in 1501, William de la Pole had also been apprehended and thrown into the Tower, leaving Elizabeth and her daughter-in-law, Katherine, alone at Wingfield. Henry had presumably decided he was not going to take the chance and allow three de la Pole men to band together and act against him. William de la Pole was just 23 at the time of his arrest; given he was living at Wingfield, the king's men must have come to Elizabeth's home to take him into custody, an incident that would be truly terrifying for all involved. William de la Pole, thankfully unbeknownst to his mother, would go on to earn the unwanted accolade of being the longest-serving prisoner in the Tower; he remained there for thirty-seven years until his death in 1539.

As the year 1502 breathed its last breath and the new year 1503 began, it would bring with it the shadow of death for three Yorkist women. The first to succumb was Queen Elizabeth, the woman who through her marriage to Henry Tudor had brought together the Houses of York and Lancaster. Pregnant with her seventh child, at the end of January

1503 she travelled by boat to the Tower in order to spend Candlemas with Henry and then enter her confinement. As she journeyed down the Thames, the heavily pregnant queen reclined on cushions, seated by burning braziers, filled with sweet herbs, trying to keep as comfortable as she could against the chilly winter air.[47]

Just a few days later, however, on the occasion of Candlemas itself, 2 February 1503, Queen Elizabeth was delivered suddenly of a girl. It seems she had unexpectedly gone into labour and the baby arrived much earlier than anticipated.

The king and queen named their new baby daughter Katherine. But just a few days after the birth, the queen fell seriously ill and Henry hurriedly sent into Kent for a physician to attend her. But even with medical help, she was unable to beat whatever ailed her. She had been ill after several of her births, but this time she was not strong enough and she died on 11 February 1503, her thirty-seventh birthday.

The country fell into mourning, grieving for their popular queen, as did the king, who, despite their differing allegiances, seemed to have loved and cared for her deeply. No doubt Elizabeth and Margaret of York also grieved for their niece when the news of her death reached them.

Elizabeth of York would begin 1503 unaware that she would never see any of her sons again. She too would surrender to death during 1503, but the exact date of her passing is not known. Elizabeth lived eleven years as a widow and died at the age of 59; it is believed at least six out of her eleven children predeceased her.

She was laid to rest alongside her husband at St Andrew's Church in Wingfield. Today their alabaster tomb stands proud on the north side of the sanctuary, directly opposite the tomb of Michael de la Pole, second Earl of Suffolk and his wife Katherine de Stafford. Elizabeth and her husband John lie next to each other for eternity, hands in prayer and their feet resting on stone lions. Elizabeth is wearing a simple dress, belted at the waist, her head resting on a pillow supported by angels. The duke's head rests on a helmet and Saracen's head. Today's visitors to their tomb can break their journey and take refreshment at the De La Pole Arms, opposite the churchyard.

Margaret of York, across the sea in Flanders, would surely have received the news of her sister's death with great sadness. They had perhaps not seen each other since Margaret's visit to England in the

1480s, but presumably kept in contact. A pamphlet in Wingfield church states that Elizabeth paid a visit to Margaret in her widowhood; I can find no evidence to corroborate this but it is not beyond the realms of possibility that she decided to take a trip to see her younger sister sometime in the 1490s, a chance for the last two remaining children of York to catch up and reminisce once more.

Margaret herself was also ailing in 1503 and she was no longer the political figure she had once been, preferring to live a quieter life. Her advice and direction were still received with love and gratitude from her step-grandchildren, Philip of Burgundy and Margaret of Austria, and she remained a respected figure in her adopted homeland. The fact that during his second exile, Edmund, Earl of Suffolk, headed for Maximilian's court in support of his rebellion, rather than to Flanders, perhaps indicates that he knew his aunt was no longer up for the fight.

Spending her last remaining years at Binche, she owned two properties there: the Hotel of the old Abbey at Lobbe and the Hotel de Salle. Margaret spent around 2,500 crowns renovating the latter, adding a new tower, chapel and great hall, along with a gallery and reception rooms overlooking the beautiful gardens.

Margaret also spent many of her later years with her step-granddaughter Margaret of Austria, perhaps happy to be in constant female company once again. Having left for Spain in 1497, Margaret of Austria returned home in 1499 after the death of her husband, Prince John, at just 18 years of age. The couple were seemingly well matched with a mutual attraction and love for each other and she likely returned to Flanders and to Margaret of York, requiring care and comfort to work her way through her grief. In 1501 the two women made a pilgrimage to Halle, before late that year Margaret of Austria set off for her third marriage, this time to Philibert of Savoy.[48] As the 24-year-old Margaret of Austria said goodbye to the woman who had been a constant in her life since birth, even though she had spent many of her early years in France, she could not know it would be the last time she saw her.

Margaret of York died on 23 November 1503. At the beginning of the year she had spent some time with Maximilian when he came to visit his grandchildren at Mechelen. Philip of Burgundy and his wife, Juana, had travelled to Spain just a month after Margaret of Austria had left Burgundy, leaving their children Eleanor, Charles and Isabella in Margaret's care at Mechelen. After the death of Prince John and the eldest Spanish princess, Isabella, Juana (and Philip, by marriage) were now heirs to the Spanish kingdoms.

Margaret still resided at Binche but kept a close eye on the ducal household and travelled there personally to greet Maximilian when he came to visit. The year 1503 had begun with a very harsh freezing winter and was followed by a very hot summer, during which Margaret took Philip and Juana's three children to Ter Elst Castle, which was in the countryside and boasted a more temperate climate than the towns. They spent July in Ter Elst and returning to Mechelen, Margaret was clearly ailing as on 21 October she signed her will. She died just as Philip arrived back in the duchy at the end of November. Her death plunged the city of Mechelen and the Burgundian court into mourning. Her home, the Hotel de Salle at Binche, was draped in black and remained so for a long period afterwards.

Margaret of York was buried in the church of the Franciscan Grey Friars in Mechelen as directed in her will. Both her tomb and memorial were destroyed in the sixteenth century, but there were reportedly two alabaster statues of her, erected by Philip and Margaret in her memory; one of her kneeling beside St Margaret, her namesake, and the other showing her laid out in a shroud with a crown on her head. Three friars were depicted watching over her. On the inscription itself were the arms of England and Burgundy, surmounted by a crown and supported by an angel.

By 1503, the Tudors had been on the throne for nearly twenty years and Elizabeth and Margaret of York, alongside their mother Cecily, had been the great survivors of an earlier era. When they died, small pockets of Yorkist supporters still existed and there may still have been hope that one day they would reclaim the throne. In hindsight we know that would never be; just six years after their death, Henry Tudor's son became the great and infamous Henry VIII and he would be followed by three other Tudor kings and queens before their line too would die out; time continuously rolling as it does, making way for another era, that of the Stuart kings and queens.

# Chapter 11

# Legacy

## Anne

In August 2012, a team of archaeologists and researchers from Leicester University discovered the bones of a king in a car park in Leicester. The car park had been built on the site of the old Grey Friars church in Leicester. That king was Richard III.

Richard's eldest sister, Anne of York, died much earlier than her other two sisters, Elizabeth and Margaret. But although her life was the shortest, Anne played a hugely significant role in this twenty-first-century dig as it was her pedigree that helped identify her brother, the king, some 550 years after their deaths.

Anne's only surviving daughter, Anne St Leger, was disinherited by her uncle, Richard III, after the rebellion of her father, Thomas St Leger, and the majority of the Exeter estates were granted to Margaret Beaufort in the reign of Henry VII. At the age of 14, Anne St Leger was married to Sir George Manners. Together they had eleven children and when Anne died in 1526, she was also buried in St George's Chapel, near to her mother and next to her husband who had died in 1513. George Manners, later known as Lord Roos, was an ancestor of the Dukes of Rutland, and the couplie lie at rest in the Rutland Chapel within St George's. The inscription near their monument reads:

> Here lyethe buried George Maners Knyght Lorde Roos who decesed the xxvii daye of Octobre in the yere of our Lorde God MVCXIII and Ladye Anne his wyfe, daughter of Anne Duchess of Exetur, suster unto King Edward the fourthe and of Thomas Sentlynger, Knyght. The wyche Anne decessed the xxi day of Apryl in the yere of our Lord God, MVCXXVI. On whose soulls God have mercy. Amen.[1]

The Grey Friars church in Leicester was a Franciscan priory on the west side of Leicester. After the Battle of Bosworth, Richard III's body was taken to Leicester and reportedly put on display for two days to prove to the populace that he was dead. He was then interred in an unmarked grave within the priory, possibly on the same day that Henry Tudor departed Leicester for London. The priory itself was closed during the dissolution of the monasteries under Henry VIII and was subsequently demolished. The site itself was acquired by the Herrick family, who constructed a house and garden over the eastern part of the site, where the choir of the church would once have been. In 1612, Christopher Wren, whilst working as a tutor to Robert Herrick's nephew, saw a stone pillar, three feet high, with the inscription 'Here lies the body of Richard III, sometime king of England'.[2] The pillar had reportedly been erected by Robert Herrick to mark the location of Richard's grave. Subsequent redevelopment over the centuries means that the Herrick family manor now also lies under modern concrete developments, and over time Richard's last resting place was lost.

However, in the late 2000s, the author Annette Carson voiced that from her research she believed that Richard's grave may, in fact, lie under the car park of the social security offices in Leicester.[3] A few years later in 2011, the University of Leicester Archaeological Services (ULAS) was approached by Philippa Langley, a member of the Richard III Society, with the idea of starting an archaeological dig to try and find the skeleton of Richard III, working on the assumption that the belief he was buried in the Grey Friars after Bosworth was the truth. In collaboration with the university, the Richard III Society and Leicester City Council, the project was agreed and in September 2012, in the best possible outcome, the archaeological dig revealed a skeleton of a male in what was believed to be the choir area of the Grey Friars church.

To confirm they had discovered the lost king, the team needed to conclusively prove the bones they had found belonged to Richard and this they believed they could do by using mitochondrial DNA, a gene that is passed down through a female line. To achieve this, they would need to find an unbroken female line in Richard's family from the fifteenth century down to the twenty-first.

Unbelievably this existed, and historian John Ashdown-Hill was able to trace a line of descendants beginning with Richard's sister, Anne of York, through Anne St Leger and down to Anne of York's

13x great-granddaughter, Joy Ibsen, in Canada. Joy had sadly died just before Richard's bones were discovered, but she had a son, Michael Ibsen, living in London. As a male he could carry the gene but could not pass it on. From Michael Ibsen back to Anne of York, the gene was identified and using this DNA, along with other scientific processes such as radiocarbon dating and bone analysis, the team was able to conclude they had indeed discovered Richard's last resting place. Nearly three years later, on Thursday 26 March 2015, Richard III was re-interred at Leicester Cathedral. During his lifetime, Richard would have known Cardinal John Bourchier, Archbishop of Canterbury, who held the position from 1454 to 1486. His twenty-first-century burial was in the presence of the 105th Archbishop of Canterbury, Justin Welby.

## Elizabeth

When Elizabeth died, two of her sons, Edmund and Richard, were still in exile and her son William was in the Tower of London. Out of her other known sons, Geoffrey had died young and Edward, who was made Archdeacon of Richmond in 1484, had died in 1485.[4] Humphrey de la Pole did outlive his mother; it is thought he took Holy Orders and was seemingly not seen as any threat to the Tudor regime as he was allowed to live in peace, dying a few years into the reign of Henry VIII.

Out of Elizabeth's four known daughters, two were seemingly still alive to mourn the death of their mother in 1503. The two who had pre-deceased her were Dorothy, who had not survived infancy, and Anne de la Pole, who was so nearly married to the Duke of Rothsay, during the reign of her uncle Richard, and eventually became a nun at Syon Abbey, dying in or around 1501. Elizabeth of York's eldest daughter, Elizabeth de la Pole, married Henry Lovell, Lord Morley, and when he died in 1489, she lived her remaining years as a widow. Described as a 'woman of more than common beauty', she lived until around the age of 52 and is buried in the church of Halingbury Morley in Essex, where an inscription to her memory begins 'Elizebetha, Ducis Suffolcie Filia' (Elizabeth, the Duchess of Suffolk's daughter).[5] Elizabeth's youngest daughter, Katherine, was thought to have married William, Lord Stourton, and a passage in *Buck's History of Richard III* claims she was also sent to the Tower during the reign of Henry VIII and that she, like her brother William, remained there until she died: 'The sister of these Princely de la Pools, the Lady Katherine, was kept close prisoner in the Tower, until grief and sorrow bowed her to the grave'.[6] If true, and she was arrested before Elizabeth's death, this must have been a cause of high stress to Elizabeth in the last years of her life. Was Katherine her one daughter with rebellion in her bones, perhaps the closest to her brothers, joining them in their fight for the House of York? Elizabeth may have accepted that her sons would continue the Yorkist fight and was probably even proud of them even as she worried for their safety, but she would surely have been incredibly upset at the imprisonment of her daughter.

As for Edmund, Earl of Suffolk, now calling himself 'The White Rose', he and his brother Richard were surely disappointed when, in July 1502, Maximilian agreed not to harbour English rebels within his territories – he too had lost the desire to unseat the English king. Maximilian did help in a small way though, perhaps out of respect for Margaret of York as the earl was her nephew, and although he agreed to expel Suffolk from his domains on 12 February 1503, he continued to financially maintain him for several months more. But without financial backing for an invasion, Edmund found it almost impossible to raise a rebellion; armies and ships needed money and a powerful backing.

In the parliament of January 1504, the two de la Pole brothers were attainted and stripped of their lands and titles. Elizabeth's homes of Ewelme, Wingfield and Westhorpe came into the possession of the Crown. In later years, Henry VIII appointed William Stafford as Keeper of the Castle at Wingfield, followed by a man named Sir John Sharpe. In 1510 it was granted to Thomas Howard, later 3rd Duke of Norfolk, and his wife, Anne. Norfolk would go on to build and live in a Tudor mansion at Kenninghall, and Wingfield gained new tenants in the shape of Henry VIII's sister, Mary Tudor, and her husband, Charles Brandon. During Henry VIII's reign they also held the titles of Duke and Duchess of Suffolk.

Edmund de la Pole eventually left Aachen at Easter 1504, leaving his younger brother Richard de la Pole behind as hostage for their debts. Captured by servants of the Duke of Gueldres whilst heading to seek protection from George, Duke of Saxony, he eventually realised the game was up. On 24 January 1506 he sent two of his servants to negotiate with Henry VII for his return to England. Suffolk was delivered to Henry VII at Calais, who promised him his life would be spared if he surrendered. On his return to England, Edmund was sent straight to the Tower, arriving there on 24 April 1506.[7]

Meanwhile, Elizabeth's youngest son, Richard de la Pole, was still at loose on the continent. Upon the accession of Henry VIII, in April 1509, Richard, Edmund, and William de la Pole were excepted by name from the general pardon issued by the new king. By 1512, rumours reached England that Richard was being sponsored by Louis XII as a claimant to the English Crown and an angry King Henry ordered Edmund's execution, which took place on 4 May 1513 on Tower Hill. William de la Pole remained in prison, but somehow escaped with his life. The date of their sister Katherine's death also went unrecorded.

Following the execution of his brother Edmund, Richard de la Pole claimed his rights to the title of Duke of Suffolk, and also openly stated his entitlement to the English Crown. He reportedly recruited disaffected Englishmen to his service and although France and England reached a peace deal, Louis XII refused to hand him over. Richard would remain overseas for the next twelve years, attempting to mount an English invasion, interspersed with fighting in various wars on the continent and always under the protection of the French kings and nobility. He was eventually killed in one of those battles, in February 1425, fighting alongside the French king.[8] The white rose never did return to England's shores, although perhaps in the shape of Elizabeth of York, daughter of Edward IV and the first Tudor queen, she was already here.

## Margaret

Margaret's beloved son-in-law, Maximilian, had become Holy Roman Emperor in 1493 after the death of his father, Frederick III. Handing over the Duchy of Burgundy to his son Philip, he spent most of the rest of his life in Germany, dying there at the age of 60 in 1519.[9]

After the death of Isabella of Castille, her Spanish lands were left to her daughter, Juana, and she and Philip travelled from Burgundy to Spain again in 1506, where Philip was recognised as King of Castille by right of his wife. However, Juana's father, Ferdinand of Aragon, also had his eyes on the prize of Castille and Philip collaborated with him to exclude Juana from her Castille inheritance, declaring her mad and incapable. The story of Philip and Juana is a fascinating one – the elder sister of Katherine of Aragon, Juana was deeply in love with Philip and yet her stubbornness and strength of passion was seen as madness, or declared as a madness of spirit by the men in her life desperate to control her. What Margaret of York would have thought of the treatment of her daughter-in-law by her beloved step-grandson, given she herself was a perfect example of how females could rule, can only be guessed at.

Philip died in 1506 and although they had a tempestuous marriage, Juana genuinely loved him, refusing to be parted from his body if reports are to be believed, which perhaps didn't help her case in disproving her madness. Philip's son with Juana, Charles, would become Holy Roman Emperor after the death of Maximilian in 1519 and play an integral role as the nephew of Katherine of Aragon during her divorce proceedings from Henry VIII.

As for Margaret's step-granddaughter, Margaret of Austria, after the death of her brother, she became a successful ruler of the Low Countries with a court at Mechelen. Her third husband, whom she had truly loved, died in 1504 and she never remarried, dying herself in 1530 after agreeing to let her surgeons operate on a case of gangrene, which resulted from her cutting her foot on a piece of glass. They gave her a dose of opium which was too strong and she never woke up.[10] Margaret's court at Mechelen would, in 1513–14, be frequented by a young lady named Anne Boleyn, who would spend nearly two years in the service of Margaret of Austria, living in the shadows of Margaret of York.

Margaret of York's final resting place of the Franciscan church in Mechelen still survives today as part of the Malines Cultural Centre. Her tomb and monument were destroyed, however, just half a century after her death at the start of the Beeldenstorm in August 1566 which saw the destruction of Catholic religious buildings, statues and funeral monuments. More troubles and destruction occurred in 1572 and again on 9 April 1580 when the part of the church that contained Margaret's monument and remains was razed to the ground. According to several seventeenth- and eighteenth-century chroniclers, the destruction of the church went deeper still and Margaret's lead coffin in which she was buried was broken up and her bones scattered.

Since then, there have been several attempts to recover Margaret of York's last resting place. The first suggestions to dig up Margaret's bones came in the later 1800s when a Brussels newspaper expressed the desire to excavate and find them, and rebury her with her husband, Charles the Bold, in the Church of Our Lady at Bruges. Permission was obtained but the work never began. Excavations did take place in 1936, when a double burial chamber was discovered and the remains of three skeletons were found, one of them apparently female. On 20 September 1936 a report was presented to the town council, convinced that they had located Margaret's bones, mixed up with parts of two other skeletons. The council, not wishing to categorically declare they had discovered Margaret's skeleton, had the bones carefully examined. The results were that one skeleton belonged to an adult male, the second skeleton was of a person of at least 50 years of age and of an indeterminate sex, and that the third possibly belonged to a female between 50 and 60. The results were therefore fairly inconclusive.

However, nearly twenty years later, on 3 February 1955, some workmen digging in the choir of the church accidentally came across a lead coffin with the remnants of a skeleton. The coffin lay in the centre of the choir and had been put straight into the ground; there was no burial chamber. Once again the bones were examined and it was concluded that they were the remains of a woman of about 50 years of age, tall, with relatively narrow shoulders, a wide pelvis and slender limbs. The skeleton revealed a long and narrow face with a thin nose; comparison was made with surviving portraits of Margaret, and it was decided that there were resemblances. Over the years several more excavations claim to have found Margaret's bones but none have ever conclusively proved they have located either her remains or her exact burial place.[11]

In 2000, the Richard III Society put up a bronze plaque at the former priory, on the outside of the wall of the choir, with the text of Margaret's epitaph and her coat of arms held by an angel. Just twelve years later, the bones of her brother, Richard III, were found and identified, also in the choir of a priory. Margaret is now the only sibling where uncertainty lies over the exact location of her remains.

\*\*\*

The stars of the family of York burned brightly, but as is the case with history it was the brothers of York whose story travelled down the centuries; their sisters, just as real, just as alive, deserve as much credit as their more famous brothers for their persistence in keeping the Yorkist cause alive and fighting for their family name. The title of Duke of York is still in existence, reserved usually for the second son of a monarch, yet arguably Richard of York is still the most famous Duke of York, not quite attaining the throne for himself but paving the way for two of his sons to take the ultimate seat of power. Yet the House of York thrived not just through the males but through the women, beginning with Cecily Neville, the strong and pious matriarch of the family. Traits of her strength and tenacity continued through her daughters.

Anne, Duchess of Exeter, who against all the odds managed to find financial security as a widow and happiness with a man she loved, before losing her life in childbirth, was sadly dealt an ending that was not uncommon to women in the fifteenth century. Elizabeth, Duchess of Suffolk, the mother, the dissembler, was perhaps the quiet rebel who managed to create a life for her family and keep them safe until in the end they were old enough to make their own choices. That four of her sons died either in captivity or fighting for the York cause perhaps illustrates the pride that she had instilled in them as they grew up in the family that they belonged to. And then Margaret, Duchess of Burgundy, the youngest but by far the most powerful, who lived longer in her adopted land than she did in her birth country but who never forgot her roots and her family. Margaret, along with Edward and Richard, showed that she had the traits required to lead, to be respected and to govern fairly and although her one great sadness may have been that she never had children of her own, she still managed to build a family around her in the shape of her stepdaughter, Mary, and her step-grandchildren, Philip and Margaret.

The daughters of York may have been outshone by their more famous brothers in the pages of our history books, but brought up alongside them, they more than matched them as representatives of their name, their lineage and as champions of the White Rose of York. This book is dedicated to them.

# Bibliography

Ashdown-Hill, John, *Cecily Neville: Mother of Richard III* (Pen & Sword, 2018)

Ashdown-Hill, John, *The Full Itinerary of Edward IV* (Amberley Publishing) (Available to download as a pdf from johnashdownhill.com)

Baldwin, David, *Elizabeth Woodville: Mother of the Princes in the Tower* (Sutton Publishing, 2002)

Baldwin, David, *The Kingmaker's Sisters* (The History Press, 2009)

Carson, Annette, *Richard III: the Maligned King* (The History Press, 2013)

Dean, Kristie, *On The Trail of the Yorks* (Amberley Publishing, 2016)

Gregory, Philippa, Baldwin, David, and Jones, Michael, *The Women of the Cousins' War – the Duchess, the Queen and the King's Mother* (Simon & Schuster Ltd, 2012)

Gristwood, Sarah, *Blood Sisters: The Women behind the Wars of the Roses* (Harper Collins, 2013)

Halstead, Caroline Amelia, *Richard III: As Duke of Gloucester and King of England* (Longman, Brown, Green and Longmans, January 1844)

Harris, Barbara J., *English Aristocratic Women, 1450–1550: Marriage and Family, Property and Careers* (Oxford University Press, 2002)

Hicks, Michael, *The Family of Richard III* (Amberley Publishing, 2015)

Higginbotham, Susan, *Margaret Pole: the Countess in the Tower* (Amberley Publishing, 2016)

Hodder, Sarah J., *The Queen's Sisters* (John Hunt Publishing, 2020)

Hodder, Sarah J., *The York Princesses* (John Hunt Publishing, 2021)

Hodder, Sarah J., *Cecily Bonville-Grey, Marchioness of Dorset* (John Hunt Publishing, 2022)

Johnson, P.A., *Duke Richard of York 1411–1460* (Oxford University Press, 1988)

Jones, Dan, *The Hollow Crown: The Wars of the Roses and the Rise of the Tudors* (Faber & Faber, 2014)

Jones, Dan, *Summer of Blood: The Peasants Revolt* (Harper Collins, 2009)

Langley, Philippa, and Jones, Michael, *The King's Grave: The Search for Richard III* (John Murray, 2016)

Leyser, Henrietta, *Medieval Women: A Social History of Women in England 450–1500* (W&N, 2005)

Lewis, Matthew, *Richard Duke of York: King by Right* (Amberley Publishing, 2017)

Lewis, Matthew, *The Survival of the Princes in the Tower: Murder, Mystery and Myth* (The History Press, 2018)

Licence, Amy, *Cecily Neville: Mother of Kings* (Amberley Publishing, 2014)

Licence, Amy, *Edward IV and Elizabeth Woodville* (Amberley Publishing, 2016)

Licence, Amy, *Elizabeth of York – Forgotten Tudor Queen* (Amberley Publishing, 2013)

MacGibbon, David, *Elizabeth Woodville – A Life: The Real Story of the White Queen* (Amberley Publishing, 2013)

More, Thomas, *The History of King Richard III*, ed. George Logan (Indiana University Press, 2005)

Murphy, Elaine, *Wingfield Suffolk's Forgotten Castle* (Poppyland Publishing, 2021)

Okerlund, Arlene, *Elizabeth of York* (Palgrave Macmillan, 2009)

Penn, Thomas, *The Brothers York: An English Tragedy* (Penguin Books, 2020)

Ross, Charles, *Richard III* (Yale University Press, 1999)

Scofield, Cora L., *The Life and Reign of Edward IV: King of England and Lord of Ireland* (First published 1923. Ralph A. Griffiths and Fonthill Media, 2016)

Seward, Desmond, *The Wars of the Roses* (Robinson, 2007)

Sutton, Anne, and Visser-Fuch, Livia, *Royal Funerals of the House of York at Windsor* (Richard III Society, 2005)

Vaughan, Richard, *Charles The Bold: The Last Valois Duke of Burgundy* (Boydell Press, 2004)

Vaughan, Richard, *Philip the Good: The Apogee of Burgundy*, Volume 3 (Boydell Press, 2002)

Weightman, Christine, *Margaret of York: The Diabolical Duchess* (Amberley Publishing, 2012)

Weir, Alison, *Katherine Swynford: The Story of John of Gaunt and His Scandalous Duchess* (Vintage Books, 2008)

Weir, Alison, *Lancaster and York* (Vintage, 2009)

Weir, Alison, *Richard III and the Princes in the Tower* (Vintage, 2014)

Wroe, Anne, *Perkin* (Vintage, 2004)

Young, Charles Robert, *The Making of the Neville Family in England, 1166–1400* (Boydell & Brewer, 1996)

# References

## Chapter 1: A brief descent of the crown: Edward II to Henry IV

1. www.adamrutherford.com
2. Marlowe, Christopher, *Edward the Second: A Play* (Published by J.M. Dent, 1896)
3. Ibid.
4. *Ingulph's Chronicle of the Abbey of Croyland* with the continuations by Peter of Blois and anonymous writers (Henry Thomas Riley, H.G. Bohn, 1854)
5. Froissart, Jean, *The Chronicles of Froissart* (Hayes Barton Press, 1895)
6. The *Chronica Maiora* of Thomas Walsingham 1376–1422 (Boydell Press, 2005)
7. From the *Historia Vitae et Regni Ricardi II* by the Monk of Elvetham (late 14th century)
8. Tuck, Anthony, 'Lords appellant (*act.* 1387–1388)' in *Oxford Dictionary of National Biography* (2004)
9. Ibid.
10. Ibid.


## Chapter 2: All branches lead to Edward III

1. Licence, Amy, *Cecily Neville: Mother of Kings* (Amberley, 2014)
2. *The Monthly Chronicle of North-Country Lore and Legend* (Publisher: Walter Scott, Newcastle Upon Tyne for the proprietors of the *Newcastle Weekly Chronicle*, 1890)
3. Licence, *Cecily Neville*
4. Young, Charles Robert, *The Making of the Neville Family in England, 1166–1400* (Boydell & Brewer, 1996)

5. Smith. J.R., *The Chronicle of Battle Abbey, from 1066 to 1176* (Battle Abbey, January 1851)
6. Ibid.
7. Young, *The Making of the Neville Family*
8. Weir, Alison, *Katherine Swynford: The Story of John of Gaunt and His Scandalous Duchess* (Vintage Books, 2008)
9. Ibid.
10. Jones, Dan, *Summer of Blood: The Peasants Revolt* (Harper Collins, 2009)
11. Weir, *Katherine Swynford*
12. Ibid.
13. Lewis, Matthew, *Richard Duke of York, King by Right* (Amberley Publishing, 2017)
14. Ibid
15. Ibid.
16. Ibid.
17. Licence, *Cecily Neville*
18. *The Monthly Chronicle of North-Country Lore and Legend*
19. Ibid.
20. Mackenzie, Eneas, and Ross, Marvin, *An Historical, Topographical, and Descriptive View of the County Palatine of Durham* (Mackenzie and Dent, 1834)
21. Lewis, *Richard Duke of York*

## Chapter 3: A young family of York

1. Weightman, Christine, *Margaret of York: The Diabolical Duchess* (Amberley Publishing, 2012)
2. Bonney, H.K., *Fotheringhay* (1821), pp.29–30
3. Weightman, *Margaret of York*
4. Ashdown-Hill, John, *Cecily Neville: Mother of Richard III* (Pen & Sword, 2018)
5. Coulton, George Gordon, *Social Life in Britain from the Conquest to the Reformation* (Cambridge University Press, 1918)
6. *The Birth of Mankind: Otherwise Named, The Woman's Book*, ed. Elaine Hobby (Routledge, 2017)
7. Coulton, *Social Life in Britain*
8. Ashdown-Hill, *Cecily Neville*

9. Blacman, John, *Henry the Sixth, a reprint of John Blacman's memoir (with translation and notes by M.R. James)* (Cambridge University Press, 1919)

10. Lewis, Matthew, *Richard Duke of York: King by Right* (Amberley Publishing, 2017)

11. Johnson, P.A., *Duke Richard of York 1411–1460* (Oxford University Press, 1988)

12. *Saturday Magazine*, Vol VIII (January 16th 1836 and April supplement no. 246, 1836)

13. Licence, Amy, *Cecily Neville: Mother of Kings* (Amberley, 2014)

14. Gristwood, Sarah, *Blood Sisters: The Women behind the Wars of the Roses* (Harper Collins, 2013)

15. Ashdown-Hill, *Cecily Neville*

16. Ibid.

17. Ibid.

18. *Saturday Magazine*, Vol VIII

19. Ashdown-Hill, *Cecily Neville*

20. Cook, Sir Theodore Andrea, *The Story of Rouen* (Gutenberg Ebook, 2008)

21. Ibid.

22. Ashdown-Hill, *Cecily Neville*

23. Ibid.

24. Stansfield, Michael M.N., 'The Holland Family, Dukes Of Exeter, Earls Of Kent And Huntingdon, 1352–1475', Corpus Christi College Thesis submitted for the degree of Doctor of Philosophy to the Faculty of Modern History for the University of Oxford, 1987

25. Ibid.

26. Ibid.

27. Thornbury, Walter, 'Upper Thames Street', in *Old and New London: Volume 2* (London, 1878), pp.17–28. *British History Online*.

28. Venn, John, *Alumni Cantabrigienses; A Biographical List of all Known Students, Graduates and Holders of Office at the University of Cambridge, from the earliest times to 1900* (By University of Cambridge; 1834–1923)

29. Bagwell, Richard, *The Project Gutenberg Ebook of Ireland under the Tudors*, Volume I (of II)

30. Lewis, *Richard Duke of York*

31. Stansfield, 'The Holland Family'

32. Johnson, *Duke Richard of York*
33. Griffiths, Ralph A., 'Richard Duke of York and the Royal Household in Wales, 1449–50' in *The Welsh History Review*, Vol. 8, June 1976
34. *Annals Of The Kingdom Of Ireland, By The Four Masters, From The Earliest Period To The Year 1616 (Vol. 4)*. Edited From Mss. In The Library Of The Royal Irish Academy And Of Trinity College, Dublin, With A Translation, And Copious Notes, By John O'Donovan, LL.D., M.R.I.A. (Hodges, Smith and Co, 1856)
35. *Irish Penny Magazine*, Saturday 9 March 1833
36. Butler, Richard, *Some Notices of the Castle and of the Abbeys and other Religious Houses at Trim* (Henry Griffith, January 1835)
37. McNeill, T.E., *Castles in Ireland: Feudal Power in a Gaelic World* (Routledge, 1997)
38. *Irish Penny Magazine*, Saturday 17 August 1833
39. Ibid.
40. Lewis, *Richard Duke of York*
41. *Ingulph's Chronicle of the Abbey of Croyland with the continuations by Peter of Blois and anonymous writers*, tr. Henry Thomas Riley (published 1854 by H.G. Bohn)
42. Johnson, *Duke Richard of York*

## Chapter 4: The duke is dead, long live the king

1. Weightman, Christine, *Margaret of York: The Diabolical Duchess* (Amberley Publishing, 2012)
2. Ashdown-Hill, John, *Cecily Neville: Mother of Richard III* (Pen & Sword, 2018)
3. Johnson, P.A., *Duke Richard of York 1411–1460* (Oxford University Press, 1988)
4. Halstead, Caroline Amelia, *Richard III: As Duke of Gloucester and King of England.* (Longman, Brown, Green and Longmans, January 1884)
5. Bentley, Samuel, *Excerpta Historica* (published 1831)
6. Halstead, *Richard III*
7. *A collection of ordinances and regulations for the government of the royal household, made in divers reigns. From King Edward III. to King William and Queen Mary. Also receipts in ancient cookery* (Society of Antiquaries of London, 1790)

8. Lewis, Matthew, *Richard Duke of York: King by Right* (Amberley Publishing, 2017)
9. Ibid.
10. Shakespeare, William, *King Henry VI, Part 3* (1623)
11. More, Thomas, *The History of King Richard III* (Indiana University Press, 2005)
12. *Ingulph's Chronicle of the Abbey of Croyland with the continuations by Peter of Blois and anonymous writers*, tr. Henry Thomas Riley (published 1854 by H.G. Bohn)
13. Pugh, T., 'Richard Duke of York and the Rebellion of Henry Holand, Duke of Exeter, in May 1454', *Bulletin of the Institute of Historical Research*, Volume 63, No. 152, October 1990
14. Marsden, P.R.V., 'Baynards Castle', *London Archaeologist*, Vol. 1(14), 1972, pp.315–316
15. Pugh, 'Richard, Duke of York'
16. Halstead, *Richard III*
17. *Paston Letters*, Volume 3 (Project Gutenberg, online)
18. Stansfield, Michael M.N., 'The Holland Family, Dukes Of Exeter, Earls Of Kent And Huntingdon, 1352–1475', Corpus Christi College Thesis submitted for the degree of Doctor of Philosophy to the Faculty of Modern History for the University of Oxford, 1987
19. Ibid.
20. *A Short Guide to the Buildings and Architecture of Dartington Hall* (Dartington Trust; available as a PDF from www.dartington.org)
21. Bruce, Thomas (ed.), *Bridgwater Borough Archives 1445–1468* (Butler & Tanner Ltd, 1948)
22. *Ingulph's Chronicle*
23. Murphy, Elaine, *Wingfield Suffolk's Forgotten Castle* (Poppyland Publishing, 2021)
24. Hicks, Michael, 'Pole, John de la, second duke of Suffolk (1442–1492)' in *Oxford Dictionary of National Biography*
25. Napier, Henry Albert, Rev., *Historical Notices of the Parish of Swyncombe and Ewelme in the County of Oxford* (Ewelme, 1858)
26. Ewelme Manor, listed on the National Heritage List for England (historicengland.org.uk/listing/the-list/list-entry/1194482)
27. Delman, Rachel M., 'Gendered Viewing, Childbirth and Female Authority in the Residence of Alice Chaucer, Duchess of Suffolk, at Ewelme, Oxfordshire', *Journal of Medieval History*, Vol. 45, No. 2 (2019), pp.181–203

28. Johnson, *Duke Richard of York*
29. Stansfield, 'The Holland Family'
30. *Paston Letters*, Volume 3 (Project Gutenberg, online)
31. Laynesmith, J.L., and Barnfield, Marie, 'Anne, Duchess of Exeter' on Richard III Society website (Richard III.net)
32. *Paston Letters*, Volume 3 (Project Gutenberg, online)
33. Ibid
34. *Paston Letters*, Volume 3 (Project Gutenberg, online)
35. Stow, John, 'Downegate warde' in *A Survey of London. Reprinted From the Text of 1603*, ed. C.L. Kingsford (Oxford, 1908), pp.229–238 (British History Online)
36. Licence, Amy, *Cecily Neville: Mother of Kings* (Amberley, 2014)
37. No. 62. Prospero de Camulio, Milanese Ambassador to the French Court to Cicho Symoneti, Secretary to the Duke of Milan. Milan: 1461, in *Calendar of State Papers and Manuscripts in the Archives and Collections of Milan 1385–1618*
38. No. 63. Milan: 1461, in *Calendar of State Papers and Manuscripts in the Archives and Collections of Milan 1385–1618*
39. Scofield, Cora L., *Life and Reign of Edward IV: King of England and France and Lord of Ireland* (Fonthill Media, 2016)
40. No. 64. Milan: 1461, in *Calendar of State Papers and Manuscripts in the Archives and Collections of Milan 1385–1618*

## Chapter 5: Our brother, the king

1. *Paston Letters*, Volume 3 (Project Gutenberg, online)
2. No. 82. Milan: 1461, in *Calendar of State Papers and Manuscripts in the Archives and Collections of Milan 1385–1618*, ed. Allen B. Hinds (London, 1912), pp.37–106. British History Online.
3. No. 88. Milan: 1461, in *Calendar of State Papers and Manuscripts in the Archives and Collections of Milan 1385–1618*
4. No. 81. Nicholas O'Flanagan, Bishop of Elphin, to Francesco Coppino, Bishop of Terni, Apostolic Legate to England, Scotland and Ireland. Milan: 1461, in *Calendar of State Papers and Manuscripts in the Archives and Collections of Milan 1385–1618*
5. Kleineke, Dr Hannes, 'A New Dawn? The Accession of Edward IV on 4 March 1461' (thehistoryofparliament.wordpress.com)
6. *Paston Letters*, Volume 3 (Project Gutenberg, online)

7. Ashdown-Hill, John, *The Full Itinerary of Edward IV*

8. Scofield, Cora L., *Life and Reign of Edward IV: King of England and France and Lord of Ireland* (Fonthill Media, 2016)

9. *Paston Letters*, Volume 3 (Project Gutenberg, online)

10. Ross, Charles, *Richard III* (Yale University Press, 1999)

11. No. 117. Milan: 1461, in *Calendar of State Papers and Manuscripts in the Archives and Collections of Milan 1385–1618*

12. Venn, John, *Alumni Cantabrigienses; A Biographical List of all Known Students, Graduates and Holders of Office at the University of Cambridge, from the earliest times to 1900* (By University of Cambridge; 1834–1923)

13. Murphy, Elaine, *Wingfield Suffolk's Forgotten Castle* (Poppyland Publishing, 2021)

14. Ibid.

15. Scofield, *Life and Reign of Edward IV*

16. Halstead, Caroline Amelia, *Richard III: As Duke of Gloucester and King of England* (Longman, Brown, Green and Longmans, January 1884)

17. Hicks, Michael, 'George, Duke of Clarence (1449–1478)' in *Oxford Dictionary of National Biography*

18. Napier, Henry Albert, Rev., *Historical Notices of the Parish of Swyncombe and Ewelme in the County of Oxford* (Ewelme, 1858)

19. Commynes, Philippe de, and Roye, Jean de, *The Memoirs of Philip de Commines, Lord of Argenton: Containing the Histories of Louis XI, and Charles VIII, Kings of France, and of Charles the Bold, Duke of Burgundy. To which is Added the Scandalous Chronicle, Or, Secret History of Louis XI*, Volume 1 (H.G. Bohn, January 1855)

20. Hall, Edward, *The Union of the Two Noble and Illustrious Families of Lancaster and York* (*Hall's Chronicle*) (London, 1809)

21. Visser-Fuchs, Livia, *English Events in Caspar Weinreich's Danzig Chronicle, 1461–1495* in The Ricardian Online, December 1986

22. Napier, *Historical Notices*

23. Everett Wood, Mary Anne, *Letters of Royal, and Illustrious Ladies of Great Britain, from the Commencement of the Twelfth Century to the Close of the Reign of Queen Mary*, Volume 1 (Henry Colburn, 1846)

24. *Paston Letters*, Volume IV (Project Gutenberg, online)

25. *Paston Letters*, Volume IV (Project Gutenberg, online)

26. Napier, *Historical Notices*
27. *Paston Letters*, Volume IV (Project Gutenberg, online)
28. Murphy, Elaine, *Wingfield Suffolk's Forgotten Castle* (Poppyland Publishing, 2021)
29. Hall, *Hall's Chronicle*
30. Weightman, Christine, *Margaret of York: The Diabolical Duchess* (Amberley Publishing, 2012)
31. Vaughan, Richard, *Charles the Bold: The Last Valois Duke of Burgundy*, (Boydell Press, 2004)
32. Hall, *Hall's Chronicle*
33. Ibid.
34. Delman, Rachel M., 'Gendered Viewing, Childbirth and Female Authority in the Residence of Alice Chaucer, Duchess of Suffolk, at Ewelme, Oxfordshire', *Journal of Medieval History* Vol. 45, No. 2 (2019), 181–203
35. Holinshed, Raphael, *The Chronicles of England, Scotland and Ireland* (first printed 1577; Project Gutenberg, 2014)
36. Vaughan, *Charles The Bold*
37. Scofield, *Life and Reign of Edward IV*
38. Vander Linden, Herman, *Itineraires de Charles, Duc de Bourgogne, Marguerite D'York et Marie de Bourgogne* (Maurice Lamertin, Brussels, 1936)
39. Ibid.
40. Holinshed, *The Chronicles of England, Scotland and Ireland*
41. *Paston Letters*, Volume IV (Project Gutenberg, online)
42. Kren, Thomas (ed.), *Margaret Of York, Simon Marmion, And The Visions of Tondal*, papers delivered at a symposium organized by the Department of Manuscripts of the J. Paul Getty Museum in collaboration with the Huntington Library and Art Collections June 21–24, 1990 (The J. Paul Getty Museum, Malibu, California, 1992)
43. *Paston Letters*, Volume IV (Project Gutenberg, online)
44. Hall, *Hall's Chronicle*
45. Maekelberg, S. and De Jonge, K., 'The Prince's Court at Bruges: A Reconstruction of the Lost Residence of the Dukes of Burgundy', *Architectural Histories*, 6(1) (1991), p.23
46. Weightman, *Margaret of York*
47. Vander Linden, *Itineraires de Charles*
48. Licence, Amy, *Cecily Neville: Mother of Kings* (Amberley, 2014)

49. Driver, John, 'Sir Thomas St Leger, c.1439–83; the Rise and Fall of a Royal Servant During the Reigns of Edward IV and Richard III', *Surrey Archaeological Collections*, Vol. 94 (2008)
50. Napier, *Historical Notices*
51. Hall, *Hall's Chronicle*
52. Napier, *Historical Notices*

## Chapter 6: A family at war

1. Commynes, Philippe de, and Roye, Jean de, *The Memoirs of Philip de Commines, Lord of Argenton: Containing the Histories of Louis XI, and Charles VIII, Kings of France, and of Charles the Bold, Duke of Burgundy. To which is Added the Scandalous Chronicle, Or, Secret History of Louis XI*, Volume 1 (H.G. Bohn, January 1855)
2. Weightman, Christine, *Margaret of York: The Diabolical Duchess.* Amberley Publishing, 2012.
3. Scofield, Cora L., *The Life and Reign of Edward IV, King of England and Lord of Ireland* (first published 1923; Ralph A. Griffiths and Fonthill Media, 2016)
4. Commynes and Roye, *The Memoirs of Philip de Commines*
5. Vander Linden, Herman, *Itineraires de Charles, Duc de Bourgogne, Marguerite D'York et Marie de Bourgogne* (Maurice Lamertin, Brussels, 1936)
6. Ibid.
7. Ibid.
8. Commynes and Roye, *The Memoirs of Philip de Commines*
9. Seward, Desmond, *The Wars of the Roses* (Robinson, 2007)
10. Stansfield, Michael M.N., *The Holland Family, Dukes Of Exeter, Earls Of Kent And Huntingdon, 1352 – 1475.* Corpus Christi College Thesis submitted for the degree of Doctor of Philosophy to the Faculty of Modern History for the University of Oxford, 1987.
11. Ibid.
12. 'Calendar of the Patent Rolls preserved in the Public Record Office: Edward IV, Henry VI, A.D. 1467–1477' (London: Printed for her Majesty's Stationery Office)
13. Myers, Alec Reginald, *The Household of Edward IV* (Manchester University Press, 1959)

14. 'Calendar of the Patent Rolls'
15. Ibid
16. Ibid
17. Deeds: A.11101–A.11200, in *A Descriptive Catalogue of Ancient Deeds: Volume 5*, ed. H.C. Maxwell Lyte (London, 1906), 93–108, *British History Online*.
18. Napier, Henry Albert, Rev., *Historical Notices of the Parish of Swyncombe and Ewelme in the County of Oxford* (Ewelme, 1858)
19. Kingsford, Charles Lethbridge, *The Stonor Letters and Papers, 1290–1483*; ed. for the Royal Historical Society from the original documents in the Public Record Office (Offices of the Society, 1919)
20. 'Calendar of the Patent Rolls'
21. Ibid.
22. Weightman, *Margaret of York*
23. Ibid.
24. Vaughan, Richard, *Charles The Bold: The Last Valois Duke of Burgundy* (Boydell Press, 2004)
25. Weightman, *Margaret of York*
26. Von Berghahn, Barbara, *Jan van Eyck and Portugal's Illustrious Generation*. Vol. 1 (Pindar Press, 2014)
27. Emery, Anthony, *Seats of Power in Europe during the Hundred Years war: An Architectural Study from 1330 to 1480* (Oxbow Books, 2015)
28. Vaughan, *Philip the Good: The Apogee of Burgundy*, Volume 3 (Boydell Press, 2002)
29. Kren, Thomas (ed.), *Margaret of York, Simon Marmion, And The Visions of Tondal*, papers delivered at a symposium organized by the Department of Manuscripts of the J. Paul Getty Museum in collaboration with the Huntington Library and Art Collections June 21–24, 1990 (The J. Paul Getty Museum, Malibu, California, 1992)

## Chapter 7: To love and to lose

1. 'Calendar of the patent rolls preserved in the Public Record Office: Edward IV [Henry VI, Edward V, Richard III] A. D. 1461–[1485] Prepared under the superintendence of the Deputy Keeper of the Records' (London: Printed for her Majesty's Stationery Office), Public Record Office (18971901)

2. Madden, Frederic; Bandinel, Bulkeley; and Nichols, John Gough (eds.), *Collectanea Topographica et Genealogica* (John Bowyer Nichols and Son, 1834)

3. *Paston Letters*, Volume V (Project Gutenberg, online)

4. Ashdown-Hill, John, *The Full Itinerary of Edward IV*; see also *Rymer's Foedera Volume 11*, ed. Thomas Rymer (London, 1739–1745), 842–852, *British History Online*

5. *The Society of the Friends of St George with which is Amalgamated the Association of the Descendants of the Knights of the Garter* (Report to 31 December 1941)

6. www.stgeorges-windsor.org/the-roos-monument-in-the-rutland-chantry-chapel

7. *The Society of the Friends of St George* (Report to 31 December 1941)

8. www.stgeorges-windsor.org/the-rutland-chantry

9. Ross, Charles, *Richard III* (Yale University Press, 1999)

10. Weightman, Christine, *Margaret of York: The Diabolical Duchess* (Amberley Publishing, 2012)

11. Hall, Edward, *The Union of the Two Noble and Illustrious Families of Lancaster and York* (*Hall's Chronicle*) (London, 1809)

12. Giovanni Pietro Panicharolla, Milanese Ambassador at the Burgundian Court to Galeazzo Maria Sforza, Duke of Milan Nancy, 4 December, 1475. Milan: 1461, in *Calendar of State Papers and Manuscripts in the Archives and Collections of Milan 1385–1618*, ed. Allen B Hinds (London, 1912), 37–106, *British History Online*.

13. *Paston Letters*, Volume V (Project Gutenberg, online)

14. Kingsford, Charles Lethbridge, *The Stonor Letters and Papers, 1290–1483*; ed. for the Royal Historical Society, from the original documents in the Public Record Office (Offices of the Society, 1919)

15. Hammond, P.W., Sutton, Anne F., and Visser-Fuchs, Livia, *The Reburial of Richard, Duke of York, 21–30 July 1476* (Richard III. net)

16. Ibid.

17. Ibid.

18. Napier, Henry Albert, Rev., *Historical Notices of the Parish of Swyncombe and Ewelme in the County of Oxford* (Ewelme, 1858)

19. Kingsford, *The Stonor Letters and Papers*

20. Weightman, *Margaret of York*

21. Ibid.
22. Ibid.
23. *Chroniques de Jean Molinet*, Volume 2
24. *Ingulph's Chronicle of the Abbey of Croyland* with the continuations by Peter of Blois and anonymous writers, tr. Henry Thomas Riley (published 1854 by H.G. Bohn)

## Chapter 8: The final act

1. Higginbotham, Susan, *Margaret Pole, the Countess in the Tower* (Amberley Publishing, 2016)
2. Napier, Henry Albert, Rev., *Historical Notices of the Parish of Swyncombe and Ewelme in the County of Oxford* (Ewelme, 1858)
3. *Paston Letters*, Volume V (Project Gutenberg, online)
4. *Paston Letters*, Volume V (Project Gutenberg, online)
5. Dean, Kristie, *On The Trail of the Yorks* (Amberley Publishing, 2016)
6. Ibid.
7. Weightman, Christine, *Margaret of York: The Diabolical Duchess* (Amberley Publishing, 2012)
8. Kingsford, Charles Lethbridge, *The Stonor Letters and Papers, 1290–1483*; ed. for the Royal Historical Society, from the original documents in the Public Record Office (Offices of the Society, 1919)
9. Napier, *Historical Notices*
10. Kren, Thomas (ed.), *Margaret of York, Simon Marmion, And The Visions of Tondal*, papers delivered at a symposium organized by the Department of Manuscripts of the J. Paul Getty Museum in collaboration with the Huntington Library and Art Collections June 21–24, 1990 (The J. Paul Getty Museum, Malibu, California, 1992)
11. *Ingulph's Chronicle of the Abbey of Croyland* with the continuations by Peter of Blois and anonymous writers, tr. Henry Thomas Riley (published 1854 by H.G. Bohn)
12. Westhorpe Hall: British Listed Buildings (https://britishlistedbuildings.co.uk/101033105-westhorpe-hall-westhorpe#.Y8wadXbP02w)
13. Napier, *Historical Notices*
14. Ashdown-Hill, John, *The Full Itinerary of Edward IV*

15. *Ingulph's Chronicle*
16. Ibid
17. Hall, Edward, *The Union of the Two Noble and Illustrious Families of Lancaster and York* (*Hall's Chronicle*) (London, 1809)
18. More, Thomas, *The History of King Richard III* (Cambridge University Press, 1883)

## Chapter 9: A question of loyalty

1. Vergil, Polydore, *Three Books of Polydore Vergil's English History, Comprising the Reigns of Henry VI., Edward IV., and Richard III. from an Early Translation, Preserved Among the mss. of the Old Royal Library in the British Museum*, ed. Sir Henry Ellis (Printed for the Camden Society, J.B. Nichols & Sons, 1844)
2. *Ingulph's Chronicle of the Abbey of Croyland* with the continuations by Peter of Blois and anonymous writers, tr. Henry Thomas Riley (published 1854 by H.G. Bohn)
3. Jones, Dan, *The Hollow Crown: The Wars of The Roses and the Rise of the Tudors* (Faber & Faber, 2015)
4. Carson, Annette, *Richard III: The Maligned King* (The History Press, 2013)
5. Vergil, *Three Books of Polydore Vergil's English History*
6. Weir, Alison, *Richard III and the Princes in the Tower* (Vintage, 2014)
7. Ibid.
8. Cunningham, S., 'Pole, Edmund de la, eighth earl of Suffolk (1472?–1513), nobleman and claimant to the English throne' in *Oxford Dictionary of National Biography*
9. 'Calendar of the patent rolls preserved in the Public Record Office: Edward IV [Henry VI, Edward V, Richard III] A. D. 1461–[1485] Prepared under the superintendence of the Deputy Keeper of the Records' (London: Printed for her Majesty's Stationery Office), Public Record Office (18971901).
10. Hall, Edward, *The Union of the Two Noble and Illustrious Families of Lancaster and York (Hall's Chronicle)* (London, 1809)
11. Napier, Henry Albert, Rev., *Historical Notices of the Parish of Swyncombe and Ewelme in the County of Oxford* (Ewelme, 1858)

12. *Ingulph's Chronicle*
13. Ibid.
14. 'Calendar of the patent rolls preserved in the Public Record Office: Edward IV [Henry VI, Edward V, Richard III] A. D. 1461–[1485]'
15. Hall, *Hall's Chronicle*
16. Lewis, Matthew, *The Survival of the Princes in the Tower: Murder, Mystery and Myth* (The History Press, 2018)
17. Napier, Henry Albert, Rev., *Historical Notices of the Parish of Swyncombe and Ewelme in the County of Oxford* (Ewelme, 1858)
18. 'Calendar of the patent rolls preserved in the Public Record Office: Edward IV [Henry VI, Edward V, Richard III] A. D. 1461–[1485]'
19. Napier, *Historical Notices*
20. 'Calendar of the patent rolls preserved in the Public Record Office: Edward IV [Henry VI, Edward V, Richard III] A. D. 1461–[1485]'
21. *Paston Letters*, Volume V (Project Gutenberg, online)
22. Lewis, *The Survival of the Princes in the Tower*
23. Vergil, *Three Books of Polydore Vergil's English History*
24. Licence, Amy, *Cecily Neville: Mother of Kings* (Amberley, 2014)
25. Vergil, *Three Books of Polydore Vergil's English History*

## Chapter 10: The Tudors

1. Bacon, Francis, *History of the Reign of King Henry VII*, with notes by J. Rawson Lumby (Written in 1622 during the reign of James I; University Press, 1889)
2. *Chroniques de Jean Molinet*, Volume 2
3. www.richardIII.net (Titulus Regius)
4. Lewis, Matthew, *The Survival of the Princes in the Tower: Murder, Mystery and Myth* (The History Press, 2018)
5. Ibid.
6. Napier, Henry Albert, Rev., *Historical Notices of the Parish of Swyncombe and Ewelme in the County of Oxford* (Ewelme, 1858)
7. Ibid.
8. Weightman, Christine, *Margaret of York: The Diabolical Duchess* (Amberley Publishing, 2012)
9. Weir, Alison, *Elizabeth of York, the First Tudor Queen* (Jonathan Cape, 2013)

10. Bacon, *History of the Reign of King Henry VII*
11. Lewis, *The Survival of the Princes in the Tower*
12. Seward, Desmond, *The Last White Rose* (Constable & Robinson, 2010)
13. *Paston Letters*, Volume V (Project Gutenberg, online)
14. Leland, Joannis, *Lelandi Antiquarii de rebus Britannicis Collectanea*, Vol. 5 (Thomas Hearne, 1770)
15. Napier, *Historical Notices*
16. Hall, Edward. *The Union of the Two Noble and Illustrious Families of Lancaster and York (Hall's Chronicle)* (London, 1809)
17. Murphy, Elaine, *Wingfield Suffolk's Forgotten Castle* (Poppyland Publishing, 2021)
18. Hicks, M., 'Pole, John de la, second duke of Suffolk (1442–1492), magnate' in *Oxford Dictionary of National Biography*
19. Camden, William, *Britannia, or, A chorographical description of Great Britain and Ireland, together with the adjacent islands*, with additions by Edmund Gibson (London, 1728)
20. Murphy, *Wingfield*
21. Wroe, Anne, *Perkin* (Vintage, 2004)
22. Weightman, Christine, *Margaret of York: The Diabolical Duchess* (Amberley Publishing, 2012)
23. Seward, Desmond, *The Last White Rose* (Constable & Robinson, 2010)
24. Spain: 1493, in *Calendar of State Papers, Spain, Volume 1, 1485–1509*, ed. G.A. Bergenroth (London, 1862), 43–51, British History Online
25. Tremayne, Eleanor, *The First Governess Of The Netherlands, Margaret Of Austria* (Methuen and Co, London, 1908)
26. Weightman, *Margaret of York*
27. Wroe, *Perkin*
28. Weightman, *Margaret of York*
29. Ibid.
30. Weightman, *Margaret of York*
31. Wood, Mary Anne Everett, *Letters of Royal and Industrious Ladies*, Volume 1 (1846)
32. Napier, *Historical Notices*
33. Weightman, *Margaret of York*
34. Ibid.

35. Wroe, *Perkin*
36. Ibid.
37. Weightman, *Margaret of York*
38. 'Calendar of the patent rolls preserved in the Public Record Office: Edward IV [Henry VI, Edward V, Richard III] A. D. 1461–[1485] Prepared under the superintendence of the Deputy Keeper of the Records' (London: Printed for her Majesty's Stationery Office), Public Record Office, (18971901)
39. Cunningham, S., 'Pole, Edmund de la, eighth earl of Suffolk (1472?–1513), nobleman and claimant to the English throne' in *Oxford Dictionary of National Biography*
40. Tudor Chamber Books: E101/414/6 folio 119v (Obligations), 1496; E101/414/16 f93r, 1497; E101/415/3 folio 169r (Obligations), 1499.
41. Wood, *Letters*
42. Cunningham, *Pole, Edmund de la*
43. Gairdner, James, *Letters and papers illustrative of the reigns of Richard III and Henry VII* (By Gairdner, James, 1828–1912)
44. Cunningham, *Pole, Edmund de la*
45. *Paston Letters*, Volume V (Project Gutenberg, online)
46. Tudor Chamber Books: E101/415/3 folio 192v (Obligations), 1500
47. Borman, Tracy, *The Private Lives of the Tudors* (Hodder & Stoughton, 2016)
48. Weightman, *Margaret of York*

## Chapter 11: Legacy

1. Rogers, William Henry Hamilton. *The Ancient Sepulchral Effigies and Monumental and Memorial Sculpture of Devon* (1877)
2. Ashdown-Hill, John, *The Last Days of Richard III and the Fate of his DNA* (The History Press, 2013)
3. Licence, Amy, *Richard III, The Road to Leicester* (Amberley, 2014)
4. Napier, Henry Albert, Rev., *Historical Notices of the Parish of Swyncombe and Ewelme in the County of Oxford* (Ewelme, 1858)
5. Ibid.
6. Buck, George, *The History and Life and Reigne of Richard the Third Composed in Five Books* (London, 1647)

7. Cunningham, S., 'Pole, Edmund de la, eighth earl of Suffolk (1472?–1513), nobleman and claimant to the English throne' in *Oxford Dictionary of National Biography*
8. Cunningham, *Pole, Edmund de la*
9. Weightman, Christine, *Margaret of York: The Diabolical Duchess* (Amberley Publishing, 2012)
10. Tremayne, Eleanor, *The First Governess Of The Netherlands, Margaret Of Austria* (Methuen and Co, London, 1908)
11. De Win, Paul, 'The Search for Margaret's Bones: 'Danse Macabre' Around the Tomb and Bones of Margaret of York', *Ricardian*, Volume 15 (2005)

# Index